D0634162

Life of a European Mandarin

Derk-Jan Eppink

Life of a European Mandarin
Inside the Commission

For the mandarins of Europe

WWW.LANNOO.COM

This book is also published in Dutch under the title *Europese mandarijnen.*
Achter de schermen van de Europese Commissie (ISBN 978-90-209-6626-8)

Second edition
ENGLISH TRANSLATION Ian Connerty
TECHNICAL ADVISER Michael Wells
LAYOUT COVER Wil Immink
ILLUSTRATION COVER Getty Images
PHOTO AUTHOR Wouter Rawoens
© 2007 LANNOO PUBLISHERS, Tielt, Belgium
D/2008/45/32 – ISBN 978-90-209-7022-7

Contents

Introduction

The European Commission is a Princess on the dance floor of history. Her first tentative steps signal the start of the waltz towards the unification of an entire continent. The Princess is gracious, but can also be capricious. She is single-minded, but can also be fickle. She is the champion of impassioned popular ideas, but stands far removed from her people. She is generous in spirit, but often quibbles about money. She is charming to a fault, but can often be moody, even short-tempered.

Throughout the years, many mandarins have served the Princess with heart and soul. After twenty years of loyalty, the chosen few are rewarded with a medal and are honoured as 'model mandarins'. The Princess has class. Her elegance is alluring, her ideas are convincing, her energy and commitment are limitless – but, like the Lord God of Hosts, her ways are mysterious, impenetrable to the minds of ordinary mortals. The Princess is a distant relative of the Roman Empire: a throwback to the days when Rome spoke and the world obeyed.

In modern Europe, things are slightly different. If the Princess speaks, her words are merely the first chords of the overture to a very long opera. But if times have changed, the aim has remained the same. The Princess wishes to offer Europe style and colour in an era of grey drabness, prestige and influence in a difficult and uncertain world. Her inspiration is not to be found in either 'old' Europe or 'new' Europe, but rather in 'eternal' Europe.

For the first time since the Congress of Vienna in 1815, the Princess is trying to help Europe order her affairs peacefully – and with no outside interference. Much changed on the continent after 1815, but not the mentality of the Europeans. Holy Alliances and resounding declarations of universal principle masked – and still mask – the harsh reality of national (and sometimes even personal) interests.

The European politician prefers to work in the wings rather than centre stage. His utterances are deliberately vague, since clarity and precision can only limit his room for manoeuvre. Americans are still driven by the ideal of 'liberty'. Weighed down by the burden of their own history, the Europeans no longer cherish such high-flown ideals. Radical ideologies have cost them two world wars and more than 100 million dead.

Europeans are sceptical, uncertain and suspicious. They operate in the twilight zone, just like Clemens von Metternich and Charles Maurice de Talleyrand in Vienna, now almost two centuries ago. Metternich and Talleyrand created a European order which lasted a hundred years. The Princess belongs to this same tradition. She has been going strong for more than fifty years. But will she reach her 100th birthday? According to some, she is long past her best and not up the tasks bestowed upon her. She is not the heroic victor of great battles, but rather a suppressor of inconvenient details and the protectress of a number of loose principles, which are subject to daily modification or even complete denial.

For more than 7 years, I was a servant at the court of the Princess, who goes through life in the guise of the European Commission. During this period, I learnt and gradually came to understand how the work of just a handful of mandarins can affect the lives of millions of people – both for good and for ill. To outsiders, the European Commission seems to be a monolithic block, issuing directives, regulations and decisions from its headquarters in the Berlaymont Building.

However, experience has taught me that the concrete pillars on which the Berlaymont is built, are all that is monolithic about the

European Commission. The European administration is a world of open doors, closed doors, side doors, back doors, revolving doors and even trap doors – enough to confuse even the most highly-skilled Polish plumber! The truth is never absolute and intrigue is sometimes healthy. Even the deliberate flouting of the Commission's own policy is occasionally beneficial, providing it remains within limits.

The Commission is a living compromise between Northern rigidity and Latin flexibility, between Protestant right-mindedness and Catholic artfulness, between the late-sleepers of the Mediterranean South and the early-risers of the frozen East. Its chosen weapon is the rapier, not the battle-axe. At its most senior levels, discussions are friendly, even courteous. However, beneath the surface there is a desperate struggle taking place, a struggle for control of crucial economic and political interests. The roads to consensus are never consensual.

The Commission is often attributed powers of mythic proportions, a bureaucratic monster whose sole purpose is to force its poor, unsuspecting citizens into a straitjacket of uniformity. It is sometimes seen as the ultimate expression of the ideal of equality. In this sense the Commission is not the inheritor of Rome: it is the inheritor of Moscow!

In reality, this view greatly overestimates the power of the Princess's 22,500 loyal servants. They are by no means in control of everything and are frequently overwhelmed by the sheer magnitude of their task. Their motto is 'enough is enough' and 'too much' is definitely to be avoided at all costs. They have neither an army, nor a police force at their disposal and live in a world made exclusively of paper. True, they do have considerable influence on a number of economic and political matters, allowing them to affect the daily comings and goings of some 500 million European citizens. But they can rarely dictate binding legislation.

The Princess opens the dance, moving gracefully to the centre of the floor, in the hope that her Ministers and her Members of Parliament will follow. Sadly, this is not always the case. More often than not, the Princess trips over their outstretched feet. She assumes that the general public admires her unreservedly, but in this she is gravely mistaken. Her aim is the unification of Europe, whether the public wants it or not. And often, the public does not want it at all! For this reason, she sometimes dreams of a more grateful public, and she despairs when she realises that this is never going to happen.

Over the years I have seen, admired, experienced and undergone many of the plans, projects, directives, guidelines and regulations devised by the Princess's court.

I arrived with a bushel of ideals and am now leaving with a small handful of practical insights. I first set foot in the Berlaymont Building in 1984 on the 11th floor and I am departing in 2007 as a full-fledged European mandarin of the 12th floor. Notwithstanding a limited promotion of just one floor in 23 years, I am proud to say that I mastered the necessary techniques of intrigue, trickery and deceit, without which a servant of the Princess cannot hope to survive.

I learnt that in the world of the Princess honesty is not a virtue but a weakness. I discovered that there is a hidden agenda, or even two or three lurking beneath every agenda! Emotion is always dangerous: administrative autism is much more acceptable. Anger is a sign of political shrewdness, providing it is faked. Genuine anger is invariably fatal and is guaranteed to put you on the losing side. Altruism is an unknown concept and there is no such thing as a free lunch. Above all, I realised that hypocrisy is the father of all victories, while naivety is the mother of all defeats.

In short, a mandarin of the Princess must be skilled in many of the less elevating aspects of God's imperfect creation.

So, too, your most humble and obedient servant.

Brussels, March 2007

1| The Mother of all Commissions

With a degree of seriousness and anxiety appropriate to the occasion, I arrived at the European Commission one sunny spring day in 1984. The man behind the reception desk was not impressed and told me to be patient. 'Look,' he said in his best French, 'You are not the only person waiting – and you're by no means the first!'

This was the gatekeeper of the Princess's castle and his wooden sentry box and his wooden-like manner compelled a certain degree of respect. He – and he alone – had the power to decide who might enter the castle, but only after a quick phone call to the official being visited. I looked behind me and saw that he was right. There was a long queue of other people, all equally keen to get inside the Berlaymont Building: students, journalists, lobbyists, each clutching a fistful of papers which they hoped would help them gain access to the Princess's inner

The Berlaymont, the imposing palace of the European mandarins.

sanctum. I wandered to the end of the line to wait for my turn, feeling disappointed that I hadn't brought any papers of my own. Twenty minutes later I stood eyeball to eyeball with the gatekeeper.

'Well? Who have you come for?' he asked in a bored, bureaucratic voice. 'Please spell the name,' he added, pointing to the building's telephone directory, with the implication that he would soon be ringing up to check my improbable story.

'I have come for Delors,' I said. 'D-E-L-O-R-S' He gave me a penetrating stare. '*Pardon. Alors, Monsieur le Président.*' He spoke the last three words with a slightly raised voice, as if to emphasise the importance of his statement. I interrupted him. 'No, it's not Alors, it's Delors. Try under D.' My attempt to be helpful was not appreciated.

'*Monsieur*, I am not a fool,' he said in a tone which clearly suggested that I was. At the time, the Commission employed a staggering 15,000 officials, but there was only one *Monsieur le Président*.

'Do you have an appointment?' he challenged. Not everyone gets to see the President of the European Commission, and certainly not a cheeky 25 year-old reporter who referred to the president by name instead of by his exalted function. If I was trying to pull a fast one, the gatekeeper intended to make sure that I never got beyond the drawbridge. I tried to reassure him.

'Yes, I have an appointment to do an interview with Mr. Delors for my newspaper.' He shook his head sadly. 'You mean with *Monsieur le Président.*' The gatekeeper telephoned the office of *Monsieur le Président*. 'Your arrival is expected,' he said in a disappointed voice.

'Thanks,' I replied cheerfully. 'Which lift do I take?' He gasped in horror. '*Monsieur*, where do you think you are? You cannot just wander around wherever you please. Sit over there. Someone will come and escort you up.'

Seconds later an officious secretary emerged from the lift specially reserved for the use of the President, so that he did not have to share his air space with mere mortals as he ascended to the Olympian heights of the 13th floor.

'Are you the visitor?' she demanded in a stern French voice. I nodded as politely as I could. 'Follow me,' she commanded. Being an obedient boy, I stepped into the lift and we glided effortlessly to the top storey of the Berlaymont Building, from where President Delors looked out across Brussels and across Europe.

The 13th floor was the nerve centre of the European Union, the bridge of the European ship of state. It was here that Delors and his members of cabinet had their offices. And it was here that the European Commission met: the mother of all commissions.

The secretary ushered me into the President's private office, a large room with numerous windows. A short, unobtrusive man walked resolutely towards me, his hand outstretched.

'*Bonjour*, Jacques Delors,' he said lyrically. His body language was friendlier than I had expected. 'Young man, have you come alone?'

He led me to a small reception room just off his main work area and invited me to sit down. Delors had only recently been appointed to his new position as President of the European Commission and was scheduled to travel to the Netherlands in the near future. This was why he wanted to do a number of preliminary interviews with Dutch journalists, to set the right tone for his visit. I had written to his secretariat some time before requesting an interview, as I was then writing

occasional pieces for a specialised political weekly read by most leading Dutch politicians. Now my request was to be granted.

Jacques Delors, the icon of Europe. Inspired but pragmatic.

These were the years of 'Euro-sclerosis', the pessimism expressed by
many towards the process of European integration. Everybody was
criticising the Princess, complaining about the slow rate of progress,
deploring the level of bureaucracy, the lack of democracy, the fact that
there were still only 12 members, etc.

Euro-sclerosis was so deeply ingrained in the Dutch media that
none of the newspapers had any interest in interviewing the President of the European Commission, a relatively unknown Frenchman.
My letter asking for an interview had not been the most prominent
request: it was the only request. Imagine my surprise one day when I
received a telephone call from Delors' spokesman: '*Monsieur le Président* has agreed to do your interview. You may come to Brussels.'

This news was so unexpected that I suddenly became nervous at the prospect of meeting face to face the man whom I had only seen on television. I needed to think of questions – sensible questions – and, worst of all, I had to speak in French. I had learnt the language at school and luckily I was one of the rapidly shrinking group of Dutch people who still embraced the language of Molière like a lover. Even so, the challenge was a daunting one.

The opportunities to speak French in the Netherlands are almost nil and the few French phrases regularly used (such as *Tour de France*, for example) are mutilated beyond recognition by a strong Dutch accent. An ordinary conversation about the weather or cycling would have been no problem, but I was obliged to question the President of the European Commission on a wide range of internationally important issues, from agriculture to finance and from institutional reform to the future of the British sausage!

The idea made me go weak at the knees. For a week before the interview, I lay awake in bed at night, shivering with fear and covered in sweat. During the day, I looked up technical terms in a French dictionary and tried to draw up a list of questions that I was at least able to pronounce. At the eleventh hour, fear of failure finally brought me to my senses. What if Delors said something that I didn't fully grasp? The French all talk the same way, burying their message in layer after layer of philosophical references and ideological jargon, which can be interpreted in a variety of different ways. If I didn't understand, I could simply make a good guess, in the expectation that I would still be reasonably close to the truth. Comforted by this thought, I spent the last hour before my journey to the Berlaymont in my apartment in Stevinstraat. I had prepared myself like an athlete training for a marathon. I had left nothing to chance. I was ready. Bring on the mandarins!

Happily, fortune was smiling on me that day. I had hardly started my conversation with *Monsieur le Président* before we were joined by a third person, another member of the Delors staff.

'Hello, I'm Hugo Paemen,' he said in perfect Dutch. I could have jumped for joy. Paeman was from Belgium – the cultural fault line of Europe – and was therefore blessed with the gift of being able to speak both Dutch and French. He looked tired, as though he might be suffering from the effects of today's heavy lunch or last night's hangover. That being said, most European mandarins have a liver of steel and possess powers of recuperation that would be the envy of many international sportsmen.

Possibly in Paemen's case his exhaustion was caused by Delors' notorious head of cabinet, Pascal Lamy. While Delors was all French suavity and sophistication, Lamy was universally known as the Beast of Berlaymont. Others referred to him as the *Gendarme*, from his habit of telling Commissioners and even director-generals precisely what they had to do – or else. Perhaps even more appropriate was the nickname *Exocet* – a reference to the French-made missiles which had sunk the British cruiser H.M.S. Sheffield during the Falklands War of 1982. In my world, I had always seen the French as *bon-vivants*, cultured livers of the good life who had elevated food and drink to the level of an art form. Lamy was the very antithesis of this image: a thin, wiry man with the clipped accent of an executioner. His average meal was more meagre than a European food-aid package to Africa and he was often seen pounding out the kilometres in the woods around Brussels. For most European mandarins jogging was a form of self-abuse bordering on masochism – and this was the man who ruled from Delors' private office with a rod of iron! No wonder that Lamy struck fear and terror into successive waves of European officials. Any attempt to bypass him or to manipulate him was destined to fail, following which the offender was likely to be banished to one of the less pleasant European postings. Under Lamy, the European Commission was kept on a very tight rein.

Even twenty years after his departure, the mere mention of his name is still enough to cause some senior mandarins to break out in a cold sweat. Yet having said that, it must be admitted that Lamy was one of the few people who was able to control all aspects of the European administrative apparatus and give it some degree of direction.

Pascal Lamy, the super-mandarin: the gendarme *of the Berlaymont.*

Jacques Delors was a totally different kettle of fish. He took his time, listened patiently to every question and offered his opinions in elegantly-crafted sentences.

'Do you want to speak to the President in French or English?' asked Paemen quietly in my ear.

I felt my fear of failure gradually ebbing away – in an emergency I could always switch to English, while Paemen was also on hand to clarify any possible misunderstandings. The Belgians make ideal mandarins: their 'adaptability' is legendary, while their lack of backbone is a positive virtue within the context of Europe.

'I've prepared everything in French,' I replied. 'Excellent,' whispered Paeman. 'The President will really appreciate it.'

Delors inherited a Europe which was almost dead on its feet. The process of European integration is subject to almost Wagnerian cycles of euphoria and depression. The early 1980s coincided with one of the periods of depression: deep depression. In 1979 Europe had been badly hit by the second oil crisis, which had seen energy prices soar. Unemployment rose dramatically and the European Community seemed powerless to help. The Princess and her loyal mandarins were in serious trouble.

The Commission was under the leadership of Gaston Thorn, a dapper little Luxembourgian, but he was unable to exert his authority to any significant extent. The European vessel seemed to be heading for shipwreck, blocked on the one hand by the British insistence that they were paying too much and burdened on the other hand by the French demand for farming subsidies on an enormous scale.

The European budget was locked in the past: more than 50% of its expenditure still went to agriculture, even though innovative sectors such as Research and Development were crying out for funds. Europe was swamped by costly butter mountains and milk lakes, while being forced to import all its new technology from Japan and the Far East.

In 1980, the British premier Margaret Thatcher launched an offensive against Europe: she wanted the British money back. The effects of this revolutionary step were felt far beyond the confines of her island home. Behaving with the intransigence of a petulant schoolgirl, she decided to veto every serious European proposal until she got her own way.

The machinery of Europe ground almost to a halt and it was not until the summit meeting at Fontainebleau in 1984 that a compromise solution was finally worked out. Its architect was the French president, François Mitterrand, who persuaded his European colleagues that London should get rebates for a large part of its contribution, while expenditure on agriculture would be limited by a system of quotas and levies.

As French Minister of Finance, Delors had been closely involved with the Fontainebleau compromise. As President of the European Commission, it was now his task to ensure that Fontainebleau heralded a new start and a new elan for the movement towards European integration.

'After my arrival in Brussels, I visited all the member states. Everywhere I heard the same complaint: Europe's decision-making processes are inadequate. We decide too slowly and we react to new situations ineffectively. However, now that our family squabbles are at an end, I also discovered that there is at least one subject on which there is full consensus: the single market. This market gives an extra dimension to our European companies and improves their competitiveness. Equally important, the single internal market gives our citizens the feeling that we all belong to the same nation. For these reasons, I decided to make the single market my main priority. Following the past example of Jean Monnet, the father of Europe, I also decided that it was necessary to set a date for this goal. The date I chose was 1992.'

If Delors hoped to succeed in this self-imposed mission, he was first obliged to do what all great politicians must do: master the details of the political procedures and then exploit these procedures to serve his higher purpose. This is extremely boring for the outside world, but it is the bread-and-butter of modern political life.

Two hundred years ago, Napoleon conquered Europe on the battlefields of Austerlitz, Jena and Wagram. Today's battle for Europe is fought in committee rooms and conference halls. The weaponry has also undergone a significant change: instead of cavalry and cannon, the fate of nations is now decided by administrative amendment and constructive compromise.

As the European Treaty provisions existed in 1985, all 12 member states were required to agree to any proposal to create the single market. To make this rigid decision-making process more flexible, Delors persuaded the member states to introduce a system of qualified majority voting, so that the national vetoes could no longer be used à la Thatcher to frustrate progress.

At the same time, he instructed the Commissioner for the Single Market, Lord Arthur Cockfield, to start drawing up the necessary practical proposals. The British Commissioner, a loyal supporter of the Iron Lady, worked with Cartesian precision to carry out this complicated task. Whatever Cockfield might think of Delors' political ideas, he catalogued directives and regulations with the efficiency of a computer. To most of us, these rules and procedures had more in common with a knitting pattern than with a great European ideal, but Cockfield's knowledge of the nuts and bolts of the single market was legendary.

Delors' efforts to give Europe a new elan commenced with the publication of '*Objectif 1992*'. It was not universally acclaimed. For many European federalists, Delors' declaration of intent did not go far enough. It was even criticised in the European Parliament by no less a person than Altiero Spinelli, the self-appointed conscience of Europe. I asked Delors if he felt betrayed by the pro-European faction.

'I wanted to go further and it would have been very easy for me to portray myself as the standard bearer of "desirable" Europe. However, my task is to build "acceptable" Europe.' With a Gallic shrug he added: 'We are all slaves to circumstance.'

I said that I understood and agreed with his position: in the process of European integration the means must be closely linked to the goals, otherwise the whole project could de-rail. Delors listened. Paemen nodded.

'Yes, you are right,' said the President. 'You have a very realistic attitude for a man of your age.' I wasn't sure whether this was intended as a compliment or an insult, but I thanked him for his time and left for home with my taped interview in my pocket.

I transcribed the spoken text into Dutch and sent it back to Delors' office, who arranged to have it translated into French, by the Commission services in Luxembourg. It was eventually returned to me with the President's comments. It was clear that he had read every word, doing full justice to his reputation as a stickler for accuracy and detail. What else can you expect from a former minister of finance?

His visit to the Netherlands took place as planned but my interview was hardly noticed by the media, notwithstanding its impressive four-page length. Europe was out of favour with the Dutch public and the meeting between the Dutch premier and the French President of the

European Commission was a major non-event. I seemed to have been wasting my time.

Twenty years down the line, things have changed very little. In the meantime, I have also become a European mandarin and have worked closely on the process of European integration with my 22,500 other colleagues. This might sound like a lot, but in reality it is only the same number as employed by the City of Amsterdam.

After two decades of relative optimism, Euro-pessimism has now returned with a bang. In the spring of 2005, both France and the Netherlands voted in national referenda to reject the European Constitution. The Berlaymont Building might be geographically close to the borders of both countries, but in terms of prevailing mentality it is a million miles away.

In 1984, I was able to view Euro-sclerosis from the bottom up. In 2005, my job in Brussels allowed me to see it from the top down. I listened with interest to the complaints of my colleagues and their failure to understand the reasons for the Dutch 'no' vote. The mandarins have worked all their lives – and often with conviction – for the cause of European integration, but they have never understood the realities of electoral politics. In particular, they have never been exposed to the anger of ordinary voters.

To be honest, even I failed to realise until the last couple of weeks that things were starting to go the wrong way. The campaign had been conducted on the assumption that the 'yes' supporters were destined to win, albeit with a fairly small majority. The European and Dutch parliaments had both given the constitution their approval and all the major political parties were in favour. What could possibly go wrong? Just one tiny thing: the electorate.

European mandarins are often the last people to recognise popular discontent. The revolutionary mob would need to be storming up the steps of the Berlaymont before most of them would realise that something is not quite right. To my shame, I experienced something similar within my own family in The Netherlands.

At one of our regular family get-togethers I suddenly and unexpectedly found myself under attack from my nearest and dearest, who always used to be in favour of European integration. Like most Dutchmen, they reaped the fruits of Europe: work at home, trips abroad and subsidies, if need be. But something was wrong. As they started drinking more wine, their anger turned into aggression.

'Why do you lot in Brussels want a new constitution? We've already got one! And a European President? What's wrong with our own Queen?' Almost everyone was unhappy about the way Europe was developing. 'It's all going too far and too fast. Soon even the Turks will be members and then we'll have no say at all!'

As the conversation progressed, it became clear that I was the only 'yes' supporter in the room – and even I was beginning to have second thoughts! Of course, in any election there are pro's and con's to be weighed. I remained convinced that the advantages of a 'yes' vote outweighed the disadvantages, but most of my fellow-countrymen felt differently. The Netherlands voted 'no'.

The mandarins from other European countries were perplexed. They couldn't understand what had happened.

'What's going on in Holland?' they asked me. 'Why are you so against Europe?'

I tried to explain by reference to the tiny fishing village of Urk. In Urk ninety percent of the voters had said 'no', notwithstanding the fact that about ninety percent of the families are dependent on European fishing subsidies. However, on this occasion money was not the first consideration with the strongly Calvinistic Urkers. They felt that the 'yes' campaign was a direct threat to the preservation of a national identity which officials in Brussels no longer seemed to think was important.

The bigger Europe becomes, the greater the need of ordinary people to defend what they see as their homeland. Or to put it another way, the bigger 'new' Europe becomes, the greater the uncertainty amongst the peoples of 'old' Europe. The mandarins had been working for decades on the blind assumption that the process of integration would eventually – and automatically – lead to a reduction in the power of the nation states. In the spring of 2005 they were forced to wake up to the realities of the situation: the nation state is alive and well, and living in the hearts of most European citizens of whatever country.

The Princess was not happy. She had done so much for her people. The farmers had received subsidies to maintain their standard of living. The Erasmus students could study for next to nothing in exotic foreign lands. Everyone could travel freely from one end of the continent to the other, using the cheap air tickets made possible by the liberalisation of the market. To top it all, the Euro had brought us all closer together and had enhanced purchasing power in a collective area containing some 500 million souls.

The Princess expected gratitude for so many good works. But the people turned their backs on the Princess. Worse, they ridiculed her and made her look foolish. The people were discontented, but the Princess could not understand why. Even so, these were her people and she could not – even if she wanted to – replace them by more grateful citizens. Perhaps she would just have to try another way of doing things.

The enlargement of Europe: work in progress.

Between the two low points of Euro-sclerosis, much has happened and much has changed. There have been twenty years of European euphoria, heralded in by Delors' *'Objectif 1992'*. In the Europe of 1986 there were only twelve member states. Now there are twenty-seven. The Berlin Wall has fallen, resulting in the reunification not only of Germany, but also of Europe on a wider scale. The treaties of Maastricht, Amsterdam and Nice have given new powers to Europe in a whole range of different areas – areas such as justice and foreign affairs, which were once the exclusive prerogative of the nation states. The Euro has become the standard method of payment throughout the continent – a market of more than half a billion potential customers.

The Commission has framed all these social, economic and political developments within a clear European context. In fact, it would be fair to say that the 22,500 mandarins (more than 11,000 of whom are policy-makers) have become the hard disc of European integration: the central repository of ideas and information which alone makes everything possible. They make proposals. They guide these proposals through the procedural minefield. They develop the technical measures necessary for the practical implementation. They monitor the long-term consequences and implications.

While it may be true to say that the engine of European integration occasionally sputters and stalls, it is equally true to say that without the Princess the engine would not work at all. In this respect, the 'no' votes in France and the Netherlands were a major blow to both the image and the self-esteem of the Princess. Her dream has been shattered and for the time being she has lost her way. Where should she go? What must she do?

Of course, during the past twenty years the Princess has also changed. She has become older and, perhaps, a little wiser. During the 1980s the European Commission was a multi-national corporation, dominated by French ideas, German officialdom and Italian creativity. Or as the British sceptics might have put it: French intellectuals, German bureaucrats and the Italian mafia.

At the very least, the Commission was an organisation run by men in Armani suits, with a strict hierarchy and an equally strict method of working. The Commissioners were referred to as *Monsieur le Commissaire* and the director-generals were addressed as *Monsieur le Directeur-Général*.

Those at the top counted for everything. Those at the bottom counted for nothing. Even after they had passed the fiendishly difficult entrance exams, new mandarins felt themselves be little more than a very small cog in a very large wheel. The Head of Section always showed deference to the Deputy director-general, while the Deputy director-general always bowed to the opinion of the director-general. The Commission was a closed and strictly ordered administrative machine.

When Delors was appointed in 1985, the Secretary-General of the Commission was Émile Noël, who was affectionately known as Father Christmas: *Noël* means 'Christmas' in French. This amiable Frenchman had filled the post since 1958 and when he retired in the mid-1980s the Commission had some 25 director-generals. Today there are no fewer than 35, with no sign of the number shrinking.

The enlargement of the European Union and the changing attitudes of the times have also had their effect on the Princess. The arrival of new mandarins from the northern and eastern extremities of Europe has led to an influx of new cultural values.

'Participation' and 'consultation' became the new buzz words, an idea box made its appearance in the Berlaymont Building and a European Ombudsman was appointed to deal with complaints from European

A historic breakthrough. The map of Europe is redrawn.

citizens and – more often than not – European mandarins. Instead of being 'top down', this new philosophy was intended to work 'bottom up'. Mandarins who for decades had been used to the concept of 'service' were now expected to cope with the very different concept of 'empowerment' – whatever that might mean.

The new Commissioners from more egalitarian cultures no longer saw themselves as *Monsieur le Commissaire*, with a status equivalent to that of a sun god, but rather as a friend to their staff and a source of accessible information for their citizens. Many of them tried to behave 'ordinarily', which placed the existing mandarin structure under an intolerable strain.

If the Commissioners started to behave like normal human beings, it was impossible for *Monsieur le Directeur-Général* to maintain his position of lofty detachment at the top of the administrative tree. He, too, was obliged to adopt a more populist approach. The resulting changes were dramatic: a reduction of 'Frenchness' in the day-to-day business of the Commission, a more informal manner of communication, looser hierarchical structures and an increase in the number of women.

The first women were appointed to the College of Commissioners in the 1990s. By 2004 seven of the twenty-five Commissioners were women and in 2006 the Commission welcomed its first female Secretary-General. Today in the Berlaymont Building it is not uncommon to see men without ties – unthinkable in the past – while during the school holidays the children of senior women officials play football in the corridors. The times they are a-changing.

The Commission is no longer a mixture of French bureaucracy, the German military and the Italian academy of art, with an occasional British busybody thrown in. The enlargement of the European Union to 27 countries has helped to dilute national identity within the administrative structure. No single country is able to dominate.

With 80 million inhabitants, Germany is the largest country in the Union but the Princess only employs about 2,000 Germans, of whom 1,300 are policy-makers. With much smaller national populations, the French have 2,400 mandarins, the Italians 2,500 and the Spanish 1,800. The Belgians are massively over-represented. With just 10 million citizens, they provide the Princess with no fewer than 5,000 of her servants, including 1,200 policy-makers and an armada of secretaries. With a similar population, Austria has only 450 of its citizens employed by the Commission, while the 16 million Dutch are good for just 750 mandarins.

Member states of the EU which are underrepresented in numbers of officials may be compensated by a stronger representation in the higher echelons, like the level of director-general. Whatever their European credentials, all member states lobby feverishly to get their nationals employed as mandarins in the court of the Princess. Even in the heart of Europe, one's own nationals come first.

European Commission officials (permanent and temporary) by nationality

On October 1 2006:
1. Belgium: 4,932
2. France: 2,747
3. Italy: 2,582
4. Germany: 2,043
5. Spain: 1,800
6. UK: 1,429
7. Greece: 936
8. Portugal: 758
9. Netherlands: 753
10. Finland: 620
11. Sweden: 601
12. Ireland: 562
13. Poland: 539
14. Austria: 446
15. Denmark: 405
16. Hungary: 332
17. Luxembourg: 267
18. Czech Republic: 255

19. Slovakia: 166
20. Lithuania: 138
21. Estonia: 121
22. Slovenia: 121
23. Latvia: 113
24. Malta: 66
25. Cyprus: 58

On 1/1/2007:

26. Romania: 134
27. Bulgaria: 96

Source: Commission website

The mandarin system was originally developed in ancient China, where there were nine different ranks. The European mandarins have traditionally been divided into four categories: A (policy-making), B (implementing), C (secretarial) and D (drivers and messengers). Within each category there are different grades. In the old days a newly-appointed policy-maker would begin as an A7, whereas a director-general was an A1.

In theory, promotion was awarded on merit, following a regular programme of evaluation and assessment. 'Merit', however, is a flexible concept: while most mandarins think they possess a high degree of this precious commodity, their superiors often think differently.

In recent years, the grading system has been completely revised. The beginner is now an AD (Administrator) 5, while the director-general is now designated as an AD 16. The other categories have undergone similar changes. Under the policy-making level of AD is now the category AST (Assistant), which merged the former B, C and D grades.

Equally important, the barriers between the different categories have been removed. In principal, a secretary from category AST can now be promoted all the way to a policy-making job in category AD.

In practice, however, this is unlikely to happen and the differences between the categories remain entrenched. In ancient China these differences were accepted by the mandarins as being part of the natural order of things. This is unacceptable in 'egalitarian' Europe, where the pretence of equality has to be maintained at all times and in all places.

Together with Belgium, Italy provides the highest proportion of drivers and secretaries. Both these countries have a strong tradition of trade unionism and there are several union organisations to keep a close watch on the activity of the mandarins. These unions even have a Central Committee: a title which nowadays is more usually associated with the fossilised political structures of Cuba and North Korea!

The trade-unionism of the Belgian and Italian employees can sometimes have unfortunate effects when things go wrong. If a policy-maker is angry, he will usually vent his frustration on a colleague from a lower-grade. This person will respond by making life hell for his/her secretary, while the secretary in turn will take it out on the driver or the messenger. Unfortunately for them, the drivers and the messengers have no suitable targets for vengeance – and so they go on strike.

This is a regular occurrence, as a result of which I have been forced on several occasions to drive my Commissioner to official functions or the airport in my own car. The chauffeur was 'exercising his democratic right'.

Happily, the Princess is able to take all these things in her stride. She is a tough lady and throughout the years she has survived the attentions of a varied entourage: careerists, legalists, activists, socialists – even alcoholics.

But there is one type of person the Princess has always had problems with: dissidents. The Princess has never been able to accept opposition from within her own household. As the chief representative of the great European ideal, she often displays the same kind of missionary zeal as a religious leader. Anyone who does not wholly agree with the ideal, or with the manner of its implementation, is instantly branded as a traitor or a heretic.

The sanctions are clear: bureaucratic isolation, demotion and – if necessary – dismissal. It is a method of discipline based on outright intimidation and for a long time it worked amazingly well.

Towards the end of the 1990s the Princess began to have more frequent difficulties with whistle-blowers and alarmists. They were relatively few in number, but one was troublesome enough to cause the Princess to stumble – and fall. In 1999 the Commission resigned prematurely – and in my opinion unnecessarily.

The cause of all this trouble was a single dissident, who pursued a one-man campaign for greater financial responsibility within the Union. His name was Paul and he made European history – although he probably didn't enjoy it at the time!

Even before I ever met Paul, I had been warned by other mandarins to watch out for this dangerous character. He was variously reported as being mad, unreliable, paranoid, fanatical, sensationalist – and lazy.

To make matters worse, this pain in the royal neck was a mandarin from the lowly B category. The Princess was not toppled from her throne by the intrigues of a senior official but by the scare stories of a lowly water-carrier.

The administrative machine responded in a predictable manner. Paul was banished to an office in Luxembourg – Europe's bureaucratic equivalent of Siberia. He was allowed to do no work of any importance and spent most of the next few years reading newspapers.

I got to know Paul later and couldn't understand what all the fuss was about. He seemed quite a nice chap. I did, however, start wondering how he might have behaved, had he been handled with greater ease. I had just been reading Zores Medvedev's book about Yuri Andropov, who between 1967 and 1982 was director of the KGB – the notorious secret service of the Soviet Union. Oddly enough, even the Princess could have learnt a thing or two from his dealings with dissidents!

When Andropov had been appointed in 1967 he found a service which had changed little since Stalin's day. It was expert in murder and mayhem, but in little else. Andropov immediately began to make the KGB more professional – or at the very least he tried to make it smarter than the members of the Politburo of the ruling Communist Party. When dissidents had started to make their appearance in the Soviet Union during the 1970s the Politburo had responded by banishing the offenders to the icy wastes of Siberia.

Whenever the name of a prominent dissident was mentioned during the meeting, most members of the Politburo pounded on the table and shouted: 'Siberia, Siberia!' It was hoped that the almost continual sub-zero temperatures would make these hot-heads think again. If not, they could be declared insane and locked away indefinitely. After all, the Soviet Union was a model state, a worker's paradise on earth: anyone who criticised it had to be mad – or so thought the Politburo.

Andropov saw the matter differently. He gave the dissidents – at least the famous ones, the ones who were causing so much bad publicity –

Yuri Andropov, former director of the KGB. How to deal with European dissidents?

the chance to leave the country. He reasoned that they would remain in the spotlight in the West for just a few months, following which they would fade into obscurity. And he was right.

It was world news when the dissident Vladimir Bukovski was exchanged for the Chilean communist leader Luis Corvalan, but six months later Bukovski had all but disappeared from view. Even the famous dissident writer Alexander Solzhenitsyn met the same fate when he moved to the West. Gradually, the dissidents began to realise what was going on. As a result, some of them refused to go.

The best known of the 'refuseniks' was Andrei Sakharov. Andropov invited him for cosy afternoon teas, in the hope of persuading him to emigrate, but Sakharov remained adamant: he was staying. Nor was it possible to use the 'insanity' ploy in Sacharov's case. As a leading member of the Soviet Academy of Science, this would have been stretching credibility, even by Kremlin standards: Sakharov was a nuclear physicist and had helped on the Soviet atomic programme. Sakharov even refused to go to Oslo when he won the Nobel Prize for Peace in 1975, fearing that Andropov wouldn't let him back in the country. He eventually went, following a personal guarantee from the boss of the KGB. By this time Andropov had had enough and Sakharov was eventually banished from Moscow – but only as far as Gorki, just some 200 kilometres from the Russian capital. It was a mild punishment in terms of distance, considering the size of the country.

After Gorbachev came to power, Sakharov was allowed to return to Moscow. He became an elected member of the Congress of People's Deputies, where he insisted that political reforms should go much further. Sakharov died in 1989. His wife, Elena Bonner, founded an institute and a museum in Moscow named after Sakharov. He had become an icon in the struggle for human rights.

What lessons should the European mandarins draw from this Russian example? Namely that it is better to shower praise on dissidents – and preferably by the bucket-load. This is what the Princess should have done with Paul – who later, more or less by chance, became a member of the European Parliament. The lesson was eventually learnt, but much too late. It was only after years of bickering, arguments and negative publicity that Paul was finally engaged in a constructive dialogue; a dialogue which resulted in a useful and meaningful exchange of information. The troublemaker was finally brought in from the cold.

It must be admitted, however, that Paul was something of a special case. In addition to the monomania usually associated with the self-appointed advocates of righteous causes, he also showed ultra-religious tendencies. In other words, he thought that he was doing God's work. He held prayer meetings with Commission mandarins, attached crucifixes to the walls of his office and always had a bible within easy reach. To me, this was his constitutional right. But in a Europe where the cultural-political elite regard religion as irrelevant, or a private activity based on mere superstition, the mandarins scarcely knew how to deal with a troublemaker who had a direct line to the Almighty.

Even so, if the mandarins had followed the Andropov example, perhaps the Commission might have avoided its untimely resignation in 1999.

2| Into the Labyrinth

'Idiot! Of course you have to lobby for yourself!' My student friend from Leiden looked at me with the kind of sympathy usually reserved for dumb animals on the way to the slaughterhouse. I had just told him that I had sent off my application for a traineeship with the European Commission, but that I wasn't planning to take any follow-up action. Why should I? With my two university degrees, all I needed to do was to wait for a positive answer.

'Then you'll be waiting a bloody long time,' he sneered. 'You have to promote yourself, get yourself in the picture, make yourself known to the right people. If you don't do it, nobody else is going to do it for you!' He shook his head in despair. Clearly, I was beyond all hope.

'Lobbying?' I said, as though the word left a nasty taste in my mouth. 'For myself?' As a student of the Protestant Free University of Amsterdam, it somehow didn't seem quite right. On the contrary, it seemed positively perverse, a kind of prostitution with clothes on. Lobbying was for egotists and self-opinionated snobs, not for a decent Christian boy like myself. My university degrees were good ones: they would be enough to get me the job I wanted. I didn't need to employ dubious methods of doubtful morality, did I?

Unfortunately, I did. My friend was right and I was wrong. A month later I received a one-line letter from Brussels. 'I regret to inform you that on this occasion you have not been chosen to fill a traineeship with the European Commission. Yours sincerely, Head of Traineeship Office.'

In the meantime, my friend from Leiden had managed to secure his own traineeship with the European Commission – and a good one. He was employed by the Secretariat-General and was responsible for liaison with members of the European Parliament. I suspected that he had arranged this job through the University of Leiden, an academic institution with a well-respected Faculty of Law and many well-placed friends in Brussels. The same could not be said of either of the two Amsterdam universities.

The Free University did not even have a course in European Law, probably because it saw the Treaty of Rome as part of some fiendish Catholic conspiracy. The left-wing University of Amsterdam did teach European Law, but most of its lecturers regarded the European Community as a bastion of capitalism and a protector of the great multinational corporations. They were not interested in markets: they were still interested in Marx. Hardly the ideal way to gain favour with the mandarins of Brussels.

'I suppose your university got you into the Commission?' I said to my friend one day, hoping to disguise my own failure. 'No they bloody well didn't!' he replied testily. 'I did it all by myself. I got off my ass, and went and did some lobbying. I've told you before: it's the only way to succeed. Try it next time.' We agreed that I would apply for the following batch of traineeships and that I would come and stay with him in Brussels, so that this time I could do some serious lobbying. I still had no idea what this actually involved – it still sounded slightly dirty – but he promised that he would show me the ropes. Even so, it was with some trepidation that I took the train to Belgium – I had the feeling that I wasn't going to enjoy this.

By now my friend was settled into room 34 on the 11th floor of the Berlaymont. 'Room' was perhaps a slight exaggeration: it was more a kind of glorified rabbit hutch with a window the size of a postage stamp.

Even so, the postage stamp gave a stunning view over the roofs of Brussels. More importantly, it confirmed his status as a fully-fledged trainee of the European Commission. Now it was going to be my turn – or so I hoped.

Things, however, got off to a bad start. I had hardly set foot in the rabbit hutch before my friend said to me: 'Where's your jacket and tie? Don't tell me you haven't brought a jacket and tie.' I told him I hadn't brought a jacket and tie. Why should I?

'Why, why, why? Why do you think? You are about to start lobbying with some of the most important men in Brussels. Men who can put your name in the blue book. Men who can decide whether or not you get a traineeship. Men who expect you to look neat and professional – not like someone about to set off on a Himalayan mountain trek!!'

He had a point. After my three-hour train journey I did look a little shabbier than usual and it was true that everyone I had seen since my arrival in the Berlaymont looked as though they were dressed for church on Sunday. This lobbying business was obviously more complicated than I thought.

My friend had the answer to our problem. 'Here, take my jacket and tie. I'll stay in the office, while you go and present yourself to one or two officials.'

I did as I was told, but the jacket was much too small. To make matters worse, while I was getting ready one of my friend's new colleagues knocked on the door to ask him a question. In my tie-less state I was still not fit to be seen by a real European mandarin and so I dived into the room's only cupboard, while my pal conducted a valiant delaying action at the door.

Luckily, the mandarin departed as quickly as he came and I was allowed out of the cupboard just before suffocation set in. By now, my friend's jacket was on the point of disintegrating. My shoulders were much too broad and it was only by walking like a penguin that I was able to prevent the thing from bursting at the seams.

My friend was undeterred. 'You look fine. Here, put the tie on.' I had to confess that I almost never wore a tie and didn't know how to make the knot. My friend said nothing, sighed heavily, made the knot for me and sat me down next to the telephone. Like the director of a Hollywood movie, he explained the next stage of the lobbying operation.

'Now you've got to call a few senior officials and ask them if you can drop in for a brief chat. Sound confident and determined. If you don't, they'll just tell you to get lost.' He gradually began warming to his theme. 'To start with, try the cabinet of the Dutch Commissioner. The cabinets are where the real power is. They can get your name in the blue book. All the new trainees are chosen out of that book.' In spite of his relative inexperience, I could hear a note of awe and respect in his voice: one day he would make a very good mandarin.

I was not so convinced about myself. Lobbying was definitely not my cup of tea and it was only with a great effort of will that I picked up the phone and started to dial. It was difficult to get the officials themselves on the line but the secretaries sounded friendly and tried to be helpful. The Dutch ones were cool and business-like, while the Belgian ones all had soft, sensual voices that reminded me of film stars. Fifteen minutes later I had arranged a couple of appointments and I set off along the corridor in my ill-fitting jacket and tie. I looked like an advertisement for an Oxfam Shop.

I took the lift to the 12th floor, where the cabinets of the Commissioners were located. One of the secretaries was waiting for me.

'Just take a seat for a few minutes. He's still in a meeting.' I said nothing and did as I was told. The secretary must have noted a certain shyness in my demeanour and this seemed to bring out the mothering instinct in her. She tried to put me at my ease with a little friendly conversation and asked if I would like a glass of water. It was kind, but I was too nervous to hold a glass without spilling it and so I replied that I wasn't thirsty.

Suddenly, the door to the mandarin's office opened. The meeting was over: now it was my turn. I entered and came face to face with my first real mandarin, the man who held the power of the blue book!

'Where do you come from and where did you study?' he began, almost without preamble.

As a son of the Dutch countryside, without a famous name and not even having studied at the University of Leiden, I didn't think I had much chance. Princes and princesses had no such selection problems: blue blood found its way easily into the blue book. The children of the rich and famous were equally well-favoured, as were the children of existing mandarins. Some countries – France, for example – also had special quotas for exceptional students, such as those from the *Ecole Nationale d'Administration*.

The mandarin looked me straight in the eyes. 'The competition is very severe,' he said, as if wishing to crush every last bit of my rapidly fading optimism. Yet somewhere deep inside he also had some sympathy for me. Perhaps he just felt sorry for anyone with a dress sense as terrible as mine.

Ecole Nationale d'Administration *in Strasbourg. Always one step ahead of the rest, even in Brussels.*

'Do you have a director or head of section who wants to take you on?' 'No,' I replied, almost pathetically. 'You're the first person I've seen!' The man who held my fate in his hands leant back in his chair and closed his eyes in thought. After what seemed an age, he opened them again. 'Alright. I'll put your name in the blue book. But make sure you find someone prepared to give you a place. And do it quickly!'

He shook my hand and before I knew it I was back outside in the secretary's office. She did her utmost to encourage me.

'Just do your best. I'm sure you'll manage. And if you want to know anything, just give me a ring.' I had no guarantees but I had learnt that a secretary can be a useful ally in the hard world of the Berlaymont.

They can offer access to the mandarins and can also influence their decisions in cases of doubt. Their mother instinct is simultaneously their strength and their weakness – a point which I hoped I could use to my advantage.

Back on the 11th floor, I talked things over with my friend from Leiden. 'The man in the Commissioner's office told me that I need to find a place.' Like his senior colleague upstairs, my friend leant back and closed his eyes. 'What contacts do you have here?' he asked. 'None,' I replied truthfully.

He reached into his desk drawer and took out an organisation chart of the Commission and the internal telephone directory. 'Try and find a directorate that interests you, phone the director and make an appointment. Begin with the Dutch and the Belgians: that's where you'll have most chance. The other nationalities just take care of their own people.'

I was slightly shocked by this comment. I had always assumed – as I had been taught at university – that the European Commission was for all Europeans. My friend must have read my thoughts.

'Forget what you learned during your studies. You're in the real world now.' I pulled myself together and dialled the number of a Belgian responsible for regional policy. He wasn't particularly helpful, but perhaps it was something to do with his unfortunate name: Vanghinderachter. Next I tried a Dutchman whose work centred around 'article 113'. As I had no idea what article 113 was, my interview with him was even shorter than with the Belgian. Discouraged, I made my way back to the 11th floor.

By this stage, my friend was becoming equally fed up with my dismal record of failure. He had one final suggestion to make.

'Look, if you like I can introduce you to my training manager and ask him if you can take my place in the Secretariat-General when I'm finished.' It was a generous offer and I said so. 'My manager is British and his name is John. If he agrees, you'll have to go to the director and get his approval as well. He's also called John but he comes from Luxembourg. The Luxembourgers get on fairly well with the Dutch, so you might be OK.'

I reached for the phone and dialled the number of the first John, whose office was two doors along the corridor. Fully realising that this was my last chance to become a European mandarin, I put on my most professional voice and asked to make an appointment. The secretary said that she would speak to her boss and after a brief delay told me to come along as soon as I could. Thirty seconds later I was knocking on her door. 'My goodness, that was quick. You must be really keen.' I assured her that I was and she showed me into John's office.

It was a strange experience. The room was almost completely dark, since the blinds had been closed to keep out every ray of the afternoon sun. The desk was covered with two huge piles of books and a stack of loose papers. Behind this bureaucratic mountain sat a man, who I took to be John.

He looked up from his work and said: 'You must be the Dutchman. What do you think about the debate in The Hague over the deployment of cruise missiles? Aren't they a bunch of tossers?'

I was surprised that a British mandarin should even have heard of these heated discussions. To add to my confusion, I had no idea what the word 'tosser' meant – although I didn't think it was complimentary.

I decided to be non-committal. 'Yeah, it's a real mess. Prime Minister Lubbers always thinks of at least five different scenarios for every situation. So with 50 rockets, that makes a total of 250 scenarios. That should be enough to keep even the Kremlin guessing.'

The Brit laughed out loud. 'Ha. That Lubbers! He's the biggest tosser of them all!' Next he asked me whether or not the Socialists would maintain their opposition to the deployment. 'I think so,' I replied. 'Dutch socialism is just a variant of Calvinism. And if the Calvinists get something in their heads, it's very difficult to get it out again.' He jumped to his feet. 'Yes, Holland: the country of vicars!'

John clearly had a healthy sense of humour, certainly by normal mandarin standards. He said goodbye and I went back to the office of my friend from Leiden. A little later John called him on the phone. I was able to listen in to the conversation. 'Yes, he's fine with me. I had a good laugh with him: he's quite a character. But now he has to convince the director.'

This was, indeed, my next task. I had passed the first test but success was by no means assured. According to my friend, the director was a real top-brass bureaucrat. His suit was always perfect and he was fluent in French, German and English. He even spoke a little Dutch.

Above all, he was known as someone who paid great attention to order and detail. If he read a memorandum, he marked every important word with a Stabilo highlighting pen. In fact, his staff all referred to him as Stabilo. My friend set out our campaign strategy. 'We can't improvise with Stabilo. It's going to take more than a jazzy tie and a penguin suit to convince him. What we need is a really strong recommendation from a well-respected person. Any ideas?'

We decided that I needed a second round of lobbying – but this time properly prepared. I left for home to see what I could arrange, but was worried about that letter of recommendation. Who on earth could I ask?

Back in my home village of Bronckhorst, I explained the situation to my parents. 'I can only hope to persuade Stabilo with a really good letter of recommendation.' My father, who was actively engaged in local politics, said that he would take the matter up with the mayor.

The mayor ruled our village like some kind of medieval fiefdom, but he always got a good write-up in the local press. This was hardly surprising. The local correspondent of the regional newspaper, *De Graafschapbode*, also came from our village and the two of them wrote the article on the municipal council meeting together. This was then passed on to the local bus driver, who handed it in to the newspaper office in the nearby town.

This simple but effective means of self-publicity meant that our mayor acquired quite a reputation in the district. This allowed him to make numerous 'study visits' with other mayors, often to quite exotic locations. He was a supporter of European integration, which he saw as the way to the future, and one of his more successful study visits had already taken him to the European Parliament in Strasbourg.

But things didn't always go that smoothly. During a visit to South Africa in the Botha era he was once heard to remark – loudly in the bar of a Johannesburg hotel – that the problem of the black South Africans was the same as the problem of the gypsies in the Netherlands. Unfortunately, the mayor had failed to notice that the stool two places further along the bar was occupied by a journalist from the Dutch left-wing weekly, *Vrij Nederland*. This journalist was not impressed by the mayor's comparison and said so at length in his next column.

The result was a major row. In particular, the mayor was furious that the *Vrij Nederland* journalist did not apply the same 'ethical norms' as his colleague from *De Graafschapbode*, who at least submitted his articles for approval by the mayor! But he needn't have worried. The Christian-democrat majority in the village council gave him their full support: they actually thought that the Bothas were doing rather a good job in South Africa and still preferred the idea of 'white rule' to 'black chaos'.

But the mayor had learnt an important lesson. From then on he was more careful about the comments he made in bars, particularly if there were strangers about. However, there were no such problems in his own local pub, *'Den Meut'*. Here the village secretary kept a careful lookout for potential eavesdroppers and even the drive home after a glass too many was guaranteed to be trouble-free. The mayor was also head of the local police, so there was little chance of anybody stopping him for a breath-test!

From time to time I had attended council meetings and so I knew the mayor quite well. Perhaps it was for this reason that he turned to me with one of his famous plans for 'putting our village on the map'. On this occasion, the plan involved a team from our village taking part in a radio quiz organised by the Christian broadcasting service.

I was 'asked' to be a member of the team and our mission was to crush the team from a neighbouring village. This would bring credit to our village – and, of course, to the mayor who, not surprisingly, was team captain.

The radio station sent two of its assistants from Hilversum to prepare the programme, which was to be broadcast live. In this case, the assistants were two absolute stunners: blonde, beautiful and with curves in all the right places. The mayor was delighted. For a man used to dealing with farmers' wives in muddy wellingtons, this was a pleasant change. Bursting with pride, he gave them the grand tour of the council building, pausing to give special emphasis to his own office: 'the nerve-centre of the whole operation,' as he put it.

Afterwards we moved on to 'Den Meut', where the surprised landlord was persuaded to provide us with food and drink: plenty of drink. During the meal, the mayor took centre stage, regaling our guests with tales of his many good works in the village and offering his opinions on a range of political matters, including the European Community. The wine flowed freely, and even the village secretary – who was responsible for making sure that all this revelry didn't cost too much – got a little bit tipsy.

The ladies began talking about their life in Hilversum. This city is the centre of the Dutch television and radio industry, but it also has a reputation for sexual promiscuity: it is popularly nicknamed 'The Mattress'. One of the blondes explained the problems faced by a pretty young woman in a city of this kind. 'The men only take you out because they want to go to bed with you.' The mayor pricked up his ears, while the secretary cleared his throat uneasily. The drinkers at the bar put down their glasses and turned to listen. The blonde carried on regardless. 'You just have to make things clear to them. That's why I always tell them: "I'm happy to have something to eat with you but I'm not going to have sex with you..."'.

It was one of those moments when time seems to stand still. The barman stood with mouth wide open. The card-players sat frozen in the middle of their game. The secretary spluttered into his beer. We were not used to this kind of public confession in Bronckhorst – and certainly not from a woman. After a silence which seemed to last for ever, it was the mayor who spoke first, trying to rescue a hopeless situation: 'I see. Dinner yes; sex no! Well, that is fairly clear...'.

Following this debacle, I suppose it was inevitable that we would lose the quiz – and we did. We were soundly thrashed by a village from Twente, but I had at least 'done my bit' for the mayor. Now it was his turn to do something for me.

The mayor was happy to help me with my letter of recommendation, but felt that it might be better coming from someone more closely linked to the European set-up. 'What you really need is a member of the European Parliament to write the letter for you. And I think I know just the man to do it!'

The man in question was the Euro-MP for Zutphen, who was known both to the mayor and to my father. After a couple of introductory phone calls, it was agreed that I should meet him at a local political rally. He seemed only too willing to lend a helping hand to someone from his own region. 'Of course I'll write a letter for you. Just let me know where I have to send it and when. And let's meet up when you get to Brussels.' Delighted and relieved, it was with renewed confidence that I set off for Brussels for my second round of lobbying: this time with the dreaded Stabilo.

Immaculately dressed in suit and tie, I climbed the steps of the Berlaymont and took the lift to the 11th floor. My friend from Leiden was in an optimistic mood. The letter from Zutphen had already arrived and had made a good impression. 'Stabilo is responsible for relations with the Parliament, so a letter from a Euro-MP can work wonders. You're in with a good chance now,' he added. 'The rest is up to you.' He disappeared quickly into his office, in case our 'conspiracy' should become too obvious to others working in the section. I wandered down the corridor and knocked on the door of Stabilo's office. It was opened by a charming secretary, who told me that I had ten minutes to make my case. I would have to work fast.

Stabilo's office was much as I had expected it: neat piles of papers, neat rows of pens, no nonsense, no mess, everything in its proper place. And close to his right hand? A Stabilo marker.

'So you want to become a trainee?' he asked in a fatherly tone. He looked like the epitome of a senior mandarin: serious, shrewd, calculating. I was impressed by the number of windows in his office: the contrast with John's dingy room was striking. This was obviously a man who counted. 'I've read the letter from Zutphen and found it very positive. It says you come from a "sound" family.' This was positive indeed: 'soundness' is the natural ally of every mandarin. 'Good. Let's give it a try, shall we? Do your best to fit into the team, remember you are a beginner, be nice to the secretaries and try to do your job conscientiously.' I could hardly believe my ears. 'You mean, I'm in?' I stammered. 'Yes,' he replied, 'you're in.' I shook his hand and almost ran down the corridor back to the office of my friend: 'I've done it! I'm in!'

A traineeship with the Princess is a great opportunity. You have few responsibilities but learn a great deal. Everything is new, everything is interesting and you are untroubled by the office politics which are a source of constant worry to the real mandarins. You get a broad view, albeit of a relatively limited field.

My particular field was relations with the European Parliament, a task I carried out under the guidance of John and Wouter, a fellow Dutchman but a true Anglophile. At this time, the Parliament contained some great names, such as Willy Brandt who was almost never there, Barbara Castle who was a furious critic of a federal Europe and Altiero Spinelli who was its most enthusiastic supporter.

This colourful talking-shop was headed by Piet Dankert, who managed to combine a Latin lifestyle with Calvinistic stubbornness. His French wife had helped to turn him into a *bon-vivant*, but in money matters he was still as tight-fisted as your average Friesian farmer. On one occasion Dankert wanted to dismiss a French official who had

Piet Dankert, a past chairman of the European Parliament, combined Friesian stubbornness with French style.

used the Parliament's money to speculate on the stock market. This wasn't as easy as it might seem. The Frenchman – with the appropriate name of *Monsieur* Le Compte – received support from the entire French delegation, under the leadership of the legendary Simone Veil. Pressed hard by Veil, Dankert was forced to back down and the two remained enemies for life.

The day-to-day work of the average Commission mandarin was far less dramatic and consisted largely of making notes about the discussions of the various parliamentary committees. These notes were checked and corrected by Stabilo, before being passed up the hierarchical chain. I never discovered on whose desk the notes eventually landed but that hardly seemed to matter. The Commission has a collective memory which is fed from many different sources – including my little notes!

Commuting as I did between the Commission and the European Parliament, I quickly noted a difference in atmosphere between the two institutions. The Commission had a strict hierarchy and a business-like approach. In contrast, the Euro-MPs ran around the corridors of the Parliament, frantically searching for lost papers and chasing missed appointments The Commission used formal methods of address (for example, the *vous* form in French), whereas everyone in the Parliament was quickly on first name terms, even the assistants and translators. The Commission was a political machine. The Parliament was a political club.

The informality of the Parliament perhaps found its best expression in the famous Copper Bar, which was situated next to the plenary chamber of the Council of Europe in Strasbourg. So named because its serving counter was actually made of copper, this bar was a favourite haunt of both politicians and officials alike.

It was invariably packed with people carrying sheaves of impressive-looking papers, stopping for a coffee or a Perrier before moving on importantly to their next meeting. In reality, it was a kind of central station, which grew busier and busier as aperitif hour approached. The atmosphere was conspiratorial, almost sultry. Little wonder that the Copper Bar was the starting point for many romantic liaisons and illicit relationships. Armed with a *kir royale*, it was the ideal place to see and be seen, to hunt and be hunted. This was not exactly John's scene (he preferred books!) but Wouter and his friend Han (who worked for the Council of Ministers) felt right at home. They were soon joined by a third partner-in-crime: Henk, whose deep, sonorous voice could always be heard above the general din of the Copper Bar.

The droves of young female assistants were easy targets for these skilled, shrewd hunters. If their charm, easy manner and *Wichtigteuerei* didn't work, the large quantities of booze could generally be relied upon to do the trick. Perhaps inspired by these young bucks, ministers and MP's also frequented the Copper Bar to see if there were any 'leftovers'. Night-time sessions inside Parliament were often followed by night-time sessions outside Parliament. It is certainly true to say that the Copper Bar did very little to promote the family values which were so frequently preached during the parliamentary debates!

Gradually, I began to appreciate this informal approach and started more and more to join in with the fun and games of the three musketeers. It gave me new insights into the structure of the European hierarchy: mandarinism with a human face. That being said, if I ever went too far in the wrong direction, there was always the strictness of the Commission to bring me back down to earth with a bump.

I experienced this one weekend, when I was working on an essay for the Japanese Embassy. Each year the Japanese organise an essay contest, centred around a theme relevant to their country. The main prize was a free trip to Japan, a land I had never visited. I decided to give it a try and wrote an essay over the arms race in Europe and its impact on Japan.

At this time, many European politicians hoped to persuade the Soviet Union to transfer the bulk of its SS 20 missiles to Asiatic Russia, a prospect which hardly filled the Japanese with delight. I therefore suggested that a dialogue was necessary between Tokyo and the EU before any such drastic decision was taken. I knew it was an idea likely to appeal to the people marking the essay!

I wrote the essay one weekend and went into the Berlaymont to type it out, since I didn't have a typewriter in my apartment. At the reception desk, I had to check in by noting my name in a register: that was the rule. Since there was almost nobody in the building, it hardly seemed important. Instead of my own name, I wrote 'Vladimir Ulyanov; 11th floor, room 34, 11 o'clock.'

I thought this was clever, a personal one-man protest against the futility of bureaucratic procedures. Apparently, not everyone shared my sense of humour. At five o'clock, I heard footsteps in the corridor outside my room. A head appeared around the door and asked: 'Mr. Ulyanov, are you finished? My shift is nearly over and it's time to leave.' It was the guard doing his last security check before he went home, making sure that the man with the suspicious-sounding name really was in room 34. He didn't seem to know that Ulyanov was the real name of one Vladimir Ilyich Lenin!

I was interested to see how long I could get away with this, and so the next day I signed in as Lev Bronstein, who was better known to history as Leon Trotsky. Precisely the same thing happened. At five o' clock a new head appeared and asked: 'Are you staying much longer, Mr. Bronstein?' 'Just an hour or so,' I replied. He nodded and left without complaint. Clearly, the Commission's guards had never studied the Russian Revolution at school!

On Monday, I told John about my schoolboy prank, thinking he would find it amusing. On the contrary: he was furious. To tease him, I said that next time I was planning to sign in as Joseph Vissarionovich Dzhugashvili (Joseph Stalin, of course), although I doubted whether I could get the long Georgian name into the space provided!

It was then that I realised that John was really mad. 'You stupid fool! You could lose your job for this!' I said I didn't believe him: if the guards were typical of the Commission's security service, then I didn't think I had much to fear. To underline my point, I showed him the page in the internal telephone directory headed '*Securité*': 'Look,' I said triumphantly, 'Just one name: De Haan!' 'What do you expect?' he countered. 'De Haan is the director, but he has a whole department under him. Their names are kept secret.'

Now I did start to worry and for the next few anxious days I sat waiting for a new knock on the door: this time from Mr. De Haan or one of his colleagues! Luckily, I got away with just a bad scare and to get back on good terms with John, I asked if he would look at my essay. He said he would be happy to. After he had changed my Euro English into British English, I sent it off to the Japanese Embassy in The

Hague, never expecting to hear anything more about it. To my amazement (and John's) I won: at the end of my traineeship I could go on a study tour to Japan!

During my time at the Berlaymont a whole new batch of candidate trainees arrived, all intent on lobbying their way into a job, just as I had done. I was paid a visit by a young man from Nijmegen called Peter, who was clearly interested in my position in the Secretariat-General. I rather liked him and it was arranged with John that Peter should take over from me when I left (I had recently been appointed as a personal assistant for several Euro-MPs).

Peter was the sort of person everybody notices and he was even more 'difficult' than I was. Even though he came from the Catholic south of the Netherlands, he possessed a strong streak of Calvinist stubbornness. If Peter got an idea in his head, nothing – and I do mean absolutely nothing! – would get it out again.

During this period the Commission's trainee office always used to arrange for the trainees to visit Berlin. The idea was that the young mandarins-to-be would be impressed by the freedom of West Berlin and horrified by the drab uniformity of the Communist East. The director of the training office was Herr Strauss, himself a German, and he accompanied what he called *Meine Kinder* (My Children) throughout the visit. I had been on the visit myself and had written a glowing report which highlighted the 'ups' of the West and the 'downs' of the East. One day, Herr Strauss stopped me in the corridor. 'About your report. I see that you have understood. We are the representatives of the free West. Every generation must understand this.'

As might be expected, Peter saw things rather differently. 'It's nothing more than a propaganda visit,' he complained. 'What's the use of that? We really should be going to East Berlin as well.' I tried to calm him down and told him that a short, half-day trip across the border to sample the smog-filled East German air was always included in the itinerary. 'But they'll only let us see what they want us to see! That's just a waste of time!' Like I said, if Peter got an idea in his head...

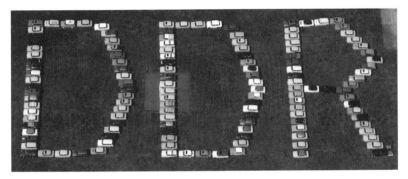

European Commission trainees: welcome to East Germany!

A couple of evenings later I was sitting with John in the bar of the European Parliament on the sixth floor of the Belliard Building. In those days the Belliard housed the entire Parliament; now it is home to the Committee of the Regions and the Economic & Social Committee.

Peter came in, carrying a piece of paper, and sat down next to us. 'Hello Peter,' said John cheerfully. 'Which tossers have you got in your sights tonight?' 'My target is Erich Honecker,' Peter replied seriously. John laughed out loud. '*Herr Honecker of the Deutsche Demokratische Republik?*'

John imitated the voice of the East German president, who was famed for pronouncing his country's name with a strong Saarland accent. 'Yes, that's the one,' confirmed Peter. He showed me a piece of paper, which was indeed a draft of a letter to Honecker, asking if he would be willing to receive a delegation of trainees during their visit to Berlin.

'Nice joke, Peter, but what do you really hope to achieve by all this?' I asked. 'I've told you. I want to visit Honecker with the other trainees – to hear the other side of the story.' By now, John was in hysterics. 'What is it with you Dutch people? If you're not impersonating Lenin, you're dropping in for tea on Erich Honecker!'

But Peter persisted. 'No, I mean it. The Strauss trip is just a propaganda thing.' Realising that he was serious, I decided to help him. The first thing we had to do was tidy up his draft letter, which was written in a mixture of Dutch and German. But how to begin? How do you address the president of a totalitarian regime? We agreed that *Herr Honecker* sounded too bourgeois. His fellow Communist Party members called him *Genosse* (Comrade), but that was too informal for Western capitalists like us. From my studies of the Kremlin, I remembered that the communist leaders all love their official titles. We therefore decided on *Sehr geehrter Staatsratsvorsitzender der Deutschen Demokratischen Republik* – 'To the Esteemed Chairman of the Council of State of the German Democratic Republic'. East Germany was then known as the Democratic Republic, whereas the West was referred to as the Federal Republic. Twenty minutes later the letter requesting the visit was finished and we dropped it in the post box as we left for home. 'And that's the last you'll ever hear of it,' said John. 'Unless you get a visit from the Stasi!'

Two weeks later, John and I were again sitting in the Parliament bar, when Peter rushed in. He seemed out of breath and a little confused.

'Well, Peter, has Erich called yet?' I mocked. He looked at me earnestly. 'I had a visitor this morning. A man claiming to be a diplomat from the DDR embassy. He said that the *Staatsratsvorsitzender der Deutschen Demokratischen Republik* would be delighted to receive us.' I could hardly believe it. Even John remained silent. What had started out as a joke now looked like turning into a serious political issue.

The European Community (EC) had still not recognised the German Democratic Republic: an official visit by an EC delegation, even if it was only by a group of trainees, could be seen as a first step along the road to such recognition. The implications were staggering. I shook my head and turned to look at Peter. 'How on earth are you going to get yourself out of this?' I asked. 'I'm not,' he said. 'I told them that we're coming. There's only one real problem: how the hell am I going to tell Strauss!'

The next morning Peter took the lift to Strauss's office, intending to tell him all about the visit to Honecker. Strauss, however, was busy and had no time to see him. The secretary told him to come back later. She probably thought that he was just another trainee trying to get an extension to his contract, so Peter decided to leave a note. The text was short and simple: 'I have arranged that the trainees' delegation to Berlin will also visit the DDR leader, Erich Honecker.'

Before he had even reached his own office, Peter's name was being paged through the public address system. 'Please report immediately to Mr. Strauss's office!' Peter arrived to find Strauss in a cold sweat.

'Tell me that this is a joke! Just some kind of warped student prank!' Peter told him that it was nothing of the kind. 'It's all perfectly true. We're going to see Mr. Honecker in East Berlin.' The director of the traineeship office was speechless. He had no idea what to say or do. As Peter left, he could hear Strauss muttering to himself over and over again: *Das is unmöglich, das is unmöglich*...(Impossible! Impossible!)

I laughed as Peter told me this story, but we both knew that he was in danger of getting out of his depth. Commission trainees simply do not visit the heads of state of non-recognised governments without prior approval from the very highest political level. Sooner or later, some very serious political heavyweights would be getting involved in this matter.

I suggested that he should take the bull by the horns and go straight to the top mandarins himself. This meant bypassing Strauss, because I was certain that Strauss would sack Peter before the visit if the matter was left up to him. From my own trainee days I remembered some conversations with a certain Herr Beck. He was one of the real mega-mandarins, who in his earlier career had worked closely with Chancellor Helmut Schmidt. There was even a photo of Schmidt on his desk, wearing one of the pork-pie hats for which he was so famous (still known in Germany as a 'Helmut' hat). Another name which sprang to mind was Gunter Burghardt, a member of the Delors cabinet. I suggested that Peter should contact these men as soon as possible. They would know all about the Commission's approach to *Ostpolitik* and could give him all the advice he needed.

Surprisingly, the Commission's most senior German mandarins replied much less negatively than Strauss, who was still appalled at the prospect of *Meine Kinder* visiting the enemy. It goes without saying that the Commission could have cancelled the visit if they had really wanted to. But they didn't want to! They had been looking for some time for a suitable way of thawing relations with East Germany – and by a stroke of pure luck Peter had given them a perfect opportunity.

And so it was that later that year Peter and his delegation crossed the famous Friederichstrasse checkpoint and entered East Berlin. They were met by a fleet of limousines, which drove them in almost presidential style to the residence of the *Staatsratsvorsitzender der Deutschen Demokratischen Republik*. It was from a balcony in this same building that Rosa Luxemburg and Karl Liebknecht had proclaimed the very first German republic in 1918. The trainees were warmly welcomed by the East German leader, who, like the good Communist he was, gave them a long speech on the achievements of the DDR.

But this was not what Peter had come to hear. And if Peter got an idea in his head...

Interrupting the president in full flow, he suddenly asked: 'Mr. Honecker, could you please tell me about the human rights situation in your country...'

This seemed like a very good way of finding out by personal experience precisely how bad the human rights situation was in the DDR, and the East German mandarins, surrounding their party leader, held their breath. Some citizens of the so-called First Farmer's and Worker's State on German soil have probably been executed for less. But Honecker was not to be thrown off balance. He smiled a deathly smile in Peter's direction and began a new diatribe, this time against the evils of unemployment within the European Community.

National-Zeitung

Das Blatt
der National-
Demokratischen
Partei
Deutschlands

JAHRGANG 39 · NR. 20 /   BERLIN, FREITAG, 24. JANUAR 1986   ISSN 0466-5678   15 PFENNIG

Erich Honecker empfing Gruppe von Praktikanten der EG-Kommission

Information über politische, ökonomische und soziale Entwicklung unserer Republik

BERLIN (adn). Der Generalsekretär des Zentralkomitees der SED und Vorsitzende des Staatsrates der DDR, Erich Honecker, empfing gestern eine Gruppe junger Praktikanten bei der EG-Kommission aus verschiedenen westeuropäischen Ländern zu einem Gespräch.

Erich Honecker begrüßte das Interesse der jungen Wissenschaftler für die Fragen der Friedenssicherung in den Ost-West-Beziehungen sowie für die politische und ökonomische Entwicklung der DDR und ihre Außenpolitik. Er hob hervor, daß der jungen Generation in der DDR immer Verantwortung übertragen und Vertrauen entgegengebracht wurde. Deshalb engagiere sie sich auch in allen Bereichen des gesellschaftlichen Lebens. Voller Stolz könne er feststellen, daß die Jugend der DDR überall dort besonders aktiv wirke, wo es um das Wohl des Volkes und den Frieden geht.

Erich Honecker im Gespräch mit der Gruppe junger Praktikanten bei der EG-Kommission aus verschiedenen westeuropäischen Ländern
Foto: ZB/Mittelstädt

Während der Zusammenkunft informierte Erich Honecker seine Gäste über die politische, ökonomische und soziale Entwicklung der DDR und beantwortete deren Fragen. Dabei würdigte er die hervorragenden Produktionsergebnisse, die von den Werktätigen in allen Bereichen der Volkswirtschaft erzielt wurden, als Ausdruck des sich ständig vertiefenden Vertrauensverhältnisses zwischen Volk und Regierung der DDR. Er hob hervor, daß die auf hohes ökonomisches Wachstum und steigende soziale Ergebnisse für das Volk gerichtete Politik langfristig fortgesetzt wird.

Die Gesprächspartner stimmten darin überein, daß alle Politiker und Staaten in Europa wie in der ganzen Welt die große Verpflichtung haben, im Interesse ihrer Völker zur Beseitigung der Gefahr eines nuklearen Krieges und zur dauerhaften Friedenssicherung beizutragen.

Erich Honecker hob hervor, daß die DDR auch künftig alles Fortsetzung auf Seite 2

Erich Honecker welcomes the European trainees. The first contact between the GDR and the European Community.

NEUES DEUTSCHLA[ND]

Proletarier aller Länder, ve[...]

ORGAN DES ZENTRALKOMITEES DER SOZIALISTISCHEN EINHEITSPARTEI DEUT[...]

Begegnung im Hause des Staatsrates

Erich Honecker empfing Gruppe junger Praktikanten bei der EG-Kommission

Gesprächspartner betonten Verpflichtung aller Länder Europas und der Welt zur Beseitigung der Gefahr eines Nuklearkrieges / Sowjetische Initiative zeigt dafür die konkreten Wege

Berlin (ADN). Der Generalsekretär des Zentralkomitees der SED und Vorsitzende des Staatsrates der DDR, Erich Honecker, empfing am Donnerstag eine Gruppe junger Praktikanten bei der EG-Kommission aus verschiedenen westeuropäischen Ländern zu einem Gespräch.

Erich Honecker begrüßte das Interesse der jungen Wissenschaftler für die Fragen der Friedenssicherung in den Ost-West-Beziehungen sowie für die politische und ökonomische Entwicklung der DDR und ihre Außenpolitik. Er hob hervor, daß der jungen Generation in der DDR immer Verantwortung übertragen und Vertrauen entgegengebracht wurde. Deshalb engagiere sie sich in allen Bereichen des gesellschaftlichen Lebens. Voller Stolz könne er feststellen, daß die Jugend der DDR überall dort besonders aktiv wirke, wo es um das Wohl des Volkes und den Frieden geht.

Während der Zusammenkunft informierte Erich Honecker seine Gäste über die politische, ökonomische und soziale Entwicklung der DDR und beantwortete deren Fragen. Dabei würdigte er die hervorragenden Produktionsergebnisse, die von den Werktätigen in allen Bereichen der Volkswirtschaft erzielt wurden, als Ausdruck des sich ständig vertiefenden Vertrauensverhältnisses zwischen der DDR und ihrer Regierung. Er hob hervor,

daß die auf hohes ökonomisches Wachstum und steigende soziale Ergebnisse für das Volk gerichtete Politik langfristig fortgesetzt wird.

Die Gesprächspartner stimmten darin überein, daß alle Politiker und Staaten in Europa wie in der ganzen Welt die große Verpflichtung haben, im Interesse ihrer Völker zur Beseitigung der Gefahr eines nuklearen Krieges und zur dauerhaften Friedenssicherung beizutragen.

Erich Honecker hob hervor, daß die DDR auch künftig alles von ihr Abhängende tun werde, um gemeinsam mit ihren Verbündeten zur Lösung der Hauptfrage der Gegenwart beizutragen, ein atomares Inferno abzuwenden und den Frieden zu sichern, das Wettrüsten auf der Erde zu beenden und es nicht auf den Weltraum auszudehnen. Das von Michail Gorbatschow vorgeschlagene sowjetische Programm zur Befreiung der Welt von Atomwaffen sei eine Initiative von wahrhaft historischer Bedeutung. Sie weise konkrete Wege, um die Menschheit von der Angst vor der nuklearen Vernichtung zu befreien und die Konzentration

ihrer geistigen und materiellen Ressourcen auf die ausschließlich friedliche Nutzung der Ergebnisse von Wissenschaft und Technik zu ermöglichen.

Es sei zu hoffen, daß alle Macht und Einfluß ausübenden Kräfte mit Verantwortungsbewußtsein diese konstruktive Initiative aufgreifen und mit ernsthaftem politischem Willen an ihrer Verwirklichung mitarbeiten. Ein erster Schritt könnte ein gemeinsames Moratorium über die Einstellung aller Kernwaffentests sein. Die Deutsche Demokratische Republik unterstütze voll und ganz die Initiative Michail Gorbatschows, mit der Bewegung in die Weltpolitik in Richtung Friedenssicherung in Gang gekommen sei.

Im Verlaufe des Gesprächs bekräftigte Erich Honecker den Standpunkt der DDR, daß die Aufnahme offizieller Beziehungen zwischen dem RGW und der EG die Zusammenarbeit auf der Grundlage der Prinzipien der friedlichen Koexistenz und des gegenseitigen Vorteils fördern kann. Sie wären geeignet, den

Handels- und Warenaustausch sowie die wissenschaftlich-technische Zusammenarbeit zu beleben. Eine vom Rat für Gegenseitige Wirtschaftshilfe vorgeschlagene gemeinsame Deklaration über die Entwicklung der Zusammenarbeit zwischen RGW und EG wäre ein großer Beitrag zum friedlichen Zusammenwirken der europäischen Völker.

Des weiteren wurden Fragen des Umweltschutzes und möglicher Initiativen der Jugend dafür, des Reiseverkehrs, der 750-Jahr-Feier Berlins, der Vollbeschäftigung, Helsinki, der Vollbeschäftigung, des Bildungswesens und der Berufsausbildung, der Gründe für die dynamische Entwicklung der Volkswirtschaft der DDR, der Wissenschaft, Technik und Technologie erörtert.

Die Gäste dankten abschließend für die Begegnung und die Beantwortung ihrer Fragen.

Zum Abschluß ihres Aufenthaltes in der Hauptstadt der DDR besuchten die Gäste das neue Schauspielhaus und führten Gespräche mit leitenden Vertretern der Humboldt-Universität.

The communist party newspaper Neues Deutschland *applauds the arrival of the trainees. What started as a joke in the bar of the European Parliament, ended as front-page news in the East German national press.*

The East German media gave the visit blanket coverage. It was the leading story on the evening news, accompanied by the usual peons of praise for the country's leadership. The process was repeated the next morning, when photos of the delegation were splashed all over the front page of *Neues Deutschland*, the Communist Party newspaper.

What had started out almost as a joke had turned into the first serious contact between the DDR and the EC – and without loss of face for either side! The only person who failed to see the irony of the situation was poor old Strauss. He never got over the 'betrayal' of *Meine Kinder* and asked for a transfer to another job. He ended his days serving the Princess's Delegation in Tunisia.

3| The Return

The telephone rang at around 3 o'clock in the afternoon. I wasn't expecting anything special. It was a sunny July day and most people were outside enjoying the weather: this was certainly the case in Leuven, where I was living at the time. 'Hello, how are you?' I recognised the voice of the Dutch candidate for a Commissioner's post with the European Union. He was calling from his holiday home in Northern France. 'You've probably heard that I have a good chance of getting the Commissioner's job,' he said. 'I'm busy putting my cabinet together and I was wondering whether or not you might be interested?'

I wasn't expecting the question, but I was pleasantly surprised. I didn't need much thinking time and said 'yes' more or less immediately. I had left the European fray 12 years earlier to work as a journalist, first in the Netherlands and later in Belgium. I remembered the words of my old friend from Leiden: 'the cabinet is where the real power is.' I didn't know if he was right, but now I was going to get the chance to find out. The Commissioner-designate remained formal: 'Good, I am pleased that you are prepared to accept. Please make an appointment to see my head of cabinet. He will tell you what to do.' And that was that! After an absence of 10 years, I was catapulted back into the European arena in 2 minutes on a Sunday afternoon.

Given my varied experience with the European Parliament through the years, I suggested to my new boss that I might perhaps be made responsible for parliamentary affairs in his new set-up. He seemed to agree and it was with this aim in mind that I set off to meet his head of cabinet at lunchtime one Thursday afternoon. Our meeting was scheduled to take place in the Breydel Building, which had become the new headquarters for the Commission following the temporary closure of the Berlaymont for renovation. It was thought that the cleaning of the Princess's Palace would only take a couple of years, but the work lasted until 2004: primarily because of the large quantities of asbestos which needed to be removed. The final cost was far higher than originally anticipated, but that was a problem for the Belgian government and their creative accountants.

As in the Berlaymont, the Commission also occupied the top floors in the Breydel. The very top floor housed the cabinet of the President, as well as the conference room for Commission meetings. My head of cabinet had an office on the 11th floor and it was there that I found him waiting for me. As I entered, I saw before me a dignified, formal and somewhat distant man: in short, a typical mandarin as I remembered them from a decade before. He said very little, only asked relevant questions and had a way of using the word 'yes', so that you didn't really know whether he meant 'yes' or 'no'. Possibly, he even meant both at the same time. It was like being interviewed by a real mandarin in the court of one of the Chinese emperors, where the conversations were conducted through a silk screen. There was no substance, nothing you could really get hold of.

At this time, I was working as a political journalist in Belgium, a world where the use of language could best be described as 'colourful'. Terms such as 'liar', 'bastard', 'thief' and 'cheat' were all part of the daily vocabulary and I had just come from a debate in the Belgian Parliament where most of these terms had been used. Imagine the culture shock I experienced when just 20 minutes later I stepped into the refined world of the European Commission. The use of the word 'bastard' would have caused most mandarins to faint, and I found myself having to watch very carefully what I was saying. The head of cabinet remained coolly non-committal as I stumbled on through the story of my life. His only contribution to our conversation was an occasional 'indeed' or 'how interesting'. When I eventually ran out of things to say, he brought the interview to an end with a brief: 'Thank you for coming. We'll keep in touch.'

As I left the Breydel, I was no longer sure that I had the job. Our conversation seemed more exploratory than confirmatory: it was as though I was just one of a dozen other candidates, the rest of whom he still had to see. I began to have doubts and so I said nothing to anyone about Sunday's telephone call and Thursday's interview. In circumstances of this kind, a single word, even if spoken to a friend in confidence, can be misinterpreted or used against you. In negotiation situations, keeping your own counsel is one of the golden rules. If the negotiations are about your own personal future, it is the only rule!

A few days later my curiosity finally got the better of me and so I phoned the Commissioner-designate to ask him what was going on. To my relief he answered: 'I've spoken to my head of cabinet and he was happy to have you in the team. That means that we have three of the six people we need. He's still looking for the other three.' Clearly, the head of cabinet had been more positive with his boss than he had been with me during our conversation. Never mind. I was in: that was the main thing. Putting together the rest of the team might not be such an easy matter as it seemed. There were strict rules about this kind of thing. The Commissioner's cabinet had to consist of six members of staff, of whom at least two had to be women and with no more than three members of the same nationality as the Commissioner.

To make matters even more complicated, the cabinet had to reflect the regional diversity of the European Union. Our cabinet eventually started off with three Dutchmen and a Dane, the female representation coming from Germany and France. However, the composition changed fairly regularly, so that after five years I was the only 'original' who was still in post.

A few days later the Commissioner-designate came to Brussels for discussions with me and the head of cabinet. We agreed to meet in a restaurant just off Schuman Square. We asked for a quiet table apart and this we were given. Unfortunately, it was right next to the door, so that we could be seen – and heard – by everyone coming in and going out. This made me uneasy, because the chances of being recognised were high. At the time, I was still writing for *De Standaard* newspaper about Belgian politics, yet here I was sitting at table with a Commissioner-designate discussing European politics. If word got back to my employer, the cat would be well and truly among the pigeons...

I didn't have long to wait before my fears became fact. The very same afternoon I received a call from a journalist from the Belga press agency, asking me if I was planning to join the cabinet of the new Dutch Commissioner. I was sitting in our editorial office, surrounded by listening colleagues, and so I had little option but to answer honestly 'Yes'. The moment I put the phone down I went to my editor and gave him my resignation. 30 minutes later the news was already being announced on Teletext. The news raced with even greater speed through the *De Standaard* offices, spread by e-mail: the fastest and most efficient way to pass on gossip in this modern day and age. Some of my colleagues were so anxious to inform their fellow-reporters of this earth-shattering development that they even forgot to delete my name from their 'send' list. As a result, I received several mails about myself! 'Have you heard? Our Dutchman is going to Europe. Three times his current salary!'

These announcements were, of course, still premature. I might have agreed to work for the Commissioner-designate, but his appointment still had to be confirmed by the European Parliament. And this was by no means certain. A Commissioner-designate with enemies – and let's be honest, which politician doesn't have enemies! – is most vulnerable during his hearing before the European Parliament. This was the moment when old opponents could attempt to settle old scores. A subtle suggestion here, an unsubstantiated rumour there: it didn't take much to ruin a candidate's chances and obtain a 'no' vote from the Parliament. My new boss had been a controversial figure in Dutch politics and there were plenty of past rivals lining up to take pot-shots at him. If they succeeded, the Commissioner-designate would be out of a job. Worse still, if they succeeded, *I* would be out of a job. I would be banished from the Princess's court for ever and my European adventure would be over before it had even begun.

In keeping with his character, the head of cabinet was not overly optimistic about the outcome. 'We're not out of the woods yet. There are still plenty of bandits out there, waiting to ambush us.' By his normal standards, this was almost a torrent of emotion. However, the Commissioner-designate remained relaxed and calm. After many years of close-quarter in-fighting in Dutch politics, he was used to this kind of thing. Even so, the head of cabinet was correct in his assessment. The candidacy was hotly contested from beginning to end.

One of the fiercest opponents was Hanja, a leading light in the Dutch Christian-democrat movement. She even went to see the new President of the Commission, in the hope of torpedoing her fellow-countryman's chances. She had wanted to be a Commissioner for years, but her party was then in opposition in the Netherlands. In addition to this jealousy, she had also had a famous bust-up with the Commissioner-designate during the 1990s, when he had been leader of the liberals in the Dutch Parliament. In the face of the political correctness of the time, the liberal leader had dared to set immigration and integration on the political agenda. Hanja accused him of responding to 'racist gut feeling' and had compared him with the French politician, Jean-Marie Le Pen. Sadly for her, this attack did not have the effect she had planned. The liberal party became the largest party in the Netherlands and the Christian-democrats lost heavily. Hanja was blamed for this electoral defeat and was banished to the political backwaters of the European Parliament.

Not to be deterred, Hanja set about making a new career for herself and she was soon a well-known figure in European circles. Even I had come across her during my training period in the 1980s. She was hard-working and imperturbable, but she had one major failing: her sense of humour had been surgically removed at birth. She never ever laughed. She was also ultra-suspicious of outsiders: her daughters all worked for her as assistants and were her most trusted confidantes. The three musketeers – Wouter, Henk and Han – started a Hanja fan-club. The club song was *I Did It My Way* by Frank Sinatra. There were even members of Commission cabinets who wanted to become members of the fan-club, but the membership committee – i.e. Wouter, Henk and Han – were very choosy about who they let join. During

Hanja: I do it my way!

'meetings', which usually took place in one of the Parliament's many bars, there were special – normally alcohol-related – prizes for the best imitation of their heroine. The members even had their own special greeting.

It was only later that I came into contact with Hanja, when I chaired a public debate about Europe in the European Parliament. She sat to my right on the podium, while an English professor of European Law from the University of Groningen sat on my left. Hanja couldn't resist a jibe in my direction before the debate started. 'Of course, I maintain contact with ordinary people through the local press. I don't need long and learned pieces in the NRC Handelsblad to flatter my vanity – not like some politicians I could mention.' I was impressed by the subtlety of this well-aimed blow under the belt: in one short sentence she had managed to insult me, my old newspaper and my new boss!

However, I soon discovered that I had an unexpected ally in the shape of the British professor. He had once been employed by the Commission as an expert in the free movement of goods and he spoke exceptionally good Dutch. He soon had Hanja tied up in knots, even in her own language. 'Madam,' he asked, 'Do you know how the free movement of goods was forced through in the United Kingdom?' As a Euro-MP, Hanja thought she knew the answer to this one: the 1978 Court of Justice ruling in the Cassis de Dijon case. The professor shook his head and went on to explain. 'Madam, in my office in Groningen I have an inflatable rubber doll. Do you know why?' Hanja looked as though she found the question distasteful: she certainly had no interest in the sordid answer! Not knowing what to say, she muttered an incoherent reply and allowed the perverted professor to continue. Apparently, the doll was a 'souvenir' from one of his important legal triumphs. During the 1980s, the British company Conegate wanted to import rubber dolls from Germany. The British Customs impounded the dolls and Conegate took the matter to court, basing its case on articles 30 to 36 of the Treaty of Rome. The Court of Justice agreed with

Conegate. The rubber dolls – providing they were made in accordance with recognised quality criteria – fell under the Treaty rules for the free movement of goods. The British had to let them in! By this time the professor was enjoying himself. 'Of course, the dolls had to meet the required standards. Imagine the problems if the valves were faulty, so that the dolls lost air and began flying around the room. The customers wouldn't be very pleased!' Hanja's face showed that she wasn't very pleased either and for the rest of the debate she referred to him as 'our professor' – she couldn't even bear to speak his name.

But this was nothing in comparison with the displeasure she showed towards my boss when he was put forward for the position of Commissioner. Her early efforts to blacken his name by a personal appeal to the President of the Commission had failed. Following discussions with the Dutch Government, the President had already approved the candidacy. He couldn't now change his mind, not without causing serious problems with The Hague. This meant that Hanja's last chance was the hearing before the European Parliament. In a final effort to block the candidacy, she set about rallying all her political allies on the centre-left. The Dutch left-wing liberal Loesewies – also a Euro-MP – began a letter campaign against my boss, while the leader of the Dutch Green Party even went so far as to draw up a 'Black Book' about his previous political career. This is typical of my country – if a Dutchman tries to make a name for himself in the international arena, he can always rely on the opposition of his fellow-countrymen! The Commissioner-designate began to sense that things might be going wrong and launched a counter-campaign, the central pillar of which was a letter of support signed by prominent Dutchmen and women.

However, we decided that this was not enough. It wasn't our supporters we had to win over: it was our enemies.

The Commissioner-designate, the head of cabinet and myself devised a strategy which we hoped would undermine the solidarity of our rivals. We clearly saw this as a 'hearts-and-minds' campaign: our aim was to conquer with kind words, not with confrontation. The Commissioner-designate's first move was to visit the Green group in the European Parliament. The Greens always protest about everything – that is their nature – but they seldom show personal animosity towards their opponents. They love debates, but for this they need debating partners. We decided to give them one. The Commissioner-designate attended one of their meetings, discussed with them his opinions on crucial 'green' issues and even formed a close relationship with the charismatic Danny Cohn-Bendit, the figurehead of the Paris 'revolutionaries' in 1968. It was an attraction of opposites, but the combination clicked. The 'Black Book' disappeared without trace and the Commissioner later took part in two large-scale debates with Cohn-Bendit, one about the legacy of 1968 and the other about the problems of globalisation. The Greens had become his friends.

I expected that Loesewies would be a more difficult challenge. I didn't really know her all that well, but from a distance she gave the impression of being wild and uncontrolled: a 'loose cannon' is the modern expression. In Brussels she had left a trail of discarded lovers in her wake and a number of well-deserved nicknames served unmistakably as references to the voraciousness of her physical appetites. She was irrepressible, irresponsible and always went straight for the jugular of her opponents, irrespective of the consequences. I thought about doing a nice little anti-campaign on her, leaking information about her activities as a *femme fatale* to the press at an appropriate moment. As it turned out, this wasn't necessary.

Daniel Cohn-Bendit, the young revolutionary in 1968.

Daniel Cohn-Bendit, experienced European politician and charmer.

Loesewies had been putting negative letters about the Commissioner-designate in the post boxes of her Euro-MP colleagues. She had been in the habit of doing this kind of thing from the very start of her parliamentary career, but while she was still relatively unknown a telephone call from her party boss was usually enough to pull her back into line. But not for long. She had an almost irresistible impulse towards self-destruction. After just six months in the European Parliament, she claimed that she was 'tired' of Europe. She wanted to make a name for herself in national politics and even cherished ambitions of becoming party leader. These ambitions came to an end one memorable evening in The Hague, when she managed to destroy the government, her party and her own political career within the space of a single parliamentary sitting. My planned anti-campaign became redundant. As my head of cabinet had wisely predicted: 'All we need to do is point her down the road to destruction: she'll do the rest herself.'

With the Greens and Loesewies effectively neutralised, there was little to stand in the way of the boss's candidacy. The hearing before Parliament passed off smoothly and the majority in favour of his confirmation was comfortable. Hanja tried to claim differently, arguing that he had just scraped through 'by the skin of his teeth', a claim which was repeated in the Dutch press. It was her only consolation: the boss had won a clear victory.

Not that our troubles were over. Our next problem was the aforementioned Dutch press. 'As long as we have no official spokesperson, perhaps you should deal with the press,' said the head of cabinet. 'After all, that's right up your street.' Like every European mandarin, he was afraid of the press: an alien world which was beyond control and beyond understanding. The chances of getting into trouble with the fourth estate were statistically high, so that each mandarin had developed his own method of covering his back when dealing with this unpredictable entity. There is a huge difference between a mandarin and a genuine politician. The politician wants change, whereas the mandarin wants continuity. The politician wants to stand in the spotlight; the mandarin prefers to remain in the shadows. The politician wants to be popular; the mandarin wants to be anonymous. The politician wants to read his name in the newspaper every day; the mandarin wants to be in the newspaper just twice: when he is born and when he dies. The relationship between the politician and the press – generally a mixture of mutual fascination and revulsion – is a constant source of misery for the mandarin. Politics and the press create uncertainty, whereas the mandarin wants absolute control.

Almost immediately after the confirmation of his candidacy, things started to go wrong for the Commissioner. The Commission wished to present a 'clear public image' of the new Commissioners and therefore asked the Information Directorate-General to make a short promotional film. The idea was that each Commissioner should be filmed going about his normal business. This seemed harmless enough and even the head of cabinet was, for once, confident about the outcome. The Commissioner was shown walking across the inner court of the Binnenhof, the Dutch Parliament building, with one of his assistants, following which they sat on a bench to 'discuss' some important political matter. It was almost like a holiday film. The head of cabinet and myself were in complete agreement: after all the fuss and bother of the parliamentary hearing, there couldn't possibly be any harm in this innocuous piece of footage. The press probably wouldn't even use it, we thought. Well, we thought wrong.

One evening I was watching the news on the television. Normally, I only watch with one eye but on this occasion I recognised the familiar figure of the Commissioner. I leaned forward and turned up the volume. The reporter had obviously received our film and had played it through in the studio. There he had noticed from the sound levels that the cameraman had forgotten to turn off the camera microphone when he was making the recording of the 'discussion'. The Commissioner's every word had been recorded and it didn't make good listening. 'The last few months I've had nothing but trouble with those bloody journalists. And the Dutch reporters are the worst of the lot. Bunch of wankers.' I could hardly believe what I was hearing, but I knew that it meant trouble. The last thing we needed was a war with the press, and certainly not over an idiotic propaganda film.

Next morning the head of cabinet was the first to call. 'You'd better get in here. Things are getting a bit warm.' Coming from him, the term 'a bit warm' implied something only marginally less disastrous than a nuclear attack. The film had confirmed all his worst suspicions about politicians and the media. 'They can't even make a stupid film without messing it up.' Immediate action was required, otherwise the newspapers would be full of the story. 'The Commissioner even called the reporters a bunch of wankers!' he said with distaste. I could sympathise with his feelings. It was difficult to imagine a worse start to our relations with the Brussels press corps, the largest in the world. In fact, this wasn't so much a bad start as a non-start. 'We've got to nip this thing in the bud. There's only one thing for it. He's got to apologise – publicly.' The head of cabinet was right, of course, and I fully agreed with him. There was just one small problem: getting the Commissioner to agree with him. Grovelling public apologies were definitely not his strong point. It was my job to make him see differently.

Our conversation didn't get off to a good start. 'It's typical of the Dutch,' he complained. 'Nobody else would think of making headline news out of something as trivial as this, except perhaps the British. Haven't they got anything better to do?' I tried to make him see the reality of the situation. 'You and I both think that the reporter who made this story is a pin-head and we're probably right. But that's not the point. The fact of the matter is that you called him and his colleagues 'a bunch of wankers'. On the television. In front of millions of viewers. Whichever way you look at it, this is not good for your reputation.' This last word did the trick: most politicians would sell their own mothers if they thought it could enhance their reputation. Grudgingly, he admitted that I was right: decent people, and certainly decent politicians, do not use words like 'wanker' – or at least not in public. Later the same afternoon, the reporter who we both thought was a pin-head arrived to ask for the Commissioner's comments on the story. The Commissioner apologised for his 'improper use of language': thereby implying that he didn't regret what he had said, just the manner in which he had said it! But it was enough. Honour was satisfied on both sides and the story died a quick and silent death.

This incident confirmed what I had known for many years: European mandarins do not like passion and emotion. Anticipation, discipline and control are their key words. The head of cabinet was pleased that the problem was now behind us but he was determined that there should be no repetition in the future. 'What we need is an official spokesperson,' he said. Once again, he was right. Until now, I had been acting as temporary spokesman but I was unable to combine my other duties with the deluge of telephone calls from the press corps. My mobile phone rang about every thirty seconds, often for the most trivial enquiries. However, finding a suitable full-time spokesperson was not likely to be an easy task. The Press Directorate had a list of candidates, but the best ones had already been snapped up by other Commissioners. Those who remained were either useless or didn't want the job. We would have to find someone ourselves and the Commissioner – who is a confirmed Anglophile – wanted a Brit.

After much searching, I eventually found someone called Peter, but he turned down our offer. A second candidate, a German, showed more interest. He at least came for an interview with the head of cabinet, who wanted to know 'what kind of joker we are getting'. Michael showed himself to be an enthusiastic supporter of the internal market and I really thought that he was the man for the job. But a few days later he called with the news that he had taken a job as spokesman for the Competition Commissioner. Bye-bye, Michael.

I had no idea what to do next. The Commissioner wanted a spokesman. The head of cabinet wanted a spokesman – if only to protect the Commissioner from himself. And I wanted a spokesman – if only to protect myself from the press. As a last resort, I telephoned the British official responsible for making the press releases for the Directorate-General, a man named Jonathan. Once upon a time he had worked for the *Sunday Times* and he had the ability to express the most complex subjects in plain, easy-to-understand language. Suddenly, the light dawned on me: an ex-journalist and a Brit, who was now a mandarin and who could write simply and easily – he was perfect, just what we were looking for! I asked him straight out: 'Would you like to be our spokesman?' He was surprised and asked for some time to think it over. I rang the head of cabinet to put him in the picture, but he wasn't enthusiastic. The director-general was also a Brit and had appointed Jonathan himself. 'Even if he comes, how can we trust him to be impartial? We don't need a Trojan horse inside our own cabinet.' I thought he was being too negative and told him so. Besides, we weren't really in a position where we could afford to be so choosy. Minutes later, Jonathan phoned back – to my great delight, he wanted to do it. I introduced him to the Commissioner the same day and, as usual, the boss came to a quick decision. Five minutes later we had ourselves a new spokesman!

Jonathan had my full confidence, but he didn't immediately have the trust of my other colleagues. On Friday evenings I used to enjoy a salad and a glass of good wine on the terrace of the Falstaff, a restaurant in central Brussels with a Jugendstil decor. I had just taken my first sip of Burgundy when I was called by a panic-stricken Jonathan. The press were calling with questions, but his colleagues wouldn't give him the information he needed to reply with plausible answers. The spokesmen needed an LTT – line to take. Without it, he couldn't do his job. However, all he got from his colleagues was TCS – the cold shoulder. Jonathan was upset and rightly so. 'If I don't get any co-operation, then I have no option but to resign.' I was shocked. It had taken us ages to find a spokesman and now it looked like he was going to quit in less than a week! That could only be damaging to the reputation of the Commissioner and would lead to needless speculation about relations within our cabinet. I phoned the Commissioner straight away and explained the situation to him. As a politician, he understood that a spokesman without information is not in a position to speak about anything. Shortly thereafter, he sent an instruction to all his staff: 'Our spokesman must be allowed to know everything. This doesn't necessarily mean that he has to tell everything – but he at least has to know everything. I hope that this is understood.' This made life a lot easier for Jonathan, but there were still occasional difficulties: it is hard to preach a policy of openness in an organisation which for so long has practised a culture of secrecy.

Now that we had an official spokesman, I hoped that I would finally have time to get down to my own work. Fat chance. The following storm was already brewing. On a Monday morning I was summoned to the office of the head of cabinet: never a good sign. From the manner in which he was moving papers from one well-ordered pile to another, I could see that he was not happy. 'Is the Commissioner under control?' he asked in English. 'Yes,' I answered, 'Quite under control.' The head of cabinet picked up the morning newspaper, which I had not yet seen. He threw it on the table: 'I'm afraid not.' The headline read: 'Journalist takes Commissioner to court.' I was surprised and puzzled. I had heard nothing about this, and so I picked up the paper and began reading. Apparently, the Commissioner had given an interview at his home to the Dutch weekly *Vrij Nederland*. In the course of the interview he had suggested that a TV reporter from the Catholic broadcasting company – a man who had been a thorn in his side for years – had deliberately submitted false declarations to the tax authorities in order to incriminate him and destroy his political career. The reporter in question felt that his good name had been tarnished and so he took out a summons against the Commissioner for libel. The head of cabinet was not amused. 'Commissioners need to be protected from themselves. They should never be allowed to give interviews alone, and certainly not at home. They're too relaxed at home – and that's when they start saying things they shouldn't. All the interviews should be done here – where we can keep an eye on him.' He had a point, I suppose, but in this instance we had clearly been overtaken by events.

A summons against a Commissioner – one of the Princess's most senior servants – is no laughing matter. It must be notified to the President, since a court case can easily damage the reputation of the Commission as a whole. After our problems with the European Parliament and the 'wankers' incident, this was the last thing we needed. It was vital to get the whole sorry affair settled as quickly as possible, but this was not going to be easy. The Commissioner had an unreasoning hatred for this particular journalist – or 'hedgehog-head' as he called him, a reference to his tormentor's US Marine-style haircut. The dislike was deep on both sides and a compromise solution seemed unlikely.

The Commissioner consulted his lawyer and went off to attend a conference on European taxation policy in the Italian city of Bolzano. I was left behind to deal with hedgehog-head. I called the lawyer, an extremely well-paid man from The Hague. I got the impression that he was taking things a bit too easily. 'Of course we'll win the case,' he said. 'No problem. All we need is a little bit of patience.' He seemed to have no idea that this particular case had three distinct aspects: a legal aspect in the Netherlands, a media aspect in the Netherlands and a political aspect in Europe. He only seemed concerned with the first of these three elements. I asked him what he was planning to do. He told me that, seeing it was Friday afternoon, he was planning to go golfing!

The media aspect was clearly the most dangerous – certainly on a Friday afternoon. The incident between the Commissioner and the journalist threatened to get out of hand, which meant that it could be news all weekend – especially if the media had no other news worth reporting. By Monday morning the story would have attracted international attention, at which point there would be no chance of sorting things out in a reasonable manner. The situation was a delicate one for the Commissioner and might even endanger his political future – which was probably what hedgehog-head had been planning all along. He already had a reputation for this kind of thing. He had once sabotaged the election campaign of the leader of the Dutch Christian-democrats, who had been favourite to become the country's next prime minister. Due to the hedgehog-head, his political career ended in utter failure.

If our lawyer was planning to do nothing, apart from improving his golf swing, I decided that I had better try and sort the matter out myself. I telephoned one of my other colleagues in the cabinet. He was a jurist by training and would have made an excellent director-general of the Legal Service. I knew that he would give me the advice I needed – and he did. 'Look, it's as simple as this. If you want to play a role in public life, whether as a politician or as a journalist, you must expect to have the occasional run-in with other people. Sometimes you win and sometimes you lose. You just have to learn to take the knocks and get on with it. And this is usually how the courts see things as well. The problem in this case is that the Commissioner has accused your prickly friend of a false declaration to the tax authorities, which is a criminal offence. We have to try and soften the words 'false declaration', so that they no longer have legal implications.'

I had hardly put the phone down before it rang again. It was a reporter from the *Volkskrant*. She asked whether the Commissioner had any comment to make about the summons against him. 'What time is the deadline for your article?' I replied. 'Eight o'clock this evening. Why?' Why? Because I had a plan. 'I'll get back to you,' I told her.

It was no easy task getting in touch with the Commissioner in rural Bolzano. When I finally got him on the line he at least seemed in a cheerful mood. 'The conference catering must be good,' I thought to myself. His mood became less cheerful when we started to discuss the summons. It became positively icy once I mentioned the name of hedgehog-head. 'Look, Sir,' I tried to reason, 'The facts of the matter are this: you have accused a leading journalist of a criminal act, for which you have no real proof. We have to retract or at least distance ourselves from the words 'false declaration'. If we don't, we're in big trouble.' At long last, the message finally seemed to be getting through to the Commissioner. 'OK. Perhaps I got a bit carried away during that newspaper interview, but I am not going to apologise to that hedgehog-head. Draw up a statement to get us out of this mess – but no apologies!'

I called back my legal friend and within half an hour we had come up with a text which we thought would do the trick. 'In my interview, I didn't mean 'false declaration' in the legal sense, but in the sense of providing the tax authorities with information which might help to create a false impression about my tax situation.' It seemed like the perfect solution. We had managed to substitute 'false impression' for 'false declaration', but still made the journalist look like the devious little rat he was. Moreover, the Commissioner's statement also expressed 'regret at the problems which this incident has caused.' This was very clearly not an apology to the journalist, but it might seem enough like one to convince the courts. I phoned the Commissioner in Bolzano and read him our proposed text. To my great relief, he gave it his full approval. He didn't change a single word. At a quarter to eight, just fifteen minutes before the deadline, I faxed the statement to the *Volks-*

krant, who used it as the basis for the leading article on the front page of their Saturday edition. The editorial comment made clear that in their opinion 'the allegations have been withdrawn.'

It was not an opinion shared by hedgehog-head. He pressed his summons and the case eventually went to court. But the Commissioner won! The judge decided that the case was 'without cause', since the Commissioner's press statement had effectively withdrawn his 'accusation' and expressed his 'regret'. He even went on to tell the journalist that 'in public life, you must expect to take some knocks!' It was a great victory. The Commissioner's reputation was saved, the President of the Commission was relieved and I – at last – would now get the chance to do the job I was actually paid for: making policy in the name of the Princess.

4| On the Treadmill

Like the other 22,000 plus mandarins, I drove every morning into central Brussels, to the enclave around Schuman Square, where the Princess reigns supreme. My fellow mandarins arrived from all different directions, most of them living in the well-to-do suburbs which surround the Belgian – and European – capital. With the discipline of worker ants, we each made our way to our respective buildings and offices, where we each 'did our bit' for the future of the continent. The mandarins are the foot-soldiers in the battle for European integration. Each mandarin manages his own set of dossiers and each dossier is a small spoke in the giant wheel of 'Project Europe': the Princess's master-plan for a better world. The leading mandarins – from director-general to head of unit – ensure that the wheel turns smoothly, while the Commissioners and their cabinets (private offices) give political direction to Europe in a stormy world. Or that, at least, is the theory.

I have always thought of the Princess as a unique figure in history. She is the only ruler ever to have created an empire without an army or secret police. The Chinese Empire, the Roman Empire, the Ottoman Empire and the Hapsburg Empire all possessed an efficient administrative machine (just like the Princess), but from time to time they all had need of an army to keep their tiresome subjects in check. The mandarins formed the backbone of the imperial system; in fact, they form the backbone of every governmental system! This is the lesson that the Americans happened to forget in Iraq. Having conquered the country and disposed of Saddam, they then dismissed the entire civil service, as well as the political elite and the entire military. Thousands of unemployed people were turned onto the streets and this in a country where weapons are as easy to come by as crack in the Bronx. Not surprisingly, public order quickly disintegrated and chaos reigned thereafter.

The Princess has only one weapon: the law. It is no coincidence that her headquarters are located in the Rue de la Loi (Law Street). She alone has the right to make legislative proposals on an EU-wide basis. Sometimes, these proposals will be directives, which must be transposed into the national legislation of the member states. Sometimes they will be regulations, which must be applied directly. In certain cases, the Princess can even make decisions of her own. Her empire is not an empire of the sword; it is an empire of rules and regulations. And for the last 50 years, she has been very busy. The combined legislation of this period – known as the *acquis communautaire* – amounts to some 90,000 pages. This is enough to fill a bookcase more than a dozen metres wide. Translated into the Union's 23 official languages, the figures become even more mind-boggling: a staggering two million pages. By any standards, that is an awful lot of legislation. The Chinese and Roman mandarins must have been glad that they only had to work in a single language!

There is almost no aspect of a European citizen's life which is not in some way influenced by the contents of the magical *acquis*. From the free movement of goods to food safety, from chemical production to the Euro, from VAT to medicines, from the labels on bottles to international relations: you name it, the mandarins have a directive or a regulation for it. Their laws are more powerful than any French, British, German or Russian army which ever swept across the continent. Their work is felt and seen in the most far-flung corners of Europe, the cement which binds together an empire created by free will. Moreover, it is an empire which has never conquered another land. On the contrary, many countries are still queuing up to join: not only from

Europe, but also from Africa, Asia and the Middle East. Such is the appeal of the mandarins and their book of rules.

Most of the mandarins who work for the Princess are unaware of this unique historical dimension to their work. This was certainly the case with me. I was given an office (room 39) next to the Commissioner on the sixth floor of a building in the Kortenberglaan in Brussels. The Berlaymont was still temporarily out of service – it really did take an awfully long time to get rid of all that asbestos – and so the President of the Commission moved his centre of operations to the Breydel Building.

Here the European mandarins guard the single European market of 500 million people.

However, departing from normal practice, he decided not to group all the Commissioners together on the eleventh and twelfth floors of the Breydel, but instead sent the individual Commissioners (and their cabinets) to work in the building in which their directorate-general (DG) was housed. This sounded like an interesting idea to me, but the Commissioners were appalled. Split up between different buildings, they felt that they would become isolated from their colleagues. The only time they would see their fellow Commissioners would be during the weekly meeting on Wednesdays. This would not only mean that they would gradually lose touch, but also – and much more importantly – that it would be far more difficult to devise the plots and conspiracies which are such a part of the Commission's way of doing business. Backstage meetings, which previously had happened 'by accident', now had to be planned and arranged. As a result, telephone calls and e-mails would leave tracks which could easily be traced back to the sender. The plotters would run the risk of detection; an unattractive prospect for any high-ranking mandarin. The President who devised this ingenious strategy was an Italian, a professor who was probably familiar with the intrigues of the Roman Senate. Clearly he thought that *divide et impera* was a tactic not just applicable to the Roman Empire.

At first, I couldn't understand what all the fuss was about. It seemed to make sense to have the political leadership and the administrative services in the same building. That is how every national ministry is organised throughout the world. But not in the world of the mandarins. There, everything has to be different. The enforced confinement of the two branches – the directorate-general and the Commissioner with his cabinet – in the same building led to a kind of 'prison-er's dilemma'. Instead of working with each other, everyone worked against each other. The cabinet tried to limit the influence of the directorate-general on the Commissioner, while the DG's staff tried to limit the influence of the cabinet on their administrative procedures. The Commissioner, his head of cabinet and I sat on one side of the corridor. The director-general and his two assistants sat on the other side. The corridor itself served as a kind of uneasy no-man's-land. It was as if the Berlin Wall had been transferred to central Brussels.

One Monday morning we held a meeting of our cabinet. The head of cabinet ran through the agenda for the week, not only for the Commissioner, but also for the Commission as a whole. He put down his papers and sighed. From the look on his face, it was clear that the 'services' of the DG had been up to their old tricks.

'There's only one thing for it. We have to do everything we can to make sure that the DG stops telling the Commissioner what to do. It's time to teach those devious services a lesson. They never miss a chance to stab us in the back.'

The 'services', as the DG staff are known within the Commission, try to influence the decision-making process by making sure that the necessary briefing documents for the Commissioner arrive as late as possible and are as thick as possible. This means that the Commissioner usually drowns in a sea of useless detail and that there is no time left for him to do anything about it. Result: the Commissioner is forced to accept the version of the facts prepared for him by the DG, whether he likes it or not. The excuses are predictable.

'The briefing is so thick,' said the director-general with a look of innocence on his face, 'because it is complete. You wouldn't want an incomplete briefing, would you?'

Another old favourite was 'unexpected last-minute developments.' The head of cabinet reacted angrily every time this kind of thing happened, but it was difficult to do much about it. The director-general acted by the book and he was perfectly safe in his bureaucratic trench.

And while we conspired against the services, so the services conspired against us. As we sat in our meeting room that Monday morning, I looked through the window and saw the director-general and his staff holding precisely the same kind of meeting in their meeting room (the curved shape of the building allowed me a perfect view). I could imagine the pep-talk the director-general was giving to his troops: how it was important to stop the Commissioner from changing anything they had prepared; how they could best achieve this through the clever timing and presentation of draft directives; how the real danger came from the Commissioner's cabinet; the Trojan horse on the territory of the DG. He was right about this last point. The cabinet staff acted as a kind of bodyguard for the Commissioner and on more than one occasion we had phoned up DG staff and given them new instructions, without going through their boss, the director-general. Naturally, this made the director-general mad and we knew in advance that his two assistants would soon be on the warpath. These assistants were actually both quite pleasant in normal circumstances, but if they smelt treachery within their own ranks they could quickly turn into vicious Rotweilers. Collaboration with the cabinet was the worst crime that a DC mandarin could commit – and the assistants made sure they knew it. How would the director-general ever get his next promotion if his staff were 'sleeping with the enemy'?

This situation led to a more or less permanent state of war; thrust and counter-thrust, meeting and counter-meeting. Matters were not helped by the rather vague division of responsibilities between the cabinet and the services. In theory, the services were responsible for technical preparation and the cabinet was responsible for political guidance. In reality, the services wanted to do their share of the guiding and the cabinet wanted to do its share of the preparing. The Commissioner was not always aware of this rivalry, since bureaucratic intrigue was often conducted behind the scenes and always with the required level of polite discretion. The Princess's mandarins – whether they work for the services or the cabinet – do not scream, yell and shout at each other. Instead, they make their displeasure known by sending each other 'notes'. Or rather, the figureheads of both respective hierarchies, the director-general and the head of cabinet, send each other notes – even though their offices were only five metres apart! And of course, once a note has been received, there has to be a meeting to prepare a counter-note: and so the merry-go-round continues.

Both sides tried to win the support of the Commissioner for their cause. The Commissioner's word was law. He was always right: a point which the director-general and the head of cabinet were monotonously keen to confirm during joint meetings. This was a weekly ritual which saw the director-general arrive with a whole armada of mandarins in the office of the Commissioner. Needless to say, the cabinet staff, the Commissioner's 'Praetorian Guard', were also present in force. There were so many people around the table that we often had to go and find extra chairs. As soon as the Commissioner spoke, there was silence. He was the source of all wisdom. More importantly, he was the source of all decisions. The Commissioner liked short meetings. If anyone spoke for too long, he began drumming his fingers impatiently on the table. If the mandarin continued to drone on, he would look pointedly at a small Swiss clock. But often to no avail. Unfortunately, most mandarins like to hear themselves speak, especially in front of their boss. In particular, it was important to try and win the Commissioner's ear, even if this required a degree of sycophancy not seen since the days of the Emperor Caligula. 'You're absolutely right, Commissioner,' grovelled the head of cabinet. Not to be outdone, the director-general would add: 'I couldn't agree more, Commissioner.' It was almost like a cabaret.

The Commissioner decided, but he didn't always know precisely what he had decided, since each dossier contained a mass of technical detail. This allowed the mandarins plenty of room for further discussion and dispute. I often asked myself why the DG was so stubborn and awkward. It was like a horse determined to go its own way, no matter how hard you pulled on the reins.

Originally, I saw the DG as being similar to a ministry in a country. Later, I realised that this is not so. A national ministry is the product of an administrative culture from just one country. A DG is an amalgamation of mandarins from several different countries, each with a different administrative culture. Moreover, they all represent different national interests, which the government back home expects them to defend. The situation is complicated further by the fact that the director-general is a political appointment, often from outside the Commission. There is only one way to hold all these various different elements together: a DG needs a common mission. The aim is twofold: a directorate-general wants to stand at the top of the DG pecking order and wants to produce an increasing amount of legislation which unmistakably reflects the importance of its own DG mission.

DG Internal Market wants to liberalise. DG Taxation wants to harmonise. DG Transport wants to mobilise. DG Environment wants to regulate. DG Development wants to develop. DG Enlargement wants to enlarge. DG Trade wants to trade. DG External Relations wants to talk. DG Information wants to inform.

They are all determined to carry out these 'missions', almost irrespective of the Commissioner and his wishes. This means that the Commissioner needs to be both knowledgeable and tough to force through any change in policy. Only a leader with a strong personality can change the thinking of the DG. But the reverse is also true. A weak Commissioner can always rely on the competence and experience of the DG, without his or her weaknesses becoming apparent. The system has its own dynamic. The Commissioner is the rider. The DG is the horse. Only one of them can be the boss.

I saw this internal mechanism at work within the DG Taxud, covering taxation and customs union.. As previously mentioned, this DG had the harmonisation of taxation in its genes. They have only one goal: namely, that taxes in Europe must be harmonised; a typically French wish. Unfortunately, the Commissioner wanted tax competition: for example, in the field of company tax. He thought that healthy competition between the tax systems of the different member states would actually reduce the rates of company tax, rather than increase them. This could only be good for the economy, he reasoned. This was a mental leap too far for the DG, which continued to produce policy documents advocating still greater harmonisation. In paper after paper, they included paragraphs about the need for 'uniformity' and 'co-ordination'. In paper after paper, the cabinet staff removed these paragraphs and replaced them with their own. The Commissioner asked the director-general of the DG to write a political document in which all the advantages of tax competition were summarised. He couldn't do it. His staff couldn't do it, either. The Commissioner ended up writing the paper himself, at home.

In our Internal Market directorate, the DG and the cabinet eventually reached a mutually-agreed balance of power. The top people in the DG gradually got to know the staff in the cabinet and a truce was agreed, because there was no point in endless bickering. As a member of the cabinet, there are lots of things you wish to accomplish, but you remain dependent on the services with their technical knowledge – which, in all honesty, is immense. By and large, this truce between the DG and the cabinet worked well, but there was always one unknown factor capable of upsetting the apple cart: the Commissioner. As always, he was *hors categorie*.

One day he said to me: 'That business about Lloyds Insurance Company: it's a complicated matter.' He often dropped into my office for a brief discussion, with the emphasis on 'brief'. 'Lots of small investors have lost all their money and legally there's nothing we can do about it. Could you ask the case officer to come and see me. Perhaps he can explain it.' Initially, this seemed like a simple enough request. I knew the case officer, a sympathetic Scot who spoke good Dutch. We often chatted over coffee. His office was just down the corridor and so I popped along and asked him if he would go and see the Commissioner. 'No problem,' he said and he trotted off to explain the collapse of Lloyds in language that even a Commissioner could understand. 'Mission accomplished,' I thought. I was mistaken.

Unfortunately, one of the assistants to the director-general saw the Scot entering the Commissioner's room and instantly set the alarm bells ringing. He went straight to the director-general and informed him that one of his staff was in conference with the Commissioner: alone!

The senior mandarin almost fell off his chair at this hideous breach of etiquette and stormed into the office of the head of cabinet, demanding an explanation. As he had no explanation to give, the head of cabinet then stormed into my office, clearly not in a good mood.

'There are rules,' he hissed, 'and those rules must be respected! The Commissioner is now alone with that man, unprotected. Good God, they might even decide something between themselves, without consulting us!'

For once, the head of cabinet and the director-general were in complete agreement: this was a serious situation. When he left the office, the Scot received an immediate rocket from his boss. You would think he'd been selling secrets to the Russians instead of talking to his own Commissioner. The head of cabinet explained matters to me, as though he was talking to a two year-old.

'The Commissioner can only function with his body guard – and that's us. Try and remember in future!'

There were, of course, further meetings between the case officer and the Commissioner, but only in the presence of strong delegations from both the cabinet and the DG. Minutes were made of the discussions, to protect both sides from 'misunderstandings' at a later date. And, of course, to protect the Commissioner from himself.

Independent action on the part of the Commissioner was always the main source of worry for the DG and the cabinet. Each week in the cabinet we discussed the 'Commissioner's Agenda', which was guarded by his two secretaries like the crown jewels. It was difficult for outsiders to find out what was going on. As chance would have it, my office was just across the hall from the secretariat, so I always knew who had visited the Commissioner and what kind of requests they were likely to make. The visitor's waiting room was next door to my office: here the visitors were placed in 'pre-wash', or that's how we used to describe it.

The head of cabinet was a believer in having a full agenda for the Commissioner. 'A Commissioner with nothing to do might have time to start thinking for himself. That's the last thing we want. If there are gaps in his agenda, then it's up to us to fill them.'

This was all well and good, but it was also important to make sure that we didn't waste the Commissioner's time with a succession of, to put it mildly, 'less relevant visitors'. To avoid this, the secretaries and I drew up a list of 'leeches' – people who tried to make appointments with the Commissioner on the flimsiest excuses. They kept on phoning until they got their way. For this reason, we introduced the *demande d'audience*: a request for a meeting. In theory, the Commissioner still decided who he saw and who not. But the cabinet always managed to arrange something more pressing if someone undesirable was scheduled to call. This 'guarding of the agenda' was one of the main tasks of the cabinet, but there was always a danger period: the weekend. On Saturday and Sunday the Commissioner was free and therefore beyond the control of his staff. He could do – and say – whatever he liked.

One Monday morning the head of cabinet came into the meeting room, looking distinctly pale. I thought that something terrible must have happened. A death in the family, perhaps? He slumped in his chair, staring straight ahead of him. Slowly, he explained the cause of his misery.

'This weekend the Commissioner criticised the Dutch prime minister, the French president and the President of the Commission. It's us against the rest of the world. And the score? Us nil, the rest of the world three. And it's only nine o'clock on Monday morning! Ladies and gentlemen, welcome to the week!'

The head of cabinet spent the rest of the day engaged in a damage limitation exercise. A phone call to The Hague, a phone call with the French head of cabinet and with the head of the President's cabinet. Soon everything was back under control, because ultimately high-ranking mandarins all understand each other well. They all suffer from bosses who love talking to the press.

But a member of cabinet has to be something more than just a watchdog. He also has to be a kind of internal spy. To do his job, he has to know what is going on in the DG – and this is not always straightforward. I thought that the easiest way to tackle the problem was to get to know some of the DG staff. Shortly after my appointment, I tried to make social contact with some of the mandarins who could give me background on the proposals on which the DG was working. I drank coffee with the case officers, chatted about the weather, asked about the kids. Gradually, I established a relationship of trust and after a while one of my contacts gave me 'a provisional copy of a first draft directive that might – or might not – be in the pipeline.' It wasn't much but it was a start. And there was more to follow. Much more. In return, I offered information about the political balance of power and the situation in other cabinets. In this manner, I was able to develop a 'back-channel' – an unofficial source of information, which was for obvious reasons, totally unknown to the hierarchy of the DG.

This, of course, is not how things were supposed to work. According to official doctrine, the DG draws up a draft proposal on the basis of general guidelines given by the Commissioner. When ready, the director-general sends the draft by internal post to the office of the head of cabinet. Only then are we supposed to know what the draft contains. Naturally, I had already known for some time, and so I had to feign ignorance. Play-acting is an important quality in a mandarin.

Drafts from other directorates-general were more of a problem. A Commissioner's cabinet is not only interested in its own portfolio; it also keeps a watchful eye on the portfolios of other Commissioners. Ultimately, a mandarin has to detect draft proposals of a possible competitor far in advance, because information, if timely received, is power. But how to do it?

In the Commission, there is a never-ending underground stream of draft proposals in preparation, ranging from transport to culture, from energy to immigration, from public health to development aid. The draft proposals are drawn up in the relevant directorate and are then circulated to the other directorates for 'technical comments', in a process known as Inter-Service Consultation (ISC). In practice, this often leads to arguments between directorates with conflicting interests, such as DG Transport and DG Environment, or DG Internal Market and the DG responsible for consumer protection.

This bureaucratic infighting between DGs is the moment for a member of cabinet, such as myself, to get his hands on a copy of the draft, via his own DG, which has received it for technical assessment. Using information obtained through his back-channel, he can then 'activate' his own DG colleagues to oppose the draft from the other DGs on 'strong technical grounds'. It is important to do this behind the scenes. If the cabinet of the Commissioner responsible for the draft gets wind of what is going on, revenge is certain to follow at a later date – resulting in the blocking of your own draft proposals the next time they come up for technical assessment by other DGs.

If the DG is unwilling to commit bureaucratic fratricide from within, a member of cabinet can always resort to the devious outside world to wreck the draft of the colleague mandarin. An effective way to torpedo a proposal could be to leak the text to the press during the preparation phase, accompanied by a little bit of negative spin. For example, if the DG Environment puts forward a draft relating to the pollution caused by buses, you can sabotage it by a press article entitled 'Commission plans to abolish double-deckers.' This would inevitably raise a storm of protest from Great Britain, since the famous red London buses are all polluting double-deckers. The next day, fat headlines in most Fleet Street papers would scream indignation and dismay which, in my humble view, should be enough to scupper the proposal. Alternatively, you could always do a leak to the French press headed: 'Commission wishes to privatise public bus service.' Hours later an angry telephone call from the French president will follow and the draft will never be heard of again. This is a simple and effective technique for smothering a draft at birth, but again it is important to ensure that the leak cannot be traced back to you. Because if it can...

Ideal headline to scare London: Brussels bashes Britain over buses!

LIFE OF A EUROPEAN MANDARIN

Once the consultation between DGs has been completed, the technical phase of the preparation is over. The draft is now subjected to political assessment by the various cabinets. Any possible 'landmines' in the proposal need to be removed before it reaches the College of Commissioners. This is achieved by, what officially is called, a 'process of consultation between cabinets'. For practical purposes, this consultation usually takes place in a 'special chef', a meeting attended by a member of each cabinet, the Legal Service, the Secretariat-General and, if needed, experts from the DG in charge of the file. In reality, these gatherings can turn out to be the political equivalent of a conclave of cardinals – and just as devious. The 'special chefs' are the perfect arena for some really nasty cloak and dagger work.

As soon as a draft reaches the political level – in other words, the level of the cabinets – national interests come more strongly into play. During my studies, I had been taught that a Commissioner works for the greater good of all Europeans. Like many things taught at school, this is not entirely true. In practice, many Commissioners allow themselves to be influenced by the wishes of their own national governments.

This can only have a damaging effect on the European decision-making process. The Princess wants consensus in the interests of European progress, but all too often national preoccupations are introduced into the debate via the backdoor of the Commissioner's cabinet. Perhaps this is only to be expected. The Commissioner was put forward for his job – a prestigious and powerful one – by his national government. It is only natural that they expect something from him in return. However, if national interests become too diverse, there is a danger that the Commission will become nothing more than a disparate group of national ambassadors – a kind of European United Nations.

Defending national interests – or fighting against them – tends to bring out the best and worst in people. I once had a real battle with a member of the Austrian Commissioner's cabinet. The Austrian Commissioner was responsible for Agriculture, but this particular member of his staff had a real bee in his bonnet about transport, especially road transport. Every time road transport came up for discussion, you could guarantee that the Austrian – his name was Michael – would make trouble. I come from a country where transport and logistics form one of the largest sectors of the economy. Dutch lorries criss-cross Europe from one end of the continent to the other – and that is the way the Ministry of Transport in The Hague wants it to stay. Many of these Dutch lorries pass through the Tyrol on their way to Italy and on this occasion the Austrian wanted to restrict heavy goods traffic on this route, because the roads were becoming overcrowded. It was a straight fight: I was for the lorries; the Austrian was against them.

The Austrian's opposition meant that I had to resort to alliance-forming. The art of politics is, by definition, the art of power politics. And the more friends you have, the more powerful you are. Before the 'special chef' on the transport draft, I telephoned the cabinet of the Spanish Commissioner for Transport. She had a proposal to harmonise driving and rest times throughout Europe. There is a large zone in central Europe – particularly in France, Germany and Austria – where all kinds of restrictions on transport apply. For example, in these countries lorries are not allowed to drive at weekends or on public holidays – of which there are many. Sometimes, I wonder whether Germany and Austria have more holidays than working days! This meant that for a significant part of the year the road network simply shut down.

I found this unacceptable. My basic premise was that a Dutch lorry had to be able to travel from Rotterdam to Rome and back within a week. If this wasn't possible, the Dutch transport industry would soon be on its knees. Happily, on this occasion my national interest happened to coincide with the Spanish Commissioner's national interest: for her it was also important that Spanish lorries should be able to travel from Barcelona to Hamburg and back within a week. Consequently, we were agreed that we needed to limit both the proliferation of public holidays and the restrictions on driving times. In contrast, the Austrian wanted as many restrictions as possible, in order to spare his beloved Tyrol. In this, he was supported by his traditional allies: the French and German cabinets.

I reached an agreement with the Spanish to try and blow their proposal out of the water. Not so much because I was against it in principle, but more to act as a counterbalance. We decided that our tactics should be the tactics of drama and exaggeration.

I was at my fulminating best. 'This proposal to further regulate driving and rest times represents the end of the free movement of goods in Europe. It is a step back in time. It is a shameful capitulation, etc. etc.'

I came across as the greatest lover of tarmac since John McAdam himself! We knew that this would provoke a reaction from the Austrian and it did. He was well prepared and had a note of support from the Austrian Permanent Representation to the EU. He also had the support of his Commissioner, another Tyrolean. They decided to exploit the environmental angle. The Tyrol was being smothered in exhaust fumes and consequently road transport needed to be transferred to trains! As might be expected, he was supported by the environmentally-conscious countries, whereas I had the backing of the traditional free market states of the European periphery, such as Great Britain.

Now it was time for our killer blow. Having polarised the situation nicely, we reintroduced the Spanish counter-proposal. In comparison with the extreme positions taken by the Austrian and myself, this proposal was moderate and balanced. My Spanish ally reaped the fruits of compromise: 'Some will say we have gone too far. Some will say that we have not gone far enough. We feel that we have found a happy medium.'

Not surprisingly – and as we had planned – the Spanish counter-proposal was accepted. They thanked me profusely for my near Oscar winning performance as the 'Brussels tarmac king', but I was also satisfied with the end result. We had limited the damage for the Dutch transport industry and I knew that the Spanish would do me a favour the next time I needed one.

And what of Michael, my Austrian opponent? Afterwards we became quite good friends. Just because you have different opinions doesn't necessarily mean that you have to hate each other's guts. I understood his position and he understood mine. We both did our best for our countries; it was as simple as that. We went out for lunch and he told me enthusiastically about the Tyrol. As the representative of a country much of which lies below sea-level, I promised him that I would one day visit his mountainous homeland. The nearest I ever got was to fly over it, but that was enough for me: I don't like heights, let alone huge mountains! Later, he was posted back to Vienna to take over the running of a national ministry and he invited me to his farewell party.

Sadly, it was not always that friendly. During one 'special chef' on regional policy I came into direct conflict with the cabinet of the Greek Commissioner. Admittedly, this confrontation was deliberately provoked, as part of a little piece of manipulation I had agreed to take part in. During the 1990s the Greeks were given 120 million euros of European money to set up a land register. Greek culture may stretch back for thousands of years but they had never got around to mapping land ownership. This was now to be put right using aerial photography. But aerial photography costs money. Lots of money. Ever helpful, Europe agreed to provide the necessary funds. And what happened? Well, not very much. The Greeks spent the money, but not on land registration. The area around Athens was covered, but they didn't seem too bothered about the rest of the country.

The Commissioner for Regional Policy, a Frenchman, demanded that 50% of the funding should be repaid. The Greek Commissioner, whose portfolio also covered regional matters, resisted fiercely. She defended the Greek national interest openly and unashamedly. You can always rely on the Greeks to stick together.

I had had nothing to do with this particular project and so my intervention in the 'special chef' came as something of a surprise. Once again, I sought to dramatise the situation. 'This is the Commission which spends money wisely. This is the Commission which expects results. The last Commission was forced to resign because of poor financial management. Surely we're not going to let it happen again?

We must practice what we preach. It is a simple matter of respect toward the citizens of Europe. The credibility of Europe is at stake. For all these reasons, the Greeks must pay back everything!'

The meeting room fell silent. Flowing rhetoric is not the Princess's usual way of doing business. Her use of language tends to be plain and simple, almost to the point of monotony. Appeals to the 'citizens of Europe' are acceptable, but only as a mythical concept – not as a practical means to a practical end. Nevertheless, I was supported by several of the other cabinets, who also felt that it was time for the Commission to show that actions speak louder than words. The Greek head of cabinet was furious.

'How dare you speak of our country like that!' he spluttered. 'We have started our land registry, but now you want to punish us, just because it is not yet 100% finished.'

Clearly I had touched a nerve. His outrage showed that he regarded my comments as an act of aggression against the Greek people! The French member of cabinet, who had made the proposal for a 50% refund, tried to calm him down.

'I understand the criticism about only paying back half the money, but let's give Greece a last chance to complete their land registry next year. Then the money won't have been wasted after all!'

The Greek quietened down a little, but it was plain for all to see that he was still irritated.

Then an expert from the Legal Service – apparently a Dutchman – chipped in with his contribution to the debate. He referred to what he called a 'linkage'.

'Perhaps I can remind my Dutch colleague,' he said, looking pointedly in my direction, 'that there is currently a similar procedure ongoing against the Netherlands. They have misappropriated money from the Social Fund, which now needs to be paid back.'

This was true and it also gave the Greeks a weapon to use against me: the Social Fund was part of the Greek portfolio. But I was not to be intimidated. I had started something, and now I was going to finish it.

'I am not here to plead a case for either Greece or the Netherlands. European money should not be wasted – by anybody. And if it is, it must be paid back. In this case, we are talking about Greece: so Athens must pay up.'

The Greek went bananas. He stood up, started shouting in Greek – which hardly anybody understood – and stormed out of the room. His final comment, this time in English, was: 'I wish to submit a formal reserve against the draft proposal relating to the Greek land registry.' He didn't seem to realise that he was objecting to the proposal which was actually most beneficial to his country: 50% repayment instead of 100%!

During the next meeting of our cabinet, the Commissioner was full of admiration for my performance.

'Well done, that's what I like to hear. We have to be firm. No weak knees. Europe gives too much money to countries that waste it. The time has come to draw the line!'

This was fighting talk and part of me was pleased by his words of praise. Another part of me was asking why the head of cabinet wasn't joining in with the congratulations. Normally, he is falling over himself to agree with the Commissioner.

'Yes,' he said quietly, 'But now we've got the hot-blooded Greeks against us. Sooner or later, they'll get us back.' As usual, he was right.

When the Commission demanded that the Dutch should repay the money they had misused from the Social Fund, the Greek Commissioner was implacable: the whole amount, and not a euro cent less! Once again I went into the clinch with the Greeks, but this time without result. The Dutch ambassador was able to get the amount reduced fractionally, but The Hague still had to pay back a massive sum.

Ultimate responsibility for this sorry state of affairs rested with the former Dutch Minister of Social Affairs, Adriaan Melk. When I was a journalist, I had known him as an ambitious member of parliament and a rising star in the Dutch socialist movement. In the meantime, his ambitions had become even bigger and he was now aiming at the prime minister's job. Melk was a real 'place-seeker', in the old fashioned sense of the word. He was determined to get to the top of the ladder – and he didn't care how he did it. People blocking his way ahead were simply sidelined. He loved political intrigue and nothing gave him more pleasure than to publicly humiliate an opponent – especially an opponent from within his own party. But now the boot was on the other foot. What had Melk been doing with all this European money? The press and his political enemies were only too happy to try and find out.

One day I had a visit from a journalist who worked for one of my old newspapers. I remembered him vaguely as a rather serious young man – and very good at his job. In 1994 he had written an article about how illegal drugs were being allowed into the country by the police. Two ministers had been forced to resign and the government of the time fell from power. Tom – that was his name – had always been able to do a good hatchet job, but the scalps of two ministers was impressive by any standards. Not to mention the number of senior police officers who also had to go. 'Tom the Hatchet' now had his sights set on Melk. 'Do you know anything about this Melk business?' he asked innocently. 'Can I find out how the financial control was carried out?'

I didn't really know anyone in DG Budget who had been involved in the control, but I remembered someone from the same DG who had recently been passed over for promotion and was still very angry about it. He had been in the job a long time, and so he thought that this time it was his 'turn'. Unfortunately, the promotion went to someone else, for reasons which were never clear. Hell hath no fury like a mandarin scorned – and so I gave Tom his name: I was certain he would talk. I heard nothing more about the matter until I opened my morning newspaper a few weeks later: the headlines read 'Melk milks Europe: Sicilian methods in Melk's ministry'.

This was bad news for Melk and for the government in The Hague. Melk had messed up big time and had used European money to finance projects which fell outside the scope of the European Social Fund. He was not alone in this: many national ministers regard European cash as an additional source of funding for national projects. The trick is not to be too obvious about it – and this was where Melk had slipped up. Tom's report had given him a real roasting and the Greek Commissioner intended to make sure that the fire was kept burning. She certainly seemed keen to do all she could to make things difficult for the Dutch in general and for Melk in particular: perhaps it all went back to the trouble that the Greeks themselves had experienced with Dutch mandarins – including me! It was an almost perfect example of the Machiavellian way in which the Commission sometimes works:

we were angry at the Greeks; the Greeks got angry at us; consequently, they vent their frustration on the first available Dutch target – who just happened to be poor old Adriaan Melk. The chain of events was both beautiful in its simplicity and devastating in its effect. The favourite for the prime minister's job suffered one of the biggest election defeats in Dutch history – although this was not all the fault of the mandarins. A certain Pim Fortuyn also had something to do with it.

Pim Fortuyn caused a revolution in The Hague. An opportunity that was too good to miss for the European mandarins.

Of all the 'special chefs', the most 'special' was the meeting of the members of cabinet responsible for liaison with the European Parliament: the *Groupe Affaires Parlementaires* (GAP), later renamed the *Groupe Relations Inter-institutionelles* (GRI). Commissioners sent their most politically astute mandarins to these meetings, in the hope of learning what the European Parliament was thinking. This was the main purpose of the GAP: to pick up the signals being sent out from the institution representing the 'European people'. The Parliament had the power to sink any proposal put forward by the Commission and this was the very last thing that the Commissioners wanted. Even worse, it could sack the whole Commission! The GAP was a kind of early warning system, which could give important first indications of where things might be going wrong.

The chairman of the GAP was a Greek, by the name of Margaritis. At first, I hoped that this might be some dark-eyed Mediterranean beauty, but it turned out to be a middle-aged man with a penetrating, shrewd stare. He had a reputation for not being the easiest person to work with: 'Watch out for that Margaritis. He manipulates without you even noticing. He knows all the tricks. Typical Greek!'

And he did indeed know all the tricks: depending on the circumstances, he could command, direct, flatter, manipulate or intimidate. In fact, he would have made a very good Euro-MP himself. Perhaps, one day he will even become one. His attitude depended to a large extent on the level of co-operation he got from the individual cabinets. Although the Dutch are generally suspicious of the Greeks, I got used to his style quite quickly and had few problems with him. In fact, the only problem with the GAP was the rivalry between Margaritis and Lucio, who was a member of the President's cabinet. Lucio also had ambitions to be chairman of the GAP and this led to constant underground warfare between the two of them. The matter was finally resolved when a similar consultative group was set up for liaison with the Council of Ministers. This was the GAC: *Groupe Affaires Conseil*. To everyone's great relief – not least his own – Lucio was made chairman. Now that they both had a toy to play with, peace and order could be restored. It was GAP and GAC, abbreviations which seemed to originate from an goose farm.

'Peace', however, was always a relative term with regard to the GAP. In an organisation famous for its Jesuitical way of doing business, the meetings of the GAP were the most Jesuitical of all. How did this work? On the basis of reports from the GAP, the Commission would adopt a position on amendments tabled by the Parliament to draft legislation which had been proposed by the Commission. The GAP report suggested which amendments should be accepted and which rejected. Sounds simple? The problem was that there was almost never a straight 'yes' or 'no' recommendation. Instead, the recommendations were nearly always 'yes, but' or 'no, unless'.

This allowed plenty of room for political manoeuvre – and there is nothing a mandarin likes more than room for manoeuvre – but it also left plenty of room for shady dealings behind the scenes. For example, some Commissioners tried to use the legislative procedure with Parliament to make up for lost ground in the Commission. Let's imagine that the Environmental Commissioner tries to influence a proposal of the Transport Commissioner by suggesting stricter environmental norms. The College of Commissioners rejects this suggestion, because most of them think that the boys and girls of the 'green' DG are often prone to exaggeration. The Environmental Commissioner has lost his battle and the proposal is forwarded to Parliament in its original form. But he has not yet lost the war.

Frustrated by this defeat, the Environment DG will then contact an active member of the Parliament's Environment Committee. They agree that he (or she) will submit an amendment on behalf of the Parliament suggesting the same norms that have been rejected in the

Commission. Now, the Environmental Commissioner is suddenly in the driving seat. The proposed amendment then comes before the GAP, where the cabinet of the Environment Commissioner can once again try and persuade their colleagues to accept the parliamentary amendment – which is, in fact, their own – this time appealing to democratic sentiment: 'Parliament is important: it is the voice of the people and we must listen. If not, the members of Parliament might even consider sacking us!' And as the aforementioned colleagues also have amendments which they would like to see accepted or rejected, there is scope for some serious horse-trading. In this way a Commissioner who has lost a battle in the Commission can sometimes win the war in Parliament! Of course, provided the mandarins play the game well.

Most members of the European Parliament are happy to play along with this game. The ready-made amendments actually lighten their work load, since they are prepared in advance by the mandarins or lobbyists of the relevant DG in Brussels. And if the amendment is successful, they will get a share of the glory – and all for doing nothing. Problems only arise when the matters at issue are so complex that the MEPs cannot even understand their own amendments. For example, the directive on pleasure boats contained line after line of mathematical formulae that even a nuclear physicist would have been hard pushed to understand! Needless to say, the amendment was prepared by the lobbyists representing the interests of boat manufacturers.

The GAP is also sometimes used as a setting for the traditional battles between the Commission's own DGs. There was once a Euro-MP who wanted the Commission to answer a written question on the cross-border transportation of deceased European citizens; an unfortunate event which occurs increasingly because people travel more than in the old days and retired North European citizens now often spend several months in Spain. Transportation of a dead person is actually a very complicated legal matter and our DG Internal Market wanted nothing to do with it. 'Our job is the free transport of goods; not the free transport of stiffs.'

I was sent off to the GAP meeting where the matter would be discussed, but the director-general also sent one of his assistants along, to keep an eye on me. I had been given clear instructions: there was to be no compromise. Dead bodies are not goods, so the issue of free movement of goods is not affected. I tried to push the whole question onto the DG responsible for public health. Perhaps the dead citizen had been ill before he died? Did this not make it their responsibility? Their answer was short and to the point.

'If someone is dead, the question of health no longer arises. By definition, the dead are not healthy. On the contrary, they are very unhealthy.' Well, I couldn't really argue with that. By now, the whole thing was rapidly degenerating into a farce and so I finally agreed, under pressure from the President's cabinet, to accept the question.

The DG's assistant was furious: 'You didn't put up much of a fight, did you? Not even against a bunch of corpses!' I answered that a clever person must sometimes be clever enough to realise that not always appearing to be the cleverest is sometimes the cleverest thing of all. I'm not sure if he understood me but my arguments did little to cool his anger. Our DG had suffered a defeat in the GAP: this was far more important than any compassion we might have shown to our deceased European citizens and their families.

After attending hundreds of these meetings, I gradually came to understand that each country has its own different method of negotiating. When these different cultures collide, it can sometimes lead to problems, especially in an organisation where consensus is the name of the game. This makes negotiation one of the most important skills that a mandarin can possess. I always thought that the Dutch were poor negotiators, because they ignore the concept of power. The Dutch think that 'good arguments' and 'correct behaviour' will always secure a majority for their proposals. They negotiate with the morality of a priest. Say the right thing, do the right thing and the gates of paradise will automatically open. But this is not how things work in the Princess's kingdom. The stakes are high and the fighting is correspondingly hard. When vital interests are affected, power counts for everything and morality only applies after the game has ended.

The Italian negotiator is much better. He appears sympathetic but is shrewd, even devious. He says one thing but does another. He invites you for a 'frank and open discussion', whilst at the same time making deals behind your back that will tie you up in knots. During 'special chefs' I was often driven into a corner by the Italians. They had two secrets weapons. Firstly, they operated by eye-contact. No screaming and shouting for them: they preferred to give you the 'death look' instead. Secondly, they worked as a team. No sooner had one Italian finished with an intervention than another one started. Before you knew where you were, they had you pinned down. After having got what they wanted, they would give you a friendly pat on the shoulder: *Siamo Amici!*

French negotiators prefer to rely on *la logique*. Strangely enough, this logic usually coincides with French national interest. They refer constantly to structures, to precedents, jurisprudence of the Court of Justice, to linkages and, if need be, even to an opinion of the Committee of the Regions. They are pedantic to the point of boredom, gradually wearing you down until they get the best possible results for themselves. The French are born negotiators, and the British are also better than many people think. The Dutch always make the mistake of believing that the British think the same way as they do. They don't. The British might not have *la logique*, but instead they have the 'pragmatic approach' – which once again is little more than a euphemism for self-interest. The British do not hold long philosophical discourses, unlike the French, who can go on for hours. Instead, they attempt to reach 'made-to-measure' solutions based on practical suggestions: sometimes so practical that the entire contents of a draft proposal can be turned around without you even realising it.

The Belgians are quiet negotiators, who prefer to secure their own interests via the back door. There is nothing 'up-front' about a Belgian negotiator. They lack the menace of the Italians and the subtlety of the French. There is, however, one thing that they are very good at: waiting until the last minute and then rushing to support the side they think is going to win.

The Germans are a bit like the Dutch. They are always convinced that they are right and get upset when nobody else agrees. Sometimes they are too ideological. They are either for a proposal or against it. The Italians are usually both. A Belgian will readily accept a compromise, but the Germans get moody if they don't get their own way. This can be a problem, because there are an awful lot of Germans in Europe. For a large nation with a large population, it is surprising how badly they negotiate. The origins of this shortcoming are to be found in their regional divisions. The regions have great power within the federal German state – particularly Bavaria, which has even bought a castle near the European Parliament to boost its own image. In comparison, the image of the federal government is pale and bland: plenty of German efficiency, but not much else. The Germans are also handicapped by two other important factors: they are the richest country, so that everyone expects them to pay; they are historically the most guilt-ridden country, so that they often feel obliged to pay. This has become less evident in recent years and Germany is starting to make use of its numerical strength, particularly in the European Parliament. This means that they can often win back in Strasbourg what they lose in Brussels.

The most difficult negotiators – at least, if you have to deal with them – are the Spanish and the Poles. They feel themselves superior to the smaller countries but inferior to the larger ones. Their greatest weakness is their pride – but sometimes this can also be their greatest strength. Notwithstanding their relative economic poverty, they demand to be treated like one of the big boys. They are capable of holding any meeting to ransom – even major European summits – until they get their own way. The macho Spanish approach is perhaps best expressed in the phrase: *poner los cojones en la mesa* (put your balls on the table!). The Poles go about things differently, exploiting their role as 'a victim of history'. Yet in spite of the difference in tactics, they both normally get what they want – usually with painful financial consequences for one or other European fund.

The Spanish prime minister Aznar: poner los cojones en la mesa!

These different negotiating styles are perhaps most evident in the supreme council of the European mandarins – the Hebdo. This is the weekly meeting of the heads of cabinet – a kind of solemn high mass for the people who make the whole European system tick. The meetings last much longer than the meetings of the Commissioners – as though the importance of their discussions can be measured by the number of words they use. There is something almost Oriental about the Hebdo. It is rather like one of those Javanese puppet shows with Wajang and Dalang. The Commissioners are the Wajang, the brightly coloured dolls who dance on the stage. The heads of cabinet are the Dalang, the master-storytellers who operate the strings of the Wajang from behind the anonymity of a white cloth.

Brussels is full of Wajang dolls, but who are the Dalam?

There was once a Danish Commissioner who, shortly after taking up his post, announced publicly that he had nothing to say in his own directorate, because everything was decided by the mandarins. The whole Commission was indignant. A Commissioner had never attacked the mandarins in this manner and he was made to apologise. He did, but he was right – although in this case his impotence may also have revealed his own weakness.

In a similar fashion, a German Vice-President of the Commission once complained in the *Süddeutsche Zeitung* that high-ranking mandarins had too much power. He said: 'There is a permanent struggle for power between the Commissioners and their senior officials. Some of

Kleinholz statt Kleinfeld – das Ende der heilen Siemens-Welt / Seite 3

Süddeutsche Zeitung

NEUESTE NACHRICHTEN AUS POLITIK, KULTUR, WIRTSCHAFT UND SPORT

DEUTSCHLAND-AUSGABE | HKI | München, Donnerstag, 5. Oktober 2006 | 62. Jahrgang / 40. Woche / Nr. 229 / 1,60 Euro

SZ-Interview mit Brüsseler Vizepräsident

Verheugen: Machtkampf in der EU-Kommission

Deutscher Spitzenpolitiker kritisiert Einfluss hoher Beamter / „Manchmal geht die Kontrolle verloren"

Brüssel – In der EU-Kommission haben nach den Worten von Vizepräsident Günter Verheugen hohe Beamte zu viel Kompetenzen an sich gerissen. „Es gibt einen ständigen Machtkampf zwischen Kommissaren und hohen Beamten", sagte Verheugen der „Süddeutschen Zeitung". Die Spitze der Brüsseler Behörde müsse „höllisch aufpassen", dass die Beamten, die ohne demokratische Legitimation seien, nicht wichtige Fragen unter sich ausmachten, sagte er. Es komme leider vor, dass Beamte gegenüber den Mitgliedsstaaten oder dem EU-Parlament ihre persönliche Sichtweise als Haltung der Kommission darstellten.

Von Alexander Hagelüken

Der deutsche Kommissar verlangte radikale Reformen der EU-Zentrale. „Die Entwicklung der letzten Jahrzehnte hat dem Beamtenapparat eine solche Machtfülle eingebracht, dass es inzwischen die wichtigste politische Aufgabe der 25 Kommissare ist, den Apparat zu kontrollieren", klagte Verheugen. „Manchmal geht die Kontrolle über den Apparat verloren", fügte der Kommissar für Unternehmen und Industrie hinzu. Wenn er manche Schreiben von Beamten an Mitgliedsstaaten lese, sei er entsetzt, sagte er: „Technisch, arrogant, von oben herab". Brüssel trifft ständig Entscheidungen, die tief in das Leben der 450 Millionen EU-Bürger und die Aktivitäten europäischer Unternehmen eingreifen. Damit stellt sich die Frage nach der demokratischen Rechtfertigung Brüsseler Entscheidungen. Während die Kommissare von den Regierungschefs ausgewählt und damit indirekt von den EU-Bürgern, fehlt den rund 16 000 Beamten solche Legitimation. Dennoch „müssen die Kommissare höllisch aufpassen, dass wichtige Fragen in ihrer wöchentlichen Sitzung entschieden werden, statt dass dies Beamte unter sich ausmachen", sagte Verheugen. Mancher Beamte denke sich: „Der Kommissar ist nach fünf Jahren wieder weg, ist also nur ein zeitweiliger Hausbesetzer, ich aber bleibe".

Als Beispiel für eigenmächtiges Handeln erwähnte er Regeln für den Einsatz von Pestiziden, die Europas Verbraucher, Landwirte und Industrie potentiell stark betreffen. Die Beamten hätten versucht, dies unter sich auszumachen. „Die Kommissare haben von dieser Frage nur erfahren, weil es plötzlich Streit zwischen den Beamten gab. Dabei wäre dies von vorneherein ein Thema für die Kommissare gewesen". Öffentliche Aufmerksamkeit hat der Streit um die Zukunft der deutschen Sparkassen mit ihren 370 000 Beschäftigten und vielen Millionen Privatkunden erregt. Dabei hatten Brüsseler Beamte der Bundesregierung im August nach Ansicht von Beobachtern weit strengere Vorgaben gemacht, als die EU-Kommissare zuvor beschlossen hatten.

Verheugen macht auch die Macht der Beamten dafür verantwortlich, dass die Bürokratie in Europa so groß ist: „Meine These ist, dass insgesamt zu viel von Beamten entschieden wird". Er hat es zu einem Hauptziel erklärt, die Bürokratie zu reduzieren. Dadurch könnten Europas Firmen mindestens 75 Milliarden Euro einsparen, die heute für Formulare oder Statistiken aufgewandt werden.

Um die Macht der Beamten in den Generaldirektionen einzudämmen, fordert Verheugen einschneidende Veränderungen in der EU-Zentrale. So sollten die Kommissare nach dem Vorbild deutscher Minister hohe Beamte auswechseln dürfen, was sie bisher nicht können. Auch sollen die Kommissare die Hoheit über die Geldverwendung in den Generaldirektionen bekommen. „Alles, was in Deutschland selbstverständlich ist, geht in der Kommission nicht". Verheugen fordert schlankere Strukturen: „Nicht weniger Mitarbeiter, sondern weniger Generaldirektionen" (Seite 5)

EU verliert Geduld mit Iran

Solana kritisiert harte Haltung Teherans im Atomstreit

wtr **Brüssel** – Der EU-Außenbeauftragte Javier Solana hat wegen der starren Haltung Teherans vorerst den Versuch aufgegeben, eine diplomatische Lösung im Atomstreit mit Iran zu finden. „Der Dialog kann nicht ewig dauern", sagte Solana am Mittwoch vor Vertretern des Europaparlaments in Brüssel. Damit dürfte der Fall in Kürze wieder vor dem UN-Sicherheitsrat landen. „Und dann geht es natürlich um Sanktionen", sagte ein hoher Diplomat der *Süddeutschen Zeitung*. Am Wochenende hatte Solana die USA, Großbritannien, Frankreich, Russland und China sowie Deutschland darüber unterrichtet, dass er keinen Sinn in weiteren Gesprächen sehe. Teheran sei nicht bereit, sich in der Frage der Aussetzung der Urananreicherung zu bewegen. Iran steht im Verdacht, Atombomben bauen zu wollen, was Teheran bestreitet.

Verhandlungen über das Angebotspaket, das die fünf Veto-Mächte und Deutschland im Sommer für Iran zusammengestellt hatten, werden deshalb nicht stattfinden. Stattdessen werden die Außenminister der sechs Länder vermutlich bereits am kommenden Wochenende über ihr Vorgehen beraten. Der weitere Weg ist vorgezeichnet, denn die sechs hatten sich bereits im Juli darauf verständigt, den Fall dem Sicherheitsrat zu überstellen, wenn Teheran sich nicht auf Verhandlungen einlässt.

Während die USA schon lange auf Sanktionen drängen, hat die EU in den vergangenen Wochen versucht, Teheran noch zu Verhandlungen zu bewegen. Dazu dienten Gespräche darüber, wie diese Verhandlungen aussehen könnten. Solana konferierte zweimal mit Irans Unterhändler Ali Laridschani. Weil Iran aber nicht einmal für die Dauer der Verhandlungen auf die Anreicherung verzichten wolle, sei mit ihm derzeit „kein Geschäft möglich", sagte ein Diplomat. (Seite 11)

Menschliches Versagen

Staatsanwalt ermittelt gegen Transrapid-Fahrdienstleiter

rtw **Hamburg** – Das Personal im Leitstand der Transrapid-Versuchsstrecke trägt nach Ansicht der Staatsanwaltschaft Osnabrück die Hauptschuld an dem schweren Unfall der Magnetschwebebahn, bei dem am 22. September 23 Menschen starben. Behördensprecher Alexander Retemeyer sagte am Mittwoch, die Auswertung des Funkverkehrs habe eindeutig ergeben, dass die zwei Männer im Leitstand die Strecke für die Fahrt des Transrapid freigegeben hätten, obwohl sich noch ein Servicefahrzeug auf den Schienen befunden habe. Ein Kommando an die Besatzung dieses Fahrzeugs, die Strecke zu verlassen, habe es nicht gegeben. Gegen die zwei Leitstellen-Mitarbeiter wird wegen fahrlässiger Tötung in 23 Fällen und fahrlässiger Körperverletzung in zehn Fällen ermittelt. Gleichzeitig entlasteten die Ermittler die Betreibergesellschaft des Transrapid. Die Genehmigungen für sämtliche Fahrzeuge seien in Ordnung gewesen. Auch dass sich Transrapid und Servicefahrzeug gleichzeitig auf der Strecke befunden hätten, sei vorschriftsgemäß gewesen: „Wäre die Betriebsvorschrift eingehalten worden, hätte der Unfall nicht passieren können", sagte Retemeyer.

Auf dem Tonband mit dem Funkverkehr ist nach Auskunft der Ermittler die Anweisung an das Personal im Transrapid zu hören loszufahren. Kurz nach dem Zusammenstoß der Magnetschwebebahn mit dem Werkstattzug sei die Frage zu hören: „Was ist passiert?" Darauf habe das Leitstand-Personal geantwortet: „Wir haben vergessen, das Sonderfahrzeug von der Strecke wegzurangieren."

Rätselhaft bleibt, warum der Lokführer trotz guter Sicht den Transrapid nicht rechtzeitig gebremst hat. Er habe sich zweifelsfrei im Führerstand befunden, sagte Retemeyer. Der Lokführer kam ums Leben. (Panorama)

Regierung warnt Airbus vor Wortbruch

Wirtschafts- und Finanzminister fordern Erhalt der Jobs in Hamburg / Flugzeughersteller will Milliarden sparen

Von Ulrich Schäfer
und Cornelia Knust

Berlin/München – Die Bundesregierung hat den Flugzeugbauer EADS davor gewarnt, die Produktion des größten Passagierflugzeugs der Welt, des Airbus *A380*, ganz oder teilweise aus Hamburg abzuziehen. Wirtschaftsminister Michael Glos (CSU) will Airbus-Chef Christian Streiff bei einem Treffen an diesem Donnerstag dazu drängen, dass Airbus „die im Zusammenhang mit der Entwicklung und Produktion des *A380* gegenüber der deutschen Seite gemachten Zusagen einhält". Auch Finanzminister Peer Steinbrück (SPD) forderte, der europäische Luft- und Raumfahrtkonzern dürfe nicht auf Kosten der Jobs in Deutschland umgebaut werden. Steinbrück forderte, „das europäische Gleichgewicht im Konzern" bei Wertschöpfung und Jobs müsse beibehalten werden.

An EADS sind die Staaten Frankreich, Spanien und Russland direkt oder indirekt beteiligt, und ebenso der deutsche DaimlerChrysler-Konzern. Das Bundeskabinett diskutierte am Mittwoch auch darüber, ob die deutsche Staatsbank KfW möglicherweise bei EADS einsteigen solle. Dies sei aktuell nicht geplant, aber eine „theoretische Möglichkeit", sagte ein Regierungssprecher. Die Bundesregierung will zunächst nach privaten Investoren Ausschau halten, die den deutschen Einfluss bei dem europäischen Unternehmen sichern könnten. Diese stünden allerdings „nicht Schlange", sagten Regierungsvertreter.

Der Flugzeughersteller hatte zuvor bekannt gegeben, dass er die Arbeit an seinen europäischen Standorten neu organisieren will. In wenigen Monaten soll die Entscheidung fallen, ob das Großflugzeug *A380* komplett am Airbus-Stammsitz in Toulouse gebaut wird. Hamburg bekäme die Fertigung der Kurzstreckenflugzeuge. „Wir werden auch die Tabus angehen", sagte Airbus-Chef Christian Streiff in einer Telefonkonferenz. Doppelarbeit und unnützes Hin- und Herschaffen von Teilen oder Flugzeugen zwischen Standorten will er nicht mehr dulden. Auch die Frage, wie viel Prozent eines Flugzeugs Airbus selber fertigt und wie viel Lieferanten machen, soll rein betriebswirtschaftlich entschieden werden. Zur Senkung des Währungsrisikos will Streiff künftig mehr Arbeiten in den Dollarraum verlegen. Außerdem plant Streiff ein Sparprogramm vor allem bei den Verwaltungskosten, das jährlich zwei Milliarden Euro einsparen soll.

Streiff reagiert damit auf die neuerliche Produktionsverzögerung beim *A380*. Das erste Flugzeug wird nun nicht nur ein, sondern zwei Jahre später als geplant ausgeliefert. Der Aktienkurs der Airbus-Mutter EADS sankt deshalb am Mittwoch zeitweise um mehr als zehn Prozent. An diesem Donnerstag will EADS auf einer Sitzung des europäischen Betriebsrats die Pläne erläutern. „Ich gehe davon aus, dass das Ganze sozialverträglich vonstatten geht", sagte Rüdiger Lütjen, Gesamtbetriebsratsvorsitzender von Airbus Deutschland. Er wies auf den bis 2012 laufenden Tarifvertrag hin, in dem die Beschäftigten längere und flexiblere Arbeitszeiten hingenommen hatten im Tausch für Jobgarantien. „Das Entsetzen in der Belegschaft ist deutlich spürbar", sagte er. (Seiten 2, 4 und Wirtschaft)

The greatest commandment: Thou shalt not chastise the European mandarins!

the latter regard the Commissioner as a temporary irritant: 'he'll be gone in five years, but I'll still be here'. As a result, they often defend their own vision as though it was the Commission's official position. That is the real bureaucratic problem of Europe.'

The top mandarins were infuriated by this public telling-off and decided to get their own back. They said that the Commissioner had made the comments because he was frustrated, or over-stressed, or just looking for another job in the European hierarchy. In reality, he had just come back from a difficult and exhausting visit to Poland and had

The German Commissioner was not completely wrong. Commissioners come and go; the European mandarins stay put.

given a spontaneous interview without briefing and without an LTT (line to take). Spontaneous or not, he was to regret his rash words. Because the Vice-President was vulnerable. And nobody can exploit vulnerability like an angry mandarin.

The Vice-President had a friendly relationship with his head of cabinet, a senior female mandarin. This was too good an opportunity for the joke-makers to miss. 'He's tired of being bossed about by high-ranking mandarins – except in his own office.' The Vice-President became a target of wit, if not the laughing stock of the Berlaymont. During a routine meeting I bumped into the German's deputy head of cabinet. 'My dear friend, I won't say a word,' I said, laughing. 'Thank God for that. I'm fed up of the whole business.' The expression on his face told me that he wasn't lying. 'And I'm afraid it's going to get worse. Sooner or later someone is going to leak the "friendly relationship" to the press. You can't chastise the mandarins and expect to get away with it.'

As predicted, a week after his initial interview the news of his relationship hit the headlines. There were photos in *Focus* and *Bildzeitung* – followed inevitably by questions in the European Parliament. It became even worse when *Focus* claimed to have pictures of the Vice-President and his female head of cabinet on a nudist beach in Lithuania. Apparently, the Vice-President had difficulty coping with the heat, because he was only wearing a hat! This hot news travelled fast along the corridors of the Berlaymont; the Vice-President, who was supposed to improve the economic strength of European industry, was suddenly nicknamed the 'naked chef' of European competitiveness. Some MPs, attracted by the scandal, thought there was a conflict of interest or – to put it another way – that the Vice-President had simply appointed his mistress. Luckily for the German, the European Parliament is in no position to lecture on sexual or political morality and so he got away with a bad fright. But the lesson was clear: if you mess with the mandarins, you'd better expect trouble.

The Monday meeting of the heads of cabinet is the final testing ground for draft proposals. Their cabinet staffs have already argued over the fine detail during the previous weeks' 'special chefs'. It is now up to the top brass to give their final blessing. The aim is to smooth out any last-minute wrinkles in the dossier, so that the College of Commissioners has to do little more than rubber stamp it. Every mandarin wants to make his dossier an A-point dossier – this means that there is full agreement over the contents in the 'special chef' and the Hebdo. The fewer items the Commissioners have to discuss, the better. That way there is less chance of them messing things up. The Commission's year 2000 draft proposal relating to immigration from third countries was an A-point – a decision which is likely to have major implications for several generations of Europeans was passed as though it was a mere formality, with a simple drop of the President's gavel. Much the same was true of the celebrated services directive, which later assumed Frankenstein-like proportions. Turning hotly contested issues into an A-point is not merely a craft; it is the real power of the mandarins.

To be fair, there are a number of things which can be said in defence of the heads of cabinet. It is important that the dossiers forwarded to the College of Commissioners do not contain too many contentious issues. The sheer scope of the different dossiers and their often technical content mean that it would be impossible for the Commissioners to discuss four or five problem points. They don't have the time and they don't have the knowledge required. For this reason, the number of points open for discussion in the College must be limited to one or two. Otherwise, the meetings of the College would descend into chaos.

In practice, however, even these one or two points are decided beforehand. Agreement is reached before the meeting even starts between the Commissioner responsible for the proposal and the President – and it is the President's head of cabinet who acts as the middleman. The other Commissioners can say whatever they like during the meeting – but it won't really affect the outcome. The President will announce the decision in accordance with the notes given to him by his head of cabinet. No wonder that most people think – correctly – that the President's head of cabinet has more power than an ordinary Commissioner. Everybody in the outside world knows the President, but nobody knows the head of cabinet. One stands in the spotlight, while the other operates in the shadows. He is the perfect mandarin: unnoticed, invisible, untouchable.

Mandarins oil the system. Thanks to them, everything has already been decided when the College of Commissioners meets on Wednesdays. This means that the meetings tend to be friendly, almost like the meetings of some exclusive gentleman's club. All the dirty work has been done behind the scenes by the cabinets. They have done the fighting; they have arranged the manipulations and the intrigues. All the Commissioners have to do is raise their hand in approval and then sign the draft directive. Moreover, it is not in the Commissioners' own interests to make too many waves in the Commission – if they oppose a proposal too fiercely, they know that the next proposal they make will be subject to the same fierce opposition. It is a system of 'you scratch my back, and I'll scratch yours'. Non-intervention is the best policy and the best thing to do – particularly in difficult circumstances – is to do nothing. And this is the way the mandarins like it as well – it means that all their hard work is not ruined at the last minute. Although having said that, there are occasionally Commissioners who try to swim against the current...

My Commissioner, for example, was one. He was furious when he heard that the free migration directive was to be approved as an A-point. 'What? An A-point! I don't believe it. A decision that's going to affect Europe for the next hundred years and we can't even be bothered to take five minutes to discuss it!' We were sitting in our cabinet, for our usual weekly staff meeting. The other mandarins looked at each other with anxiety, wondering what the boss was planning next.

'An A-point is good,' one of them suggested. 'It means that there is no conflict. Everybody is happy: the other Commissioners, the President, everybody.' For the mandarins, this had been a perfect directive, a procedure by the book. First meet, then discuss, then eliminate problems, then agree. Everybody happy.

'Well, I'm not happy!' said the Commissioner grumpily. 'We prattle on for hours in the Commission about petty fines for multi-national companies that can pay them a thousand times over, yet when something really important comes on the agenda, it's all done and dusted in time for lunch!' I could see that he didn't intend to take this lying down, so I wasn't surprised when he asked me to stay behind at the end of the meeting.

It was clear that he wanted to do something. But what? Officially he had to toe the line. The Commission had decided by A-point to embark on an 'open door policy' for immigrants. Europe had to become an 'Immigration Union'. An explanatory communication had been agreed and the draft directive would soon follow in the summer of 2001. We knew that the Parliament would be in favour. The press was also full of praise for the Portuguese Commissioner who designed the widely acclaimed immigration policy. However, he had devised this policy even though there was not one single policy instrument in place to steer the process: effective border control, application centres for legal labour immigration, a return policy for illegal immigrants to their countries of origin and effective legal measures against human trafficking. My Commissioner wanted action against what he called the 'mistake of the decade'.

'This directive is going to set the political agenda in Europe for years to come. I am not just going to sit by and do nothing.' He wanted another channel – and so I tried to give him one. 'There must be many national ministers who are as appalled at the prospect as you are. And a lot of their voters whose jobs are at risk aren't going to be too happy either. Perhaps we should be looking in that direction?' The Commissioner liked it – and so a strategy was born. We would approach national ministers, in the hope that we could form a counterbalance to our own Commission!

Naturally, we had to do all this behind the back of the head of cabinet: if he found out what was going on, there would be hell to pay. To him, violating Commission policy was tantamount to a sin. Equally, the spokesman had to be left out of the plot, because prior knowledge would only embarrass him.

At this time, Belgium was chairing the European Union and so I privately called a couple of my contacts in the Wetstraat: the Minister of Justice and the Prime Minister. There then followed a whole series of meetings with ministers from different countries, most of whom seemed to think the same way as we did. Gradually, our underground opposition movement began to win support. We weren't being terribly loyal towards our own Commission, but it seemed the only way to do something about this disastrous piece of legislation.

'The Commissioner is doing an awful lot of travelling lately,' said the head of cabinet one morning, probably suspecting that something was going on. 'Yes, there's a lot to discuss,' I answered. I said nothing about the nature of these discussions, and for the moment he left it at that. I always used to link the meetings to a lunch or to another subject which was related to the Commissioner's portfolio, so that it was difficult for others to guess what we were actually doing.

Did all our efforts achieve very much? To a certain extent it did, but eventually the matter was resolved by an outside event. The Belgian Minister of Justice, who chaired the Council of the European Ministers, had his doubts about the Commission proposal and he expressed his views over lunch at his office. He wanted to shelve it for a while. Procrastination would cover the proposal in dust and time would finally bury it. The Commission sent the draft directive to the Council on 6 September 2001. Five days later, two airplanes crashed into the World Trade Center in New York. Unexpectedly, the issue of immigration was put in a entirely different perspective. In fact, the draft directive never surfaced on the agenda of the ministers and in 2006 the Commission decided to withdraw the proposal and to replace it with more realistic draft legislation. But the utterly naive 'open door' policy

Immigration to Europe: an A-point in Brussels!

of 2000 had not failed to produce its effect. The press and the public only began to take notice when boatloads of immigrants started turning up on the beaches of Western Europe. These desperate people took the term 'immigration union' literally. And who can blame them? After all, the Commission had made it an A-point.

Following his tour of several European capitals, my Commissioner wanted to hold an general discussion about immigration in the College. He got his way – but only two years later. And even at this late stage, no definite conclusions were reached: it was considered 'too delicate'.

A skilful mandarin will try to bypass this long-winded decision-making process by using a 'shortcut' – a written procedure which is often used for the implementation of existing legislation. Suppose that there is an enabling directive relating to the approval of chemical products. After the directive has been passed, new products will continue to arrive on the market, also needing EU approval.

The Commissioner in charge can draw up a draft proposal and send it to the Commission using this written procedure. The proposal is sent to all the cabinets and if nobody reacts before a certain deadline, it is assumed that the proposal is accepted. After this, the proposal is dispatched to the so-called Comitology: a nebulous network of expert work groups, covering just about every subject under the sun. There are hundreds of these groups, most of them unknown, even to the members of the European Parliament. If the Comitology work group also accepts the Commission's written proposal, the proposal automatically becomes law. It is all very simple and all very efficient: the Commission can make decisions without the need to hold meetings and the mandarins can exercise policy through the bureaucratic channels they know and love so well.

This is how things would work in a perfect world. But the Princess's world is not perfect. There are so many written 'shortcuts' that nobody can keep track of them, let alone block them. The decisions are rushed through the College of Commissioners as A-points. The mandarins love the 'shortcuts', because they allow them to influence policy without anybody knowing. For example, a mandarin might use a written procedure to introduce VAT into a previously exempt sector. If nobody objects, the proposal becomes draft law. A new tax could be introduced, but nobody knows how, or why, or by whom. The decision is not announced in the press – which can sometimes be a problem, because it means the Commissioner gets no publicity. But for unpopular decisions this is not necessarily a bad thing. The best tactic is to launch a whole series of written procedures just before the summer holidays. There is no-one there to block them and success (and anonymity) is guaranteed.

In normal circumstances, the press is an indispensable part of the European circus. The most prestigious newspaper for the mandarins is the British *Financial Times*. An issue isn't an issue until it has appeared in the pink pages of Britain's premier daily. There is also the *European Voice*, but this is more suitable for the Commission's 'internal' news and the infighting it entails: the paper is widely read in Brussels EU-circles. For reaching a wider public, the mandarin will try and get his message in the *Financial Times*; for internal intrigue, he will use the *Voice*.

At the other end of the spectrum, there is the British *Daily Telegraph*. This is probably the most Euro-sceptic paper on the continent and is the standard-bearer for all European non-believers. The Commissioner once gave an interview to the *Telegraph*, working on the principle that even non-believers sometimes want to read the other side of the story. The Brussels correspondent of the *Telegraph* was a man with the impressive sounding name of Ambrose Evans-Pritchard. He came into our office one evening, shook hands, sat down and turned on his tape recorder. Jonathan, our press spokesman, also sat at the table, but he seemed worried. We could both see that the Commissioner was tired and that he didn't really feel like doing the interview. It was already late and it might have been wiser to postpone to a later date. Much wiser.

Evans-Pritchard started by asking the Commissioner why Great Britain still occupied such a special position within the EU. The Commissioner sighed, looked at the microphone and then did something that every mandarin dreads: he spoke his mind. No official EU jargon ('Europe is good, the Commission is necessary'), no Line To Take (although Jonathan had prepared him one) – these were the Commissioner's own thoughts, pure and unadulterated.

'Great Britain is the only EU country which came out of World War Two as a winner. One way or another, all the other countries were losers.' Evans-Pritchard leaned forward in his chair: this wasn't the kind of stuff he was used to hearing from a European Commissioner. 'Great Britain still thinks of itself as 'Great' because it never heard the thump of German jackboots down Whitehall.' He continued in a similar vein for another ten minutes. All the other European countries still lived in a fantasy land, as far as the war was concerned. The French think that De Gaulle liberated the country single-handed. The Dutch think that resistance fighters riding around on bicycles were a major factor in the Wehrmacht's defeat. The Belgians also see themselves as great resistance fighters, whereas in reality their political elite collaborated until five minutes before the Allied tanks arrived. The Italians are much the same: at the last minute they shot Mussolini and changed sides, to make it seem like they had really been good guys all along. The Austrians cherish the myth that Hitler was a German and Beethoven an Austrian, whereas in reality it was the other way around. Even the Danish and the Norwegians are at it: mention the name Quisling in Oslo and all you will get are blank looks. Strangely enough, the only nation to tell the truth about the war is Germany: they say that they lost and that the Third Reich was a big mistake. Only the British can say with justification that they were winners – although even they tend to forget the little bit of help they got from the Russians and the Americans.

It was an interesting theory and I could see that Evans-Pritchard was much amused by it. Jonathan and I were less amused, and we tried to interrupt the Commissioner with frantic bouts of fake coughing. It was all to no avail. The Commissioner just kept staring at the microphone and kept on talking. Only when he was finished did he look up – and then it was too late. Evans-Pritchard went whistling back to his car, with the story of the year in his pocket.

Gradually, the Commissioner began to realise what he had done. 'I've been a bit reckless, haven't I?' Jonathan, as always, remained diplomatic. 'Some of your comments were not exactly "portfolio-related".'

I said nothing: the damage had already been done. Two days later the article appeared with large headlines in the *Daily Telegraph*. The head of cabinet came and stood in front of my desk, shaking his head in disbelief. He claimed never to read the *Telegraph*, regarding it as a mouthpiece for Perfidious Albion. But he knew as well as the rest of us what had happened. 'Let me give you a little piece if advice – ignorance is sometimes the best form of defence,' – and with that, he disappeared. Two minutes later, the phone calls started. The first was from the President's spokesman.

'What the hell are you lot playing at? Are you trying to re-open World War Two?' I answered that the *Daily Telegraph* was a Euro-sceptic paper and that they had twisted the Commissioner's words to suit their own views. Remembering the head of cabinet's advice, I added: 'Besides, I didn't know they were such non-believers.' 'Then let that be a lesson to you,' he said – and hung up. As a mandarin himself, he preferred to accept the word of a fellow-believer instead of the lies of the non-believers, although in this case the latter were right for a change.

Press leaks always cause a commotion in the College of Commissioners. Sometimes an enquiry is launched to find the culprit, but this seldom meets with success. This is because the leak usually comes from one of the Commissioners or from someone in their cabinet! The targeted leak is one of the most important weapons in the mandarin's armoury. It is the perfect way to influence the wicked outside world. If a draft proposal is approved in a 'special chef', a member of the proposing cabinet will frequently leak the news to a reporter – preferably one from *the Financial Times (FT)*. A deal is quickly done. The reporter gets a scoop and all the background information he can use. The mandarin gets a positive article about the proposal on the day it appears before the Commission meeting. Everyone is happy, everyone is 'onside' – the mandarin's permanent aim.

Of course, some scoops are not really scoops at all, because the leaked documents merely have the status of discussion papers or non-papers, but the *Financial Times* will often print them anyway. Sometimes this non-news can actually become real news – simply because it has appeared in the pages of the *Financial Times*. No wonder it is the mandarins' favourite newspaper. It is the perfect tool for moulding public opinion and spreading positive spin. Moreover, it also has advantages for the journalists. Instead of having to look for a story, they are delivered on a silver platter, neatly gift-wrapped – by every cabinet in the Berlaymont! There are some people who think that there are hundreds of Chinese, Russian and American spies in Brussels, all anxious to learn the Princess's secrets. I don't know why they bother. All they need to do is buy a copy of the *Financial Times*.

I was happy to take part in this game and for many years I was one of the *FT's* best suppliers. Until the day I received a telephone call. It was a Dutchman.

'I work for the Commission's Security Service and I would like to come and have a chat with you, if that's alright.'

He announced this in a voice which suggested he would be coming anyway, whether I found it alright or not. I was surprised and shocked. I remembered vaguely that there was a Security Service, from the days when I tried to pass myself off as Ulyanov and Bronstein. Surely they couldn't have found out about that? An hour later the man knocked on the door and entered my office. He showed me his badge, just like in the films, and took a seat.

'I'm investigating a press leak in a competition case,' he said. 'An article has appeared in the *Financial Times*, with complete details about the fine, even the correct amounts. Only very few people knew this information.'

I was careful. In this case, I wasn't actually the guilty party – I had leaked nothing. But I wondered why the man from Security had come to call on me. He continued: 'You know the young reporter from the *FT* who deals with competition matters, don't you?'

He sounded polite and respectful, but his questions were well targeted. I did indeed know the reporter in question and had occasionally given him inside information about the Internal Market, in return for some positive spin. But how had the Security Service found out? I sensed that he already knew the answer to his own question and so I decided that it was best to tell the truth.

'And you had contact with him, around the time that the Commission made its decision in the case?'

This also was true, so I nodded confirmation. Suddenly, the man from Security pulled a huge pack of printed e-mails from his brief case – they had been reading my computer! I was puzzled, but tried not to let it show. The reporter from the *FT* – strangely enough, an Italian working for this most British of newspapers – was good at his job, and could paint a clear picture with very few words. But I was certain I had told him nothing about fines. I didn't know anything to tell! I denied the implied accusation and the Security man handed over his pile of print-outs. Fortunately, I was not the only person who had sent mails to the reporter and so my inquisitor left without clapping me in irons. Luckily, I heard nothing more about the matter – but I made sure I got a new e-mail address: outside the Commission and outside Belgium!

Like most politicians, the Commissioner was keen to have a 'good press'. My collaboration with the *FT* helped in part to ensure this, but sometimes the applause was more spontaneous. Every day, the correspondents from the press corps attended a daily briefing in the Commission's headquarters. Here they received information from the various Commission spokesmen about the issues which were currently being dealt with by the mandarins. I used to drop in on these briefings, partly for old time's sake and partly to find out what the press was thinking. It was here that I met the correspondent for the *Wall Street Journal*. Like most Americans, he was enthusiastic, and not afraid to show it. During a press statement by the Commissioner, he stood up and raised his hand, to ask if he could say something. The Commissioner paused.

'Mr. Commissioner,' began the American, 'I would just like to congratulate you on this excellent draft proposal. You're definitely moving in the right direction. Just keep on going, sir!'

The Commissioner wasn't quite sure how to react to this unusual intervention, but eventually managed to thank the reporter for his kind words. By this time, the Dutch reporters – who the Commissioner had once described as 'a bunch of wankers' – were falling off their chairs in laughter. The American's unintentional sycophancy gave them the perfect opportunity to have a dig back at the Commissioner. The Christian press had a field day. 'Our Commissioner was praised yesterday by the *Wall Street Journal*. Praised by the nation which believes in capitalism and greed. This must give every decent, Christian Dutchman and woman pause for thought.'

The American was, however, an exception. Most comments were critical rather than complimentary. This is not unusual – most politicians receive more brickbats than bouquets – but the Commissioner was always sensitive to criticism. For this reason, he used to send me regularly to the press room to find out what the reporters were saying about him.

Every year the journalists make a league table of the best and worst Commissioners. Every Commissioner said that this table was a lot of nonsense – but they all wanted to know where they stood! Initially, my Commissioner stood about half way, but later he rose into the top five. Oddly enough, the President was almost always in the bottom three. He used to pretend that he didn't mind, that he was happy to see the stars of other Commissioners 'shine brightly'. But it didn't stop him from sacking his spokesmen. Not that it was really their fault: the President's post is regularly occupied by someone who uses the vocabulary of a high priest, rather than the plain speaking of a born communicator.

The Commissioner often used to ask me about the mood in the press corps. I didn't always know the answer and so I used to ask our spokesman. In this way, we gradually created our own Politbureau – the Commissioner, the spokesman and me.

We had a weekly meeting to discuss press reactions and to plan interviews and debates. The head of cabinet knew nothing of all this – a Politbureau is, by nature, a very select group. Everything went smoothly until the head of cabinet saw the word 'Politbureau' in the agenda for one of the weekly cabinet meetings.

'Politbureau? What in God's name is the Politbureau?' I had little option but to explain. He was horrified at the existence of a forum beyond his control – and therefore potentially dangerous to his position. 'This cannot, shall not and must not be allowed. First of all, I know nothing about it – and I'm supposed to be the boss around here! Secondly, the cabinet has just one purpose: to keep the Commissioner under control. For his own safety!'

From then on, our Politbureau had four members – the head of cabinet came along to keep any eye on us. Yet media matters continued to occupy an important place in the Commissioner's scale of priorities. Sometimes he had problems with the Italian press, which can be a real headache, since Italy is renowned for its ability to cause trouble within the Commission.

One day I heard that a female correspondent from an important Italian newspaper had broken both her legs in an accident in Milan. 'That's a great shame,' said the Commissioner during one of our Politbureau meetings. 'Yes,' I replied, 'It's a great shame, but it's also a great opportunity. Send her a 'get well' card with best wishes for a speedy recovery.'

I bought a card from the paper shop in the Berlaymont and the Commissioner penned a few consolatory lines. That night I dropped it in the post box and waited to see what happened. Two months later, the correspondent returned to Brussels and thanked the Commissioner fulsomely for his kindness. We never had any more trouble from her newspaper. On the contrary, we had gained an ally.

Apart from the press, the other main source of irritation for the mandarins is the lobbyists. In many ways, lobbyists can be useful. They provide valuable background information and represent the voice of those most closely affected by the Commission's legislation. I never had any real problems with the 15,000 lobbyists who work in Brussels – but most of my colleagues saw things differently.

The lobbyists earn their money by clocking up 'declarable hours' – and very lucrative it can be, too. The best lobbyists are often former mandarins, because they know all the 'ins' and 'outs' of the system. Some of them can be a real nuisance; telephoning, faxing and mailing until they finally get an appointment. Once they are in your office, the 'declarable hours' start to tick. One of my first jobs for the Commissioner was to accompany him to a speech he had to give about journalistic photography. This was not the most popular, or interesting, subject in the world and I didn't expect many people to be present. Imagine my surprise when a dozen or more lobbyists turned up. They were no more interested in journalistic photography than I was: they had just come to 'make contact' with the new Commissioner and his staff. Even I was a target for their interest: by the end of the evening I had been given so many business cards that I couldn't get them all in my wallet! The telephone calls started the next week: the lobbyists wanted lunches and meetings.

The head of cabinet was suspicious. 'There's no such thing as a free lunch,' he said dismissively. 'There is always a price to pay.' And for the hundredth time, he was right. They always wanted something – and usually something I couldn't or wouldn't give. As a result, I quickly started to cut back on my number of lunches and diners. In part, this was a question of self-preservation. I was getting too fat! Like most mandarins, I began to measure my life cycle not in terms of years, but in terms of kilograms. Little wonder that the Commission doctor is one of the severest weight watchers in Brussels: he watches the weight of the mandarins!

I was even more careful with presents. Once again, the head of cabinet had warned me. 'Don't accept them: the lobbyists will have you by the short and curlies.' One day I received a telephone call from a Dutch telecommunications company, inviting me to attend the opening match of the European football championship in Brussels. It seemed like a fun idea, but I remembered the advice of the head of cabinet. I was only prepared to accept the invitation if I could pay the cost of the ticket myself.

'Pay?' said the representative of the telecommunications giant. 'I've never heard that before. I wouldn't even know how to go about it.'

I remained firm and refused to accept the invitation, unless they gave me a bank account number to which I could pay the sum required. A week later, they phoned back with the number. 'And how much does the ticket cost?' I asked. '200 euros, sir!' I almost fell off my chair. It seemed an awful lot of money, and certainly for a match involving the Belgian national football team! I paid up, but if I had known I would never have accepted the offer in the first place.

When I later moved to a new job, the network of lobbyists deserted me almost overnight. No calls, no lunches, no invitations. I no longer had any favours to bestow and there were very few 'declarable hours' to be earned in my company. I now eat alone and pay my own lunches.

5| The Widow's Best Friend

'And how do you think we should take this particular bull by the horns?' asked the Commissioner, as our official car sped along the motorway towards Strasbourg, where the plenary sitting of the European Parliament was taking place.

This regular four hour drive gave us plenty of time to talk and to catch up on our paperwork. On this occasion, the 'bull' in question was the liberalisation of European postal services.

'I haven't got the faintest idea,' I replied truthfully. 'It must be ten years since I was last in a post office.'

This was the truth, as well. Most of my incoming mail was of the 'junk' variety, which I threw straight into the bin, while the rise of the internet meant that I almost never sent an ordinary letter by post. Why should I go and stand in a long queue at the post office, when I could keep in touch with all my friends (and enemies) at the touch of a button?

That being said, I had happy childhood memories of our local village postman. He was always popping in and out of our house and was a positive mine of information. He used to sit at the kitchen table, drinking a glass of something 'just to keep him warm', telling us all the local gossip. If there was anything in the village he didn't know, then it usually wasn't worth knowing.

This information was especially useful to my dad, in his capacity as a member of the parish council. It allowed him to keep an unofficial check on changing political opinion within the local populace. At one time, everybody's political preference was common knowledge. In our village everyone was either Catholic or Protestant (with a small minority of liberals). However, when we became popular with 'second-homers' – rich people from the densely populated urban areas wanting a little house in the country – it became more difficult to keep track of voting habits.

This is where the postman came in handy. Newspapers could tell him nothing: almost everyone read the same local newspaper, the *Graafschapbode*, although a few also had subscriptions to national dailies, such as my old paper, the *NRC Handelsblad* ('a paper for university professors,' according to the postman). However, it was different with television magazines. Television and radio is politically coloured in the Netherlands – in other words, there are Catholic, Protestant, liberal and socialist broadcasting companies. These companies sent a weekly programme magazine to their subscribers, who tended to be supporters of the same political party. This allowed the postman to keep a check on who was voting for whom: information he was willing to pass on to my dad in return for the occasional glass of gin around the kitchen table.

To top it all, he also combined his postal round with the delivery of eggs, purchased at knock-down prices from my uncle. No wonder he was such a popular figure in the village!

The Commissioner was not really interested in my childhood reminiscences. He was more interested in how we could achieve a rapid liberalisation of the postal services. In theory, it was easy. Simply break the monopoly of the national post organisations on mail delivery, and the rest would follow automatically. However, the more I studied the background and the history, the more I realised that this wasn't going to be 'easy' at all. Our 'bull' was likely to put up a great deal of resistance.

The previous Commissioner for Post and Telecommunications (a German of some reputation) had also tried to launch a rapid liberalisation – and had fallen flat on his face. After German reunification, the

German postal service had been subjected to a major efficiency exercise: this amounted to the East German *Reichpost* being absorbed into the West German *Bundespost*. The problem was that the *Reichpost* just had too many staff: in the Democratic Republic, the postman didn't just deliver the post: he also kept an eye on his fellow citizens for the secret police. However, in typical fashion, the Germans bit the bullet and made thousands of these ex-informers redundant. The result was a more slim-line *Deutsche Post* which was ready for liberalisation. Much the same was true of Sweden and the Netherlands, where the old P.T.T. – known affectionately to everyone as 'Auntie Post' – had been radically reformed in the 1980s. It was on these foundations that the German Commissioner wanted to extend his liberalising plans to the rest of Europe.

Things had not gone exactly as he had hoped. He had wanted to hold an orientation debate about his liberalisation plans, but the preparatory 'special chefs' had degenerated into a raging battle between the different cabinets. In fact, after four 'special chefs' – all equally heated – he had not taken a single step forward. The key to the German's plan was the breaking-up of the monopoly which the national postal services held for the delivery of letters of less than 350 grams. Throughout Europe private companies were forbidden from processing letters beneath this magical weight, unless they charged five times the normal tariff, which made delivery unprofitable by definition. Heavier envelopes and parcels were handled (usually quickly and efficiently) by courier companies, such as DHL, UPS and TNT, but they felt that they were being unfairly restricted by the state monopoly. The justification for this monopoly was that it was necessary in order to guarantee the delivery of mail to economically 'uninteresting' districts. Deliveries to these districts were relatively costly, much more so than in the cities. The state post offices therefore needed to corner the lucrative city markets, so that they could finance the loss-making countryside markets from the profits. The French always managed to dress up these arguments in romantic imagery, defending the right of 'Grandma in the Alps' to receive letters from her darling grandchildren in Paris, Bordeaux or wherever. These arguments might once have been valid, but they were becoming rapidly less so in the age of the internet. As a result, most national services no longer needed the monopoly to subsidise their less viable deliveries. Instead, they used the money to buy up the express companies or to start other activities, such as savings policies and insurance. In short, the monopoly had outlived its social usefulness and was now simply a flagrant example of unfair competition.

The German wanted to sort out this sorry situation once and for all, but his plan had backfired completely. He didn't even get as far as an orientation debate, since the Commission was forced to resign prematurely. In the new Commission, responsibility for the postal services was allocated to DG Internal Market. DG Telecommunications was sick and tired of the endless problems with 'Auntie Post' and her relatives. They preferred to play with their bright new laptops and shiny mobile phones. Telecommunications was a growth sector, telecommunications was 'sexy' (as were most of the secretaries who worked there), whereas the post was a definite turn-off. As a result, the post was tossed into the hands of my Commissioner – and he wanted to carry on where the German had left off. Or rather, he wanted me to carry on where the German had left off.

Obediently, I went off to try and find what was left of the recently transferred postal affairs unit. To my dismay, all I found was one, not incredibly tall, Spaniard with a beard. He had been head of the postal section for years, but fortunately he seemed friendly and reasonable. 'Why don't you set up your "unit" here in this corridor?' I suggested politely. As a mere cabinet member I was in no position to tell him what to do and I didn't want to give the impression of bossing him about. I needed to work closely with this man and this would only be possible if there was mutual confidence and respect. His reply was timid, almost pathetic. 'Unit? I am the unit. All my other colleagues became so frustrated with the job that they left. Now there is only me...' This was bad news. Without experienced and specialised staff, we wouldn't have the necessary technical knowledge to make a draft proposal. This kind of proposal always needs to be accompanied by supporting documents based on a detailed understanding of the economic, financial and technological developments in the sector. All the member states – most of which were likely to be against us – had Ministries of Post with hundreds of expert officials. All we had was my short Spanish friend.

I hurried to the Commissioner's office. 'How are you getting on with that 'bull'?' he asked. 'The bull is fine,' I replied. 'But grabbing him by the horns is going to be a different matter. We haven't got a postal unit.' In typical fashion, the Commissioner took immediate action. He ordered the head of cabinet to issue an instruction to the director-general, 'requesting' that a postal section should be set up without delay. However, this was easier said than done. The mandarins with specialised postal knowledge had all moved on to bigger and better things. Nobody wanted to return to a specialisation which was widely regarded as unsexy, a recipe for stalemate and a non-starter for promotion prospects. For lack of a suitable alternative, the DG was forced to go begging to the national postal services, asking if they were prepared to lend us some experts on a detached duty basis for a couple of years.

This obviously put us in a potentially weak position. There were plenty of experts willing to come – the Princess's conditions of service have always been generous – but we knew that the national post offices would only send us staff who they thought would remain loyal to them. Several were even promised promotion on their return to the mother country, providing they kept feeding back information about the Commission's plans. In short, we now had our expertise, but we also had more moles than most secret services combined. Our postal unit was about as watertight as a sieve. Fortunately, there were some exceptions. There was an excellent British expert who worked loyally on our proposal for more than a year, until he was suddenly recalled to England. Apparently, the Royal Mail had no time for staff who were not prepared to leak all our secrets. For them, the word 'loyalty' meant 'loyalty to England', not 'loyalty to Europe'.

Not surprisingly in these circumstances, the national post organisations were extremely well-informed about our plans. Within weeks, we were deluged by an almost constant stream of lobbyists, each seeking to modify our proposals – and this was before we even had any proposals to modify! The strongest objections were raised by France.

One afternoon I received a visit from a Mr. Dayan and a small delegation. Mr. Dayan introduced himself as a representative of *La Poste*, the French national postal service. He was a short, grey man in a short,

Edouard Dayan (left), France's Monsieur Poste.

grey suit and he carried an impressively full brief case of documents. I showed him into our cabinet meeting room and invited him – and his silent colleagues – to take a seat. I soon learnt why his colleagues were silent – they simply never got a chance to get a word in edgeways. Mr. Dayan began talking – and he didn't stop. I was treated to a long lecture about precisely what I should be doing – and, more importantly, what I should not be doing: liberalising the postal services.

'*Monsieur*, you do not understand,' he said patronisingly. 'You come from a small country, but France is a large nation. Our 60 million citizens are widely dispersed. Our *patrie* is strongly dependent upon the *amènagement du territoire*. And in this respect, the role played by *La Poste* is vital!'

He pronounced the words *patrie* and *amènagement du territoire* as though they were sacred mantras, raising his voice slightly and looking upwards to the heavens in supplication. I almost expected him to make the sign of the cross! To be honest, I wasn't exactly sure what *amènagement du territoire* was, but I imagined it had something to do with town and country planning. I tried to counter him by suggesting that in a land of 16 million inhabitants, most of whom live below sea level, the Dutch also know a thing or two about *amènagement du territoire*. But it was like talking to a brick wall. Listening was not one of Mr. Dayan's strong points.

He carried on as though I had never spoken. 'There were recently severe storms in France. Whole villages were cut off. There were floods, there were power cuts, there was panic. Only one government organisation continued to function properly: *La Poste*. The postmen were the first people to reach the disaster areas.'

Clearly, I had been watching too many Louis de Funès films: I had always imagined a French postman to be a shambolic, slightly comical figure, whereas in reality he was a national hero! For Dayan, *La Poste* was the infantry of the French national administration, the backbone of the nation. Moreover, the postman was very popular: was it not he who distributed the pensions each month? Little old ladies gave him cups of coffee and little old men shared a glass of cognac with him, just like in my home village of Bronckhorst.

By now, Dayan was beginning to warm to his theme. In a monologue which seemed to last for hours, he waxed lyrical about the social dimension of the French postal service.

'In France, more than 300,000 men and women are employed by *La Poste*. It is the ally of the common man. It is the citizen's most loyal comrade. It is *l'amant des veuves*, the widow's best friend. You and your Commissioner will not break up *La Poste*. You will first incur the wrath of the French people!!'

Dayan stood up, shook my hand and left. His delegation followed him. They hadn't said a word during the entire meeting. As I rose from my seat, two of my suit buttons fell to the floor. I had been moving about so much in my chair during Dayan's endless diatribe, that

The French postman: the widow's best friend and the foot soldier of the French nation.

the threads had been worn away against the edge of the table! It was one of the most one-sided 'meetings' I had ever attended. In fact, for more than an hour I had been on the receiving end of a demonstration of finger-wagging French self-justification. Liberalism was apparently not just a political concept: in this case, it was also an attack on the immortal French soul.

The Commissioner remained calm when I told him what had happened. 'O, that's just typical French rhetoric. All mouth and no trousers, our Gallic cousins. Mark my words: we'll hear nothing more of it.'

It was not his most accurate political prediction ever: within a week the French Minister of Post had launched a savage attack on us in an interview in the *Libération* newspaper.

'I say this to the ultra-liberal Commissioner, sitting behind his fat desk in Brussels: there will never be liberalisation of the post office in France, *jamais, jamais, jamais*! *La Poste* serves our people and is crucial to our national administration. We will never accept a complete liberalisation of this great national institution.'

I placed a copy of the paper on the Commissioner's fat desk and waited for his reaction. 'Yes, it's a shot across our bows, but you have that in every negotiation process. Still, it might not be as easy as I thought.'

I could only agree with him. During the 1980s, Margaret Thatcher had liberalised almost everything in Great Britain: public transport, water, electricity and telecommunications. But even she had held back from taking on the 'widow's best friend'. 'And now we're going to attempt what she never dared!' I exclaimed. 'Dear, oh dear,' muttered the Commissioner, and carried on reading a thick brief on Basel II and the supervision of 'capital adequacy' in the European banking world!

I decided to test the water in a number of other cabinets, just to see what people were thinking. I made a round of tea and coffee visits, starting with our main source of trouble: the French. There were two French cabinets at this time: one was totally against our plan, but the other was at least prepared to discuss it.

I made an appointment with a young man called Benoit, who looked a little bit like Tintin. He was one of the few mandarins who came to work on a scooter, but he was nobody's fool. As a graduate of the *Ecole Nationale d'Administration* and a former *Inspecteur des Finances*, I expected nothing less. I wasn't quite certain what a job as a Finance Inspector involved, but I remembered from French films that it was a fairly senior post: if *La Poste* is the infantry of the French administration, *les inspecteurs* are its cavalry.

He knew the dossier thoroughly and had also received a visit from Dayan. I opened cautiously: 'We need to try and pick up the threads of liberalisation in the postal sector. The last Commissioner made a bit of a mess of it, I'm afraid.' I tried to play the role of an innocent soul who had been saddled unwillingly with a difficult dossier, hoping that he might take pity on me. Sometimes, a mandarin has to play the dupe, even if he isn't one.

The liberalisation of the telecommunications sector during the 1990s had been a great success: even the socialists had been enthusiastic. But the postal service, with its market of 90 billion euros per annum, was much more of a problem. The Delors Commission had made a modest start at the beginning of the 1990s, with the issuing of a postal directive, but the monopoly position remained strong. New private companies were given little room for manoeuvre and were forced to concentrate on express services. The national post organisations continued to employ far too many people. In countries such as France, Spain, Italy and Belgium, the post was often seen as a kind of safety net against unemployment. If times were hard, the politicians would make sure that their supporters were given a job with the post or the railways. The unions would then make sure that these surplus people were kept on, even when they were no longer needed. As a result, the post offices grew and grew, until they became a major political force in several member countries.

Benoit came straight to the point. 'I can support a gradual reduction of the monopoly, perhaps to a level of 100 grams. But it is out of the question to set a date for 100% liberalisation. That's a complete non-starter.'

He was certain that this was the most that could be achieved in France, where liberalisation is still a dirty word. Liberalising politicians in France are regarded as being only slightly better than paedophiles and when the French employers' federation timidly suggested that they were in favour of liberalising the post office, they were immediately condemned by the minister for their 'unrepublican attitude'. In other words, they were traitors, more or less on a par with Marshal Pétain.

My visits to other cabinets revealed much the same picture. Only the cabinets of the Commissioners from Germany, Italy and Sweden were in favour. Or, to put it another way, three out of twenty. The rest were either non-committal or positively against, usually for national political reasons. We were in an absolute minority and were faced by a pan-European opposition front. I kept in touch with Benoit, since he seemed to be the leader of this opposition group, although I knew that in his case there was at least some room for discussion. Besides, he was an intelligent *cabinetard* and in negotiations it is sometimes better to have a smart opponent than a stupid ally.

Notwithstanding the forces ranged against us, our DG was in an optimistic mood. Like the German Commissioner before him, the director-general wanted a 'Big Bang': a rapid reduction in the monopoly, followed by a total liberalisation within 5 years. As a Brit, he was above all interested in banking and finance, but he thought the same principles which had revolutionised these sectors could now be applied with equal success to the more mundane world of the post. He instructed our postal unit to draw up a draft proposal which would lead to a complete and high-speed liberalisation.

Originally, I, too, was a supporter of a 'Big Bang' and it was also the Commissioner's first political reflex. However, after my tea and coffee visits, I was starting to have second thoughts. My doubts were confirmed by the head of cabinet.

'If the French are against it, you'll never succeed.' Wise words, as always.

The French would fight liberalisation tooth and nail, and they had the weapons to do it. Perhaps their most important mandarin was the director-general of the Legal Service. If the Legal Service rejected a draft proposal, it was dead in the water. And for as long as anyone could remember, the director-general of the Legal Service had been a Frenchman. Consequently, in the world of the Princess any proposal could be knifed in the back by a quick stroke from a French *assassin de couloir*. Little wonder that the French always insisted on having the top man in the Legal Service.

It was only with difficulty that I was able to persuade the Commissioner that the 'Big Bang' approach was doomed to failure.

'There simply isn't a majority for it,' I told him with passion. 'And if we try to force it through, we'll end up like Napoleon at Waterloo.'

This was my dossier and I didn't want to see it miscarry. If things went wrong, I would get most of the blame, much to the delight of many of my mandarin colleagues. However, this was not what our DG wanted to hear. Spurred on by the director-general and supported – against his better judgement – by our Spanish postmaster, the directorate continued to turn out document after document in which an end date for the liberalisation was clearly mentioned. The director-general even turned up with his full armada of mandarins at a meeting in the Commissioner's office, just to convince the boss that they were right and I was wrong. Like the British in 1940, I stood alone. But would it be my 'finest hour'?

I somehow had to get closer to the 'ear' of the Commissioner. A 'special chef' on the postal question was scheduled and as part of the preparations I was called to the office of the President of the Commission. I was received by a Belgian lady with a Dutch (even Friesian)-sounding name and an Italian husband. Like myself, she had been inundated with telephone calls and visits from lobbyists. Almost every national postal service had sent its top men to Brussels, in order to argue for or (in most cases) against the liberalisation of the postal sector.

'How are things in your DG?' she asked, as we sipped our coffee on the thirteenth floor of the headquarters building. 'To be honest, they're simply doing their own thing,' I replied. 'I'm completely dependent upon them for the technical side and the preparation, but they seem to resent any kind of political input on my part.'

Suddenly and unexpectedly, she launched an attack against our director-general. 'Doesn't he realise that this dossier is politically highly sensitive? No, probably not, knowing him. As always, he's too busy concentrating on financial matters. It's easy to score points with financial matters, but if we're not careful, we could get ourselves into serious trouble with this postal business.' Then came the *coup de grace.* 'And he's really got to stop all those leaks to the *Financial Times.* I'm getting fed up with them. And so is the President ...'

I had also noticed how the director-general was appearing with increasing frequency in the press – now I knew why! Most Commissioners would have been against this type of behaviour by a director-general, but not my Commissioner. He reasoned that if the director-general explained a proposal in the newspapers, it would save him the bother of having to do it himself! But the President's cabinet had a different view. And before I left, the lady from the President's cabinet told me precisely what that view was: 'We reduce the monopoly gradually, but the President wants no fixed date for full liberalisation. Is that clear? If there's a final date, there won't even be a "special chef".' She stood up and I knew the meeting was at an end.

Back at my desk, I thought over what she had told me. As chance would have it, the director-general walked into my office at that very moment. He made a few jokes and we started chatting. He was actually quite a decent bloke, a typically British official, with the emphasis on 'British'. He would later be knighted by the Queen.

Our first meeting had been a bit of a disaster. I had just started in the cabinet, when the director-general came out of the staff canteen and headed towards the lift, with a cup of coffee in his hand. At the entrance to the lift, he stopped to talk to one of his staff and so he shouted to me to keep the lift doors open for him. As a new boy, I wasn't too familiar with how the lift worked, and so instead of pressing the 'doors open' button I pressed the 'doors closed' button! To save himself from being crushed, the director-general jumped back in alarm, spilling coffee all over his front in the process. The doors slammed shut and I went back to my floor, hoping that I would hear nothing more about the matter. Five minutes later, an angry director-general stood in front of my desk. 'I can see that I'm going to have to keep a close eye on you!' he said. His tie – which had been yellow that morning – was now a nice shade of coffee brown.

After this, our relationship gradually got better, but the postal dossier had led to some renewed friction between us. 'I've just been to the President's cabinet,' I let slip. 'Oh yes? And what did they have to say?' he asked, feigning disinterest. 'They said that they're fed up of seeing your face in the newspapers. They even think you might be leaking to the *Financial Times!*' The director-general went red with rage and the cup of coffee in his hand started to shake. I thought he was in danger of ruining another tie.

'What?! Me?! A leaker?! Never! Who dared to say such a thing! Give me their name! I'm going to call them immediately!' I gave him the name and he stormed out of my office. I sent a quick mail to the President's cabinet, warning them what to expect and then sat back to await developments. They were not long in coming. Within fifteen minutes, the President's cabinet mailed back, saying that I should expect no further trouble from the director-general. I never found out exactly what was said during that telephone conversation, but the fact that the director-general's mandate was up for renewal probably had something to do with it: a word in the wrong place from the President's cabinet can ruin a mandarin's career.

I was now back in political control, at least as far as the director-general was concerned, but there was still a risk of leaks from his department. The national postal experts who had been seconded to us continued to pass back information to their home capitals. It would be even worse if they now started to take over the director's role as press leakers. To avoid this possibility, I instructed them to leave all weight references in their documents blank. In other words, instead of '100 grams', the text must read '... grams'. I would then fill in the figures myself at the appropriate moment! It was a neat solution, I thought, but it didn't improve my reputation in the DG!

As a next step, I organised an information meeting for all the different cabinets. This took place on the day of the Schuman Anniversary, 9 May. I hoped that this would inspire some 'European' feeling amongst my listeners and was confident that my well-prepared information packs would do the rest. But I had underestimated the strength and efficiency of the opposition lobby. As I read my introductory text, all I could see on the faces of my audience was hostility. When I had finished, instead of asking questions they hurled insults and accusations.

'You want to ruin the post,' called someone. 'This liberalisation is unnecessary,' shouted another. 'You're just free-market fundamentalists,' chimed in a third.

I looked over to the representative of the President's cabinet for help, but she was examining her finger-nails. Clearly, she thought that the whole thing was a shambles – and it was. The only thing that could be said for my meeting was that it at least allowed people to let off steam. And there was plenty of steam to be let off.

The 'special chef' was approaching rapidly and I began to get nervous. I couldn't afford another failure but the prospects were not looking good. I decided to do another round of coffee and tea visits, in the hope that I might find some way to do a deal. After my visits to the two French cabinets, I noticed that their respective positions were gradually getting further apart. In particular, the chances of negotiating some kind of compromise with Benoit's cabinet now seemed a realistic possibility. I paid him a final call and decided to put all my cards on the table.

'Look, Benoit, this whole situation is getting out of hand. Are we going to help each other or not?' He repeated his cabinet's bottom-line offer: a reduction in the monopoly from 350 grams to 50 grams, with all the different types of post (letters, publicity material and cross-border mail) to be treated in the same manner, but with no final date for full liberalisation. 'Agreed,' I said. The rest was just discussion of the fine detail.

A few days before the 'special chef', I filled in all the blank spaces in my draft proposal, building in a little extra room for manoeuvre. I made the pace of liberalisation a little quicker than the French would have liked and I made the liberalisation of publicity mail total and immediate. If I could get away with these things, so much the better. If not, it gave me the option to make some cheap and easy concessions.

The next part of my plan was the traditional leak to the press. There had already been plenty of speculation in the newspapers about the proposal, but nobody had the right information. Their normal sources – the staff of the DG – were useless: nobody knew what figures I was planning to use in the blanks! I leaked first to the *Financial Times* (of course), and followed this up with the *Wall Street Journal* and the *Economist*.

These were all papers or magazines with a healthy respect for the free market and I knew that they would support us. Better still, I knew that at least one of them would argue for the pace of liberalisation to be increased. Best of all, I knew that they could be persuaded to release their articles at exactly the right moment: on the day of the 'special chef'. And this is precisely what happened.

The mood at the beginning of the meeting was still tense. I had put down my speech on paper, to make sure that my arguments came across clearly and concisely. I was reassured that I had been able to re-establish eye-contact with the lady from the President's cabinet. She might have deserted me during my information meeting, but she could no more afford a new disaster in the 'special chef' than I could.

Some of the cabinets supported me, but the majority remained against. However, I began to notice hopeful cracks in the opposition's united front. Benoit's comments, in particular, were more conciliatory than in past meetings and formed a useful counterbalance to the blatantly 'national' standpoints still being put forward by some other cabinets. Negotiation is not simply the endless repetition of the same fixed position, but rather a more fluid process. It is also a psychological process: if the pressure is great enough and is correctly applied, everything becomes fluid! This is the game I now began to play.

'I have listened to what you have said,' I told the meeting. 'I have learnt much and understood much. But now we must all be flexible and seek to reach a consensus. That is the psyche of the Commission.'

I started to juggle with the weight figures and the timescale. I obtained general agreement for a drop from 350 grams to 50 grams, but in return I had to concede that the new measures would be introduced over six years instead of four. Benoit insisted that this should also apply to publicity mail – or 'junk mail' as he called it – and to this I readily agreed: after all, it was part of my built-in room for manoeuvre.

During the meeting I was accompanied by the postal experts from our own DG. They began to squeal like stuck pigs when I started making these timely concessions.

'Don't do it!' one of them whispered in my ear. 'It's a trick!' Another even poked me in the back with a pencil. They thought that I was betraying their months of hard work. But politically, there was no other way out. It was this, or nothing. Benoit put forward the proposals we had agreed in advance and the meeting concurred. I said that I would need to consult with the Commissioner, and it was arranged that we should reconvene the next day.

At first, the Commissioner was as unimpressed with my concessions as the DG had been. He was more used to hard and direct negotiations, in the American style, and had expected me to adopt the same principled, free market approach in the 'special chef'. But this is not how the Princess works. In Europe, you must always be prepared to wheel and deal and the quickest route to success in usually via a detour! The head of cabinet supported me: he knew that we were lost unless we kept the two French cabinets divided. I was convinced that the deal would work, largely because I felt that I could trust Benoit.

'If we back his proposal, we will split the opposition right down the middle,' I argued. 'The cabinets which are already for us will stay with us. Benoit will bring ten more moderate cabinets with him. That will leave the hard-line opposition cabinets in the minority – six or seven at most.'

The Commissioner finally understood the political sense of what I was saying. Next day, I was able to inform the reconvened meeting that he gave his consent for the proposed compromise solution. Benoit thanked me for my *capacité d'écoute* (ability to listen) and the lady from the President's cabinet nodded her approval. When the vote was taken, it was almost exactly as I had predicted. We had changed a 3-17 minority into a 14-6 majority! It was a sweet moment, all the more so since the news of the previous day's inconclusive meeting had been leaked to the press, with the negative spin that the proposal was dead and buried. On the contrary, we were very much alive and kicking! Monsieur Dayan had counted his chickens too soon.

The draft proposal also survived its passage through the Hebdo. Our head of cabinet used the same arguments he had used in the past for dozens of other dossiers.

'Some cabinets will think we have gone too far. Some cabinets will think we have not gone far enough. We have chosen the golden path of moderation and compromise. Our proposal is balanced.'

Benoit's head of cabinet stuck by the agreed deal and the day was won. In all honesty, I find it fairly easy to negotiate with the French, providing you understand how they think. Admittedly, this is not an understanding granted to every nationality. Our British-dominated DG was convinced that the French would betray us – or 'drop us in the shit', as they so eloquently put it. The British have never been able to understand the French – and they probably never will.

The same story was repeated in the College of Commissioners. One of the French Commissioners was in favour, but the other was still strongly against. This was no less a person than Pascal Lamy, Jacques Delors' former head of cabinet. My Commissioner had breakfast with him before the meeting. At a distance I could see how my boss knocked back a huge cheese and mushroom omelette, while Lamy ate carefully measured spoonfuls of diet yogurt. It somehow seemed to sum up the differences between the two men: the one liberal, flexible and moderate, the other socialist, rigid and radical. 'Pascal is still against,' whispered the Commissioner, as he left the dining room. 'We'd better get ready for a missile attack!'

A missile attack from *Monsieur Exocet* was something to be feared. Lamy knew the Commission better than anyone and he was a past-master at sniffing out the smallest weakness in a draft proposal. On this occasion, he thought that we had gone too far. 'We must reduce the monopoly to 150 grams,' he suggested, 'and then wait to see what happens.'

It was one of the longest Commission meetings I can remember. All the Commissioners (apart from the Brit Neil Kinnock) wanted to have their say and the debate raged for a full two hours. But at the end of it all, there were still only three votes against: the Greeks, the Portuguese and Lamy. This time his missile was off target. We had won!

The Commission's acceptance of the postal proposal was the first big success for the Commissioner and we celebrated that evening with a drink in his office. I also invited the experts from the DG and their bearded Spanish boss. At times, they had tried to sabotage our political line, but in the small world of the mandarins there is little point in bearing grudges. Today's enemy might very well turn out to be tomorrow's ally. Better to forgive and forget. Besides, in this case, the war was still not over. We had won a battle, but the hardest fighting was still to come. And this against the fiercest opponent of liberalisation: the European Parliament.

This new stage in the conflict began less than an hour after the Commission had cast its vote. The opening salvo was fired by a British Euro-MP, Brian Simpson, who issued a press statement in which he described the Commissioner as 'a fundamentalist; he is the Hezbollah of liberalisation.'

Simpson had not yet even seen the proposal, but he had already prepared a whole string of negative comments about it. This was perhaps not surprising. Simpson was an MEP for the British Labour Party and belonged to the wing of the party known as 'Old Labour'. This wing was still strongly socialist (which you couldn't say for the rest of the party) and proudly maintained their traditional ties with the trade union movement. Simpson was effectively a spokesman in Parliament for the British National Union of Postal Workers and it was largely on Simpson's resistance that the '*Luftwaffe*' of the German Commissioner's 'Big Bang' had failed under the previous Commission. Like many Brits of his generation, Simpson still loved to talk in terms of the Second World War and it was obvious that he intended to treat us to a *Blitzkrieg*!

I realised that we had to try and get past Simpson. In particular, it was important to make sure that he wasn't appointed as the parliamentary rapporteur for our new proposal. From his EU information sheet I knew that his favourite hobby was rugby and I was anxious to avoid a 'scrum' with him at all costs. The rapporteur of a proposed piece of legislation plays a crucial procedural role within the European Parliament. He sets the basic framework, negotiates with interested parties, seeks to secure a majority for possible amendments, etc. Given half a chance, I knew that Simpson would like nothing more than to kick the 'Hezbollah' and its liberalising plans firmly 'into touch'.

There was no choice: I would simply have to find an alternative candidate to Simpson. But how to go about it? I was just a lowly mandarin in the service of the Princess. I had no real power to influence the appointments of the European Parliament. Or did I? I decided to rely on the weapons I knew best: backdoor politics. As Simpson was a staunch left winger of the old school, I decided to target my efforts on the centre-right. I phoned some of my contacts in the Christian-democrat and liberal factions, suggesting that Simpson might not be the best person for the rapporteur's job. 'He's Old Labour,' I said. 'What's more, he has no support from his party bosses in London and has no real standing in the socialist grouping in Strasbourg.' And, much to my amazement, it worked! The Christian-democrats demanded the rapporteur's job for their grouping (the largest in the European Parliament) and proposed a German MEP from Bavaria. The Germans were still in favour of a rapid liberalisation of postal services and they thought that this Bavarian would be the man to bring it about.

I thought that I had carried out a perfect piece of political manipulation, but unfortunately I had left my fingerprints behind. At the first meeting between the Commissioner and the competent parliamentary committee, Simpson stormed to the front of the room and demanded to be heard.

'I have not been appointed rapporteur,' he accused, jabbing a finger in the direction of the Commissioner. 'And the only reason is that a member of your cabinet has been conducting a dirty-tricks campaign against me. I find this unacceptable.'

I was sitting next to the boss and continued shuffling my papers, wondering how he was going to escape from this one. 'My dear sir, I couldn't agree more,' he replied. 'If true, this is indeed unacceptable. I will have your allegations investigated immediately. And I will ask my trusted colleague here to carry out this important task himself!'

It took me a couple of seconds to realise that I was the 'trusted colleague' in question. Needless to say, my investigation never really got to the bottom of the matter...In fact, it was closed without any serious findings.

We had managed to secure the rapporteur we wanted, but the draft proposal was still given a rough ride. Simpson did not intend to take things lying down and he tried to mobilise support against us from all colours of the political spectrum. And credit where credit is due, he was pretty successful. He even managed to win over a number of conservative and Christian-democrat MEP's from rural constituencies, who realised that the liberalisation of the post was unpopular with their voters. They knew all too well that the post was indeed the widow's best friend.

In the case of one Euro-MP from Luxembourg, this was probably the literal truth! Astrid Lulling was 75 years old and still very much single. She was famous in her own country for an affair she had once had with a government minister. Such was Astrid's passion that the minister had not survived one of their love-making sessions. He had died on the job, so to speak. Afterwards, Astrid had been banished to the European Parliament – the fate of many misbehaving politicians – but she had lost none of her ardour. She took part with her usual fervour in the post debate.

'Mr. Commissioner, as you know, I am a romantic soul. If I order a wedding dress by post, I want to be sure that it will arrive before my wedding day. You would not like to see me without a wedding dress on my wedding day, would you?'

He assured her that he would not, and the chamber collapsed in laughter. Laughing apart, Lulling defended the interests of the Luxembourg post office with the same fire as she had once defended the continent's wine growers – she had been one of the most vociferous opponents of the introduction of VAT on wine.

Lulling's support for the Simpson lobby was symptomatic of the wide range of opposition forces against us. Old Labour or not, the Brit had managed to persuade a varied collection of socialists, communists, Trotskyists, conservatives, social democrats and nationalists to rally to his cause. Time after time, our rapporteur found himself outvoted in the parliamentary committee. At the end of these preliminary discussions, there was very little of our original proposal left. This did not bode well for the full plenary debate to be held in Strasbourg.

In fact, this debate was a nightmare from start to finish. It was worse than even our most pessimistic worst-case scenario. I had prepared a clear, Churchillian-style speech for the Commissioner, in which (like Winston) we promised to fight on the beaches, landing grounds, etc., etc. We had no intention of giving in to the forces of reaction and narrow national interest.

The Commissioner wanted to underline exactly what was at stake: the modernisation of the European postal industry in preparation for the global market. Unfortunately, he got a bit carried away with his own rhetoric, and some MEPs took exception to some of his more colourful phrases, such as 'no surrender to the old guard' and 'fighting for the future'.

'Mr. Commissioner,' interrupted one shocked German from Hamburg, 'you are addressing the Parliament of the free European nations – not the People's Congress of the Chinese Communist Party!'

Defeat was inevitable and next day the 'Parliament of the free European nations' cut our proposal to pieces. As I left the plenary, I looked up to the public gallery, where I saw a smiling *Monsieur* Dayan. No doubt he saw himself as one of the main architects of our humiliation and he was probably right: at least for the time being. Halftime score: Dayan 1 – the Commissioner 0.

To make matters worse, on my return to Brussels I found that we were now being opposed from within our own cabinet! The deputy head of cabinet, who was a tax specialist, thought that it was time to introduce VAT on postage stamps. 'This proposal has been on the back-burner for years. But after your defeat in Strasbourg, this is the ideal moment to make it an active issue again.' His reasoning was somewhat difficult to follow. Some northern countries had already introduced VAT on stamps, but the Commission would now have to sanction these countries because they were in contravention of European legislation, whereas the Commission itself was actually in favour of the actions taken by the countries it now had to sanction. The deputy's solution? VAT on stamps for everyone! This was madness and I told him so. If we couldn't get liberalisation through the European Parliament, there wasn't a snowball's chance in hell of getting VAT on stamps through. It would mean political suicide for the Commissioner with a capital 'S'.

The Commissioner called a special cabinet meeting to hear both sides of the argument. The deputy stuck to his guns: the proposal had waited long enough and now was the time to act. Next it was my turn to speak. I likened the VAT proposal to a Patriot missile: it would blow the liberalisation plans out of the sky and would bring the Commissioner crashing down with them.

The Commissioner asked the other members of the cabinet for their opinions, but most of them just sat on the fence: they didn't want to choose between me and the deputy. The Commissioner leant back in his chair and we could all see him weighing up the different views he had just heard. Like the true politician that he was, he accepted the validity of the deputy's arguments – but then decided to back me.

'The liberalisation proposal is currently balanced on a knife edge,' he explained. 'Trying to force through VAT might just tip that balance against us. We'll do it later.' The deputy was furious. After the meeting, he cornered me in the corridor: 'You and your bloody liberalisation of the post. You'll still be stuck with that dossier three years from now.' But he was wrong. It would cost us a great deal of time and effort, but two years later we succeeded in introducing VAT on stamps, after we had first successfully completed the liberalisation proposals. Of course, we used the famous 'written procedure' to sneak it past the opposition and, as we had hoped, nobody noticed. Only the British (who else) are still blocking it in the Council of Ministers.

After the nightmare of Strasbourg and the attack from within our own ranks, we now had to take the remains of the draft proposal to the Council of Ministers, to see what could be salvaged. The Parliament had rejected the proposal in the vote on its first reading, but there would still be a new vote on the second reading, after the Council of Ministers – in this case the national Ministers of Postal Services for the different member states – had had their say. In other words, we were guaranteed a second bite of the cherry. However, it would all be to no avail, unless we could persuade the Council of Ministers to accept our way of thinking. And to do this, we needed to change our strategy.

In particular, I was convinced that the time had come to start talking with the unions. Until now, we had always been reluctant to do this, but Dayan's smile of victory from the gallery in Strasbourg had shown me that it could no longer be avoided. I knew that the Commissioner would not be happy about it – moaning about the 'bloody unions' was one of his favourite pastimes – but I tried to make him see sense.

'The unions are stirring up the entire Parliament. At the moment, there are majorities against liberalisation on both the left and the right. If we make no overtures to the unions, it will be precisely the same during the second reading. They might even go on strike – and then we can forget everything.' Grudgingly, he agreed. 'OK,' he said. 'If you think it's the only way. Go and talk to them.'

I made contact with the leader of the British postal union, a friendly man named Derek. He had once been a boxer and you could see from his physique that he had probably been good at it. He had already been in touch with our cabinet on several occasions, but only to bombard us with accusatory letters about our liberalisation plans.

According to Derek, these plans were 'a Dutch conspiracy'. Even so, he readily agreed to meet me during his next visit to Brussels for an international union conference.

'Where do you suggest we meet, mate?' he asked, as though he had known me for years. 'Let's go and have a beer in *La Mort Subite* (Sudden Death),' I answered. *La Mort Subite* is a well-known Art Nouveau-style café in the heart of Brussels. After my experiences during the parliamentary debate in Strasbourg, the name suggested that it might be an appropriate location for my meeting with Derek. 'OK, mate. I'll be there. See you soon.'

Derek's arrival at *La Mort Subite* made a big impression on the regular customers. He was the kind of man you couldn't help but notice. To begin with, he was the size and shape of George Foreman. And as if this wasn't enough to attract everyone's attention, his shoes had metal heels, so that you could hear him coming a mile off. On this occasion he had brought a friend with him: the Danish chairman of the European union of postal workers. The two of them sat down and began drinking beer as though there were no tomorrow. With a note of pride in his voice, Derek recounted his role in the struggle against the liberalisation of the postal service.

'That last Commissioner, the German heavyweight, he thought he could push through the Big Bang. Well, we soon showed him. We had the whole Parliament in uproar, mate. I told him: in terms of politics, you're in the upper class and I'm in the lower class. But in terms of boxing, we're both in the same weight class.'

Derek had a sense of humour and seemed to enjoy his role as a 'notorious' union leader. But it was soon clear that he also had a good head on those broad shoulders and I found myself growing to like him.

'Look, mate,' he continued. 'We can either carry on fighting each other – in which case your proposals will go the same way as the Kraut and his Big Bang – or else we can sit around the table and talk to each other. Who knows what might happen?'

Derek suggested a meeting with the Commissioner and I agreed instantly. I knew that a three hour discussion with the unions was not exactly the Commissioner's favourite way of spending an afternoon, but that was the point of this whole exercise: to start talking to each other.

Talking was something that Derek was good at. Talking – and drinking. The hours passed and the landlady of *La Mort Subite* began putting chairs on tables, in the hope that we might soon be going home. It seemed, however, to be the last thing on Derek's mind. Still he carried on talking and I found my concentration beginning to wander: until I heard him say something about Dayan. My ears pricked up.

'Yeah, that Dayan. He's been quite useful to us in the fight against you lot, but I don't really like him. I'm not a great lover of frogs.'

Now this was interesting news. I had assumed that Derek and Dayan were close allies – perhaps even friends. But apparently not. This meant that there was a little scope for some mandarin-like manipulation. I just hoped that I wouldn't forget it all in my drunken stupor! In the early hours of the morning, we finally rose to leave. I could hardly stand, let alone walk, and Derek guided me gently to the door. I tried to cross the road and was almost knocked down by a car I hadn't seen. Derek's arm pulled me back just in time. 'It's too early to cash in your chips just yet, mate,' he laughed.

The next morning, our postal experts came to see how I had got on with the fearsome Derek (they knew that I was planning to meet him). 'Still alive, then,' they joked. 'The famous boxer didn't beat the crap out of you, after all.' 'Yes,' I answered, 'I'm still alive – perhaps thanks to the famous boxer...'

Our strategy was beginning to take shape. We needed support from the national postal ministers and we needed support from the national postal unions. A visit to London seemed to offer the possibility of killing two birds with one stone – a meeting with the British Minister for Postal Affairs and a less formal chat with Derek. 'Do I really have to go?' asked the Commissioner like a naughty child. 'Yes, you really have to go. Or would you prefer to see striking postmen on the streets of Brussels?'

We left on a Thursday morning, travelling by Eurostar train to London's Waterloo Station. I hoped that the name was not symbolic of the likely outcome of our trip! We were met by a car from the Commission's London delegation. This delegation is the Princess's 'forward base' in 'enemy' territory and it is one of the toughest postings for any mandarin.

The British are the biggest Euro-sceptics on the continent and the delegation could do nothing right as far as the British press was concerned. Most newspapers regarded them as a kind of fifth column, secretly plotting to succeed where Hitler and the Third Reich had failed. The delegation's office was in Westminster, not far from the famous Houses of Parliament. For the pro-Europeans, this office was an island within *the* island. There was a kind of siege mentality about the place and the delegation leader had poured us a stiff whisky almost before we had taken our coats off!

His view about our prospects was sanguine. As might be expected from someone who spent all his time in England, he expressed his thoughts in terms of the weather. The 'wind' was blowing from the wrong direction and things looked 'stormy'. The British Minister for Postal Affairs, the young Douglas Alexander, was non-committal about liberalisation, even though he lived in the country which had invented the free market. The Labour Party was lukewarm about our proposals: they were scared of the unions, so everything would have to proceed slowly.

During the afternoon, Derek was our guest in the delegation building. He was in a good mood and had just come from a garden party at 10 Downing Street. 'It wasn't a bad do,' said Derek. 'I had a good chat with my old friend, John Prescott, and we sank a few beers together. He was in the papers recently for giving a reporter an uppercut. I told him: "John, you should always give an uppercut with your left hand – you get more power in the punch that way..."'

Derek eventually got around to talking about the post office and the Commissioner listened politely to what he had to say. It wasn't the most animated political discussion I have ever witnessed, but it was a start. I kept in contact with Derek and we had regular meetings at *La Mort Subite*, which became our 'local'. He told me at length about the British labour movement and about his role in the European postal sector. He liked this European role, particularly because it meant that the Royal Mail had to take greater account of him. It also meant that

La Mort Subite, the ideal place for a secret rendezvous.

he occasionally exchanged his working class pub for the tables of the rich and famous. Hence, his invitation to Tony Blair's garden party. 'You get a better class of booze with the big boys,' he said. It was a double role which suited him.

This is where I drank with Derek, far too much ...

Having appeased the unions in this manner – at least for the time being – we set about trying to pacify the member states. Germany was already on our side, but France remained resolutely opposed. The French premier had even sent the Commissioner a nasty letter, complaining about his liberalisation plans. He must have been very angry – he made three spelling mistakes in the Commissioner's name: not what I expect from a former ENA student. Things looked more promising in several of the other national capitals, and certainly more promising than things had been in Strasbourg. Many of the national postal services ran at a huge loss – largely because they were overstaffed – and there was more than one Minister of Finance who looked forward to the prospect of them being forced to run more efficiently. And if the blame for this painful operation could be passed on to Europe, so much the better.

Notwithstanding these positive signals, our first attempt to reach agreement in the Council of Ministers ended in failure. At this time, France held the Presidency of the European Union and France was only interested in a low-level agreement. A day of negotiations in the Council's headquarters in Brussels got us precisely nowhere. Besides, it was almost Christmas and most of the ministers were more interested in getting away early to finish their Christmas shopping. Yet in spite of the failure, there were some further encouraging signs. There were still a number of countries opposed to liberalisation, but there was also an increasing number in favour. This was a group with whom we could work in future.

The best chance of reaching an agreement came when Belgium took over the Presidency of the Union. For me, this was like a home match. I knew Belgium well and the Belgian Minster of Postal Affairs was a close personal friend. I had helped several times with the harvesting of grapes at his family vineyards near Aarschot. I had met his wife and child and we regularly went dining and drinking together, usually in the company of good-looking young women (one of the minister's specialities). Equally important, he was badly in need of a political success. The impending bankruptcy of the Belgian national airline, Sabena, was a major worry for both him and his party. A success story relating to another national industry – the post – might help to soften the blow – and the bad publicity.

Not that I was putting all my eggs in one basket. My aim was to build a broad coalition of support for our liberalisation package and so I began to approach a number of the most important 'social' organisations. A number of professional groups and organisations had organised a lobby against the draft proposal for purely selfish economic reasons, whereas the people who supported us had failed to make their voices heard. What we needed was an organisation of consumers and ordinary citizens who loudly applauded our plans. But how was I to achieve this? One day I received a visit from a Belgian senator, who had little to do in his own parliament. This hardly came as a surprise to me: the Belgian Senate likes to think of itself as a chamber of reflection, but in reality it is more a chamber of somnolence – or as the rest of us call it, sleeping. And this, indeed, was the complaint of my senatorial visitor: he had nothing to do, but eat, drink – and sleep. He had once been a successful businessman, but after two years in the House of Slumber he was bored to tears.

'I would like to do something in Europe,' he said during his conversation with the Commissioner. 'Perhaps I could help you with the liberalisation of the post? Maybe set up some kind of support group?' This was music to my ears.

We quickly agreed that he would set up a platform which would act as a mouthpiece for pro-liberalising organisations. He was even prepared to write an article for the newspapers, praising the Commissioner's visionary stance. To cap it all, he provided two assistants – a Frenchman and a Swede – who would run the whole operation.

These assistants were frequent visitors to my office, passing on the information they had obtained and helping to co-ordinate our spin campaign. I gave them a very specific task. 'Keep a close check on what all the opponents of liberalisation are doing. Above all, try to find out what Dayan is doing – and then stop him. Use all legal means at your disposal, but no break-ins. We don't want any Watergate situations.'

These young men set about their task with great enthusiasm, and I named them Special Agent Mulder, after the character in the *X-Files* television series. It seemed appropriate: the whole post dossier had become a gigantic *X-File*! One day, one of the Special Agents rushed into my office.

'I have news,' he said. '*Monsieur* Dayan is busy in Belgium. He is planning to lobby the national parliament – in person.'

Alarm bells started ringing inside my head. The sneaky little Frenchman was trying to tie the hands of the Belgian minister – my own personal friend – by having a resolution passed in the Belgian Chamber of Representatives. There was only one thing I could do. There was only one person I could call. I picked up the phone and dialled the number. 'Good afternoon, this is Herman De Croo speaking.'

De Croo was chairman of the Belgian Parliament and therefore 'the first citizen of the country'. We knew each other well from the years when I had worked as a political journalist in Brussels. He was a colourful politician, with a huge power base in his home region of East Flanders. De Croo was known as the 'King of the Preferential Votes' and he had personal files on more than 70,000 people he had 'helped' in the course of his political career. All he expected in return was that these people should continue to vote for him: which they did, year after year after year.

One weekend he invited me to visit him at home and I was treated to a spectacle which reminded me more of 19th century England than 20th century Belgium. We rode around his constituency on horse-

Herman De Croo receives his guests with full military honours!

back, greeting voters as if he was some kind of latter-day lord of the manor. The voters loved it – and so did he! But if his mannerisms were old fashioned, the same could not be said of his political methods. De Croo was a tough, modern parliamentarian – and I knew that he would be able to help me with Dayan.

'My dear friend, what is your problem?' he asked. I explained to him about the post dossier and about Dayan's plans to undermine it, using the Belgian Parliament as an accomplice.

It seemed that the Frenchman had found a French-speaking socialist from Wallonia who was prepared to submit a resolution supporting the French position.

'I will look into this matter immediately. I suspect that the Infra-structure Commission is the relevant body in our parliament. If so, this could be a messy business, because most of its members lack political experience. I will get to the bottom of it.'

I had every confidence that he would. De Croo has already been in the Belgian Parliament for forty years and nobody knows the system better than he does. It is his great ambition to break the record of the Flemish socialist, Camille Huysmans, who was still chairman of Par-liament when he was 94 years old. Even Huysmans would have been impressed by De Croo's deviousness. He may be a liberal in name but he is a Catholic by inclination: he knows more Jesuitical tricks than the whole Society of Jesus put together!

In the meantime, I had also telephoned the chairman of the Infra-structure Commission, a member of the right-wing Flemish Block party. He was another man I remembered well from my journalist days: a typical Flemish nationalist of the old school, complete with beard, a deep-seated suspicion of Islamic immigrants and an over-fond love of beer. The other 'democratic' parties refused to work with the Block, but parliamentary regulations said that their number of parliamentary seats gave them the right to the chairmanship of one parliamentary commission.

De Croo had given them Infrastructure, thinking that this was the place where they could do least damage. The Blocker felt honoured by my telephone call. At last, he had a political role to play!

'I think that my Commissioner should be given a chance to put his point of view to your commission in person,' I suggested.

He agreed immediately and promised to put it on his agenda. Next I phoned my contacts with the Flemish liberals and Christian-democrats, advising them to watch out for the manoeuvrings of the French-speaking socialists.

'The Walloons are up to their old tricks,' I warned. This was always calculated to cause a knee-jerk reaction amongst the Flemings and they promised to support us.

Things seemed to be brewing nicely and a few days before the meeting of the Infrastructure Commission I received a new phone call from De Croo, inviting myself and the Commissioner for a drink to discuss tactics.

On the day of the meeting, we arrived at the 'chairman's entrance'. There was a guard of honour waiting for us and they saluted as the Commissioner got out of the car and went into the Parliament Building. De Croo was standing in the foyer, accompanied by a photographer (he has always loved to be in the picture). He led us to a special reception room, decorated with regal elegance. Three perfectly-chilled glasses of champagne stood on a Louis XIV table. Say what you like about Old Herman, but he certainly knows how to do things in style!

Although we were alone in the room, he lowered his voice conspiratorially. 'I have had a quiet word with the lady from the French-speaking socialists. I know that she has ambitions to become a quaestor in our Parliament, a lucrative little job which it is in my power to grant. I pointed out to her that a position as a quaestor is hardly compatible with an anti-European stance. After all, we Belgians are good Europeans,' laughed De Croo. 'She told me that she understood...'

De Croo did not attend the meeting himself. There was no need: everything had been arranged. He had 'fixed' the lady socialist and I had 'fixed' the chairman and arranged for the necessary liberal and Christian-democrat support.

The members of the Infrastructure Commission were waiting for us in the Europa Chamber. I knew this room well: it was here that the parliamentary enquiry into the Dutroux affair had been held. I looked around and saw just two people in the public seats: *Monsieur* Dayan and, one row behind him, Special Agent Mulder. The lady socialist painted a romantic picture of the postal services in Wallonia. It was more or less what you might expect from an ally of Dayan. The postman was popular, the postman brought the pensions, the postman was the widow's best friend, etc. This passionate woman was just beginning to get into her stride, when the chairman cut her short. I had been keeping eye-contact with him throughout the meeting, making sure that opponents of postal liberalisation were quickly put in their place. Our supporters were given more speaking time, and the Commissioner was given as much time as he wanted.

Our Flemish allies had put in a number of amendments to the Dayan resolution, which the lady socialist now 'suddenly' seemed willing to discuss. The result of these amendments, if approved, would be to change Dayan's resolution into the Commission's resolution. And this, of course, is precisely what happened. De Croo's 'sting' had gone exactly according to plan. Dayan took the next train back to Paris, muttering dark curses about *ces sacrés Bataves* – which I took to be an uncomplimentary reference to the Commissioner and myself. The score after 90 minutes: Dayan 1 – the Commissioner 1.

The Belgian Minister of Postal Affairs was also delighted with the outcome and came to congratulate us after the meeting. 'Excellent,' he said. 'This is something we can build on in the future.' He couldn't stay for a celebratory glass of champagne. Instead, he had to rush off to deal with the latest episode in the continuing Sabena crisis. It was a dossier which was destined to cast a shadow across the remainder of his political career. This was a shame, because he was a good politician and Sabena's problems were not really his fault: he simply paid the price for the accumulated failure of others throughout the years.

As a result of the Sabena affair, the minister was seldom in his cabinet and he delegated the task of preparing the post dossier to two of his younger colleagues. These were clever, enthusiastic young people, but a little lacking in experience. I felt that they deserved some support – preferably, mine. I was in and out of their office all the time, offering useful advice and picking up little snippets of information. The European post ministers were scheduled to meet in Luxembourg in October, when a final decision on liberalisation would be taken. I was anxious to find out what kind of compromise solution was in the making.

At this stage, there were two main dangers to our plans: the Belgian government – because as chair nation they were the ones responsible for putting forward the proposal in Luxembourg – and the French government – because they were the ones most likely to oppose it. I decided to start with the French. I phoned Benoit and asked him what minimum limit his minister would be prepared to accept. With a sense of *déja vu*, I heard him reply: 'A reduction of the monopoly to 50 grams in 5 years, but no final date for full liberalisation.' Not exactly what I hoped, but it was a position I could live with.

What about the Belgians? The Sabena crisis was a blessing in disguise for the Commissioner and myself – and for our plans. The traditionally suspicious Belgian socialists were so preoccupied with the impending bankruptcy of the national airline that they left the minister a free hand in the postal dossier. In turn, the harassed minister left a free hand to his cabinet. And his cabinet was dependent on advice from ... me.

The Belgian proposal was finally ready on the Friday afternoon before the meeting was scheduled to take place on the following Monday. I advised the minister to say as little as possible about the proposal to the Belgian inner cabinet of vice-premiers. They would only cause unnecessary problems and there was always the risk that the Prime Minister would have one of his characteristic attacks of enthusiasm, which could ruin everything. I told him to apply the mandarin's golden rule: what a politician doesn't know can't hurt him – or me!

We circulated the text of the proposal to the national ministers on Friday evening. In essence, this text was based on the minimum French position: a reduction of the monopoly to 50 grams in five years, following which a study would be carried out to assess the impact of liberalisation on the principle of universal service provision. If this study gave the green light, the Commission would propose 2009 as a suggested dated for full liberalisation. This meant that 2009 would no longer be a compulsory legal date, but simply a desirable target.

The reasoning was as follows. Liberalisation cannot be implemented overnight via a 'Big Bang', but is a gradual process which usually takes about a decade to complete. This, at least, was the time necessary for liberalisation in the air travel, road transport, telecommunications, gas and electricity sectors. Liberalisation in the postal sector would probably need more time, partly because of its heavy reliance on manual labour (= unions) and partly because of its political sensitivity (= politicians).

However, once the process was up and running, it would gradually develop its own momentum, allowing it to set its own date for final liberalisation. In this respect, the target date of 2009 was a kind of psychological barrier for the postal industry, the date by which it must start to put its house in order: preparing for the free market, becoming profitable, seeking new niches in the market, etc. The postal companies could no longer maintain their 'Auntie Post' mentality: they needed to become modern communications and logistics enterprises, capable of competing on a global scale in Asia and America. The only thing that the Commission needed to do before 2007 was to confirm or amend the end date of 2009 via a new draft proposal.

The time frame of five years gave the negotiators some political room for manoeuvre. Moreover, we knew that a number of the major players at the Luxembourg meeting would be on our side. The Belgian minister seemed a little brighter and was prepared to back us to the hilt. For better or worse, Sabena was dead and buried and he now looked on the post as a means of polishing up his reputation. Germany would support us as well, as would the French minister (albeit with the necessary display of reluctance). The British might well be the key: their position was still uncertain. To find out which way the wind was blowing, the Belgian minister invited his colleagues from the Big Three for a preliminary discussion before the full plenary meeting. He asked them point blank how they intended to vote on the Belgian compromise proposal. The German said he had hoped that the proposal would go further, but he could live with a target date. The Frenchmen said that he had hoped that the proposal would not go so far, but he could live with the absence of a final date. To my relief, the British minister said that he could live with both the absence of a final date and the existence of a target date. The British were the 'inventors' of European liberalisation and did not want to be seen as party-poopers – especially as their own prime minister had been one of the leading figures behind the previous year's Lisbon Agenda, which called for a speeding up of the liberalisation process in Europe.

It looked like we were home and dry: with the support of the Big Three, it was almost certain that the rest would follow. At the meeting, we went through the charade of listening to everyone's point of view and we heard once again from ministers who thought the proposals were too radical and from ministers who thought they were not radical enough. But as soon as Britain, France and Germany declared their hand, the decision became a formality.

When the vote was finally taken, there was only one country which voted against: the Netherlands! The lady minister from The Hague believed that the proposal was not in Dutch interests and in typical Dutch fashion she didn't care what anybody else thought! I looked at the Commissioner and he just shrugged his shoulders. What did it matter? We had won! Not that you would think so if you listened to the French minister after the meeting. 'France has negotiated and France has triumphed!' he told the press. But we knew differently. All Europe knew differently. Final score after extra time: Commissioner 2 – Dayan 1!

Following the agreement reached in the Council of Ministers, the second reading in the European Parliament was much easier. Most

MEPs had been instructed by their national government to support the Council's position and most of them did what they were told.

Even Simpson was as quiet as a lamb. I bumped into him one day, dressed as usual in his rugby shirt. 'You know I'm only agreeing to this because I have no choice,' he said. His party leadership in London was not prepared to tolerate dissent and would have scrapped him from the candidates list for the next European elections, if he had not behaved.

'Can you give me a face-saver?' he asked. 'If you can, I'll make sure that Derek and his troops stay off the barricades.'

It sounded like a good deal to me and so I made him an offer. 'What do you think about this? During the 5 year period for the reduction of the monopoly, we'll arrange for two progress reports to be made, which we'll send to parliament for discussion. That way, you'll have the chance to shine twice in public before the next European elections. What do you think about that?' 'That sounds just fine to me, mate,' he replied. 'Just fine.'

The draft proposal was approved without difficulty on its second reading in Strasbourg and a directive was issued based almost exactly on the text approved by the Council of Ministers.

In 2006 the Commission confirmed 2009 as its preferred date for full liberalisation. As this date approaches, no doubt all the old arguments will be dusted off and given another airing. French politicians persistently oppose full liberalisation as a matter of principle and can be particularly guaranteed to do so in the presidential election year 2007. Not surprisingly, the European Parliament will also be an opposition force to be reckoned with once again.

And what of the leading players in this drama? Some went. Some stayed. Some went and then came back! Initially, Simpson was one of those who went. He failed to regain his seat in the next European election, but made a come-back in 2006 as a replacement for a retiring British MEP. He still makes himself heard (loudly) whenever the postal service is discussed.

After a brave rearguard action, the Belgian Minister of Postal Affairs finally fell victim to the Sabena affair. He is no longer in the government and now concentrates on the family grapes.

Derek was also given the order of the boot, being forced to make way for someone younger and more radical. He retired and now gives lectures on boxing.

Even *Monsieur* Dayan lost his job, being unable to cope with the new liberalising trends of *La Poste*. At first, he went to Africa, where he acted as an advisor for several national postal services. Later he became Secretary-General of the Universal Postal Union, a world-wide consultative organ for the global postal industry. From this elevated position, he is still opposing the full EU liberalisation proposed for 2009.

And which of our players managed to stay? Herman De Croo, of course. He is still in Brussels – and that's where he is planning to remain. For ever, and ever.

6| The President is always right

For all mandarins, the President enjoys the status of a deity. They never see him, but his presence is felt everywhere and everyone claims to act in his name. He is the jewel in the Princess's crown: the ultimate authority within her kingdom and also its face to the outside world. Most mandarins have never even seen the President, except on television. They work tirelessly every day towards the goal of European integration, but the man at the helm of the European ship remains unknown and invisible to them – as long as things are running smoothly. If the mandarins are unable to agree amongst themselves, there is only one person who can force them to agree; one person whose decision is final: the man on the thirteenth floor. His name is hardly ever spoken: instead, he is referred to by his title. He is *Monsieur le Président* or sometimes just 'Him Upstairs'.

The President's offices and cabinet are to be found on the thirteenth floor of the Berlaymont. The accommodation is spacious – the President's staff always have offices which are a little bit bigger than everyone else's – and there are meeting rooms for both the Hebdo (the royal council of the mandarins) and the College of Commissioners. There is even a restaurant, with the appropriate name of *La Convivialité*. Napoleon used to think that an army marched on its stomach, but the road to European integration has also made use of this culinary approach: many deals have been made in the elegant surroundings of *La Convivialité*.

In the early years, the meetings of the College of Commissioners reflected this informal way of doing business: small gatherings – there were only 10 Commissioners – held around a small circular table. With the enlargement of the union, there are now 27 Commissioners and they meet around a massive oval table in the shape of a ship. The Commission acts as the bridge of the European ship and the President is the pilot who sets the course. The bridge looks out over Schuman Square in a southerly direction, and also in the direction of Mecca; much to the alarm of those who fear the future development of Eurabia. Access to the thirteenth floor is restricted to the very top mandarins. The President's complex is sealed off from the outside world and is carefully guarded to keep out unwanted intruders, whose potential numbers have increased dramatically in recent years.

From his crow's nest on the thirteenth floor, the President enjoys the very best view over Brussels. What he does not enjoy is the undivided loyalty of his subjects. There are still many European citizens who see the Princess as a force of darkness, a giant octopus which wishes to extend its tentacles into every aspect of daily life. For these doubters, the President is a kind of glorified tax collector – true, a tax collector with a heart, but nevertheless a tax collector who expects the taxes to be paid. And like most tax collectors, the President's position is a solitary one.

He stands alone, a victim of his own power and prestige. Even the very senior mandarins refer to him as 'Mr. President' and the more junior ones edge warily away from him if, by chance, they are forced to share a lift. Within the organisation, his word is law. But if things go wrong, he is also the person who gets the blame. The buck stops with him and he may quickly find himself thrown onto the dung-heap of history which, as always in politics, lies very close to the mountain peak of success.

I was once fortunate enough to meet the President and even had the chance to speak with him. During the plenary sessions of the European Parliament, the Commissioners often travel together to Strasbourg – a French city with a German past, for meetings in the Winston Churchill Building: the European Union really is a modern Tower of Babel. Members of the College, the members of their cabinets and other Commission staff, fly on ordinary scheduled flights. Someone once remarked that if the plane were to crash unexpectedly, the Commission would be wiped out and the whole European structure would topple. Someone else – with a more realistic view of things – said the new Commissioners would already be in office before the memorial service for the old ones had taken place! This is indeed the Princess's great strength: whatever happens, continuity is always guaranteed.

On the occasions when I took this flight, the President and his staff – the head of his cabinet and a few assistants – were seated at the front of the plane, in first class. The head of cabinet sat next to the President and hardly moved from his side. He was determined that no Commissioner – and certainly no humble mandarin – should be allowed to speak to his boss without him hearing what was said. The President is a deity and deities – at least according to the head of cabinet – should not mix with mere mortals. On the contrary, the deity must be locked away in an ivory tower, the only key for which is safely in the pocket of the head of cabinet. Of course, the deity has his own retinue of servants and retainers. If he makes a joke, they all laugh. If he is angry, they all look sad. It is a closed world from which the rest of us are completely excluded.

I did occasionally see the President in the corridors of the Parliament because his office was near to the office of my Commissioner. I once even stood next to him in the gents, a place where even kings – and the President of the Commission – have to go alone. This is about as close as most ordinary mandarins ever get to the President – but it is not really the place to start a conversation!

From time to time, bilateral meetings were held between the President and my Commissioner, to discuss subjects on which no agreement had yet been reached. Strasbourg was the ideal place for these bilateral meetings. All the Commissioners were present and the President could see each of them, one by one, before handing down his personal Judgement of Solomon.

One such meeting involved a heated discussion between my Commissioner and the President on the subject of international bank transactions within the European Union. It was the first time I had seen the President at close quarters and he came across as a pleasant, jolly man – the kind of person you would like to have as an uncle for your children. He was friendly, funny and hospitable. But he was also iron-hard in negotiation. My Commissioner thought that international transactions within the EU should be paid for; the President thought that they should be free. My Commissioner argued that the situation was comparable with international telephone calls, which also have to be paid for; the President argued that the recent introduction of the euro was perceived by most Europeans as costly, and that this was a chance for Europe to give something back to the 'little people'. According to him, free transactions would increase the popularity of the Commission in general and its President in particular. My Commissioner refused to budge; so, too, did the President. It seemed like we were going to be in for a long afternoon.

I was sitting next to the President on a black leather sofa. I could see that he was tired. He had just returned from a summit with the

Chinese in Peking and in a few days time he was scheduled to fly off for high-level negotiations in the United States. In the meantime, he was here in Strasbourg, trying to persuade his troublesome Commissioners and an equally troublesome Parliament to see reason on a wide variety of different issues. The life of a President is high-energy and high-stress. He is constantly on the move, constantly in meetings, constantly reading briefings – and he has to do it all with a freshness and an enthusiasm which reflect, as he sees it, the visionary boldness of the Commission.

Yet even deities have their physical limits – and on this occasion the President was rapidly approaching his. Even at the best of times, he had the habit of speaking in staccato, half-finished sentences in a strange mixture of English and French, which was always difficult to understand. But now his speech trailed off altogether. He slumped down in the sofa and the room fell into silence. I thought he was dead and I could see from their faces that the Commissioner and the head of cabinet feared the same.

For a full minute no-one said or did anything. Suddenly, there was a loud knock at the door: it was the President of Peru! The President of the Commission sprang to his feet, instantly awake, and moved across the office to welcome his distinguished visitor. The head of cabinet shepherded the Commissioner and myself out through a side door and we made our way back to our own offices.

'So what the hell was decided?' asked the Commissioner, once he was safely behind his own desk. 'I don't know,' I replied. 'The President fell asleep before we got that far.' 'Well, go and ask the head of cabinet – he'll know.' I went and did as I was told. Europe's most senior mandarin answered with a half-smile. 'What did we decide? As always, it is the wish of the President which prevails.' I returned to my

The President slept, but his Peruvian counterpart, Alejandro Toledo, woke him up.

Commissioner and told him that from now on the citizens of Europe would be enjoying free international bank transactions within the EU. The Commissioner sighed in resignation, shook his head and kept on reading the newspaper.

Within the Commission, the President is not so much a person: he is more a political myth. Everything is done in his name – even when he doesn't know it. I have often been at 'special chefs' where there was a wide difference of opinion between the various cabinets. If there was no clear majority, the member of the President's cabinet who chaired the meeting would bring matters to a close with the words: 'The President wishes to follow this course of action...' This was enough to bring everyone into line, even though the 'losers' would continue to grumble about it afterwards.

I wasn't always convinced that the President actually did want to follow that particular course of action. I often thought that his mandarins had simply used 'the myth of the President' to get their own way. But a cabinet member of an 'ordinary' Commissioner can do nothing against this kind of power – not unless he wants to commit professional suicide. And I haven't met very many mandarins who want to do that!

If the President is God and the cabinet are his angels, his high priests are to be found in the Secretariat-General and the Legal Service. These two organisations are crucial to his efforts to keep the rest of the Commission in order.

The Secretariat-General (SG) organises meetings, draws up agendas and takes minutes. The staff of the SG are the Commission's Pharisees: they know absolutely everything about procedural matters. This is a vital role. The Commission is made up of many different nationalities and the only thing which binds them together are the Princess's procedures. In the absence of a common administrative culture, these procedures have acquired the status of a sacred rite. They are all that stands between the Commission and chaos. Every mandarin of whatever culture views chaos with distaste: consequently, the SG is accorded a semi-divine status only slightly lower than that of the President's cabinet.

Of all their tasks, the preparation of minutes is perhaps the most important. It is the ideal opportunity to 'adjust' the facts to the wishes of the mandarins. If something is not included in the minutes, it hasn't happened. It no longer exists! Long and difficult discussions can be summarised in a few bland sentences, as though all was sweetness and light. Minutes are the means by which the surreal is allowed to triumph in the Commission. You might think you said one thing, but the minutes will prove that you actually said something else!

The Director of the Minutes was for many years a gentleman with the appropriate name of *Monsieur* Bisarre. The head of our cabinet used to check the minutes of every meeting very carefully – just to make sure that our Commissioner 'isn't being stitched up by those scheming high-priests in the SG'.

It is also through the SG that the President decides which matters appear on the agenda – and which do not. At the end of the 1990s, media concentration was a hot issue in the Commission. The Internal Market Commissioner thought that the media was becoming too concentrated in the hands of a limited number of very powerful companies, allowing them to exercise undue influence on the public's thinking. He wanted to break up this concentration and to impose restrictions on companies which were monopolising both the newspapers and broadcasting.

There was an economic aspect to this dossier, but also an important democratic one. On the one hand, it was possible through cross advertising for one of the company's media outlets, for example a television channel, to promote another of the same company's outlets in a different branch of the media, such as a newspaper or a weekly: in other words, a clear example of unfair competition. On the other hand, there was a risk that public opinion – an important element in the democratic structure – would become dominated by the propaganda of specific interest groups, as was the case in Silvio Berlusconi's Italy.

There was fierce resistance to the Commissioner's proposal to tackle this problem – resistance which came from both the media itself and from the politicians. These two groups are natural allies. Politicians need the media to get themselves on television and in the newspapers, while the media needs the politicians to ensure that legal controls on press monopolies remain lax. It required no less than twelve 'special chefs' before agreement could be reached on a text to be forwarded to the College of Commissioners. Yet even then, the matter was not settled. Leo Kirch, the German media magnate, telephoned the German Chancellor to ask him to oppose the Internal Market Commissioner's draft proposal. It says much about the power of the media that the Chancellor immediately phoned the President – who instructed the SG to remove the item from the agenda. The question of media concentration was never raised again – at least not during my time.

Leo Kirch phoned Helmut Kohl, who phoned the President in Brussels. The media concentration directive was quietly buried.

The Legal Service is equal in power and status to the SG, but its area of operations is different. If the SG are the Pharisees of the Commission, the Legal Service is its Sanhedrin: its council of legal experts. They examine every issue from a very specific point of view, namely, the various treaties on which the workings of the European Union are based. Their first question is always: 'does this proposal have a legal basis?' If their answer to this question is 'no', then the proposal under discussion – no matter how well intentioned – is doomed to failure. To continue with the biblical analogy, the Legal Service is not unlike Judas Iscariot: it does a very nice line in the 'kiss of death'. It can sink any draft proposal, because each and every proposal needs legal approval before it can be passed on to the College of Commissioners.

This requirement is also useful from the President's point of view, since it allows him to quietly bury proposals which he does not like. All he needs to do is phone up the jurists and ask them to find a technical detail to cast doubt on the proposal – and finding such details is precisely their speciality. Little wonder that the policy-making mandarins hate these high priests of the treaties. The policy-makers draw up beautiful plans and frame them in elegant legislative forms – only to see the Legal Service blow them out of the water on the basis of a legal nicety. This explains why there is great amusement in almost every DG and every cabinet when an opinion of the Legal Service is overturned by the Court of Justice. In truth, however, this doesn't happen very often. The Princess's jurists are amongst the very best in Europe: I can't remember that I ever won a single battle against them. For most mandarins they remain a force beyond their control.

Both these levers – the Secretariat-General and the Legal Service – are used with frequency by the President and with even greater frequency by the mandarins who act in his name. If I may compare the Commission to something as unflattering as a horse, the SG and the Legal Service are the reins by which the President and his staff apply pressure to the bit. The horse has no option but to move accordingly.

Over the years, the President's role has evolved from a position as 'first among equals' to become more truly presidential in style. Originally, the European Union was made up of three different entities: the European Iron and Steel Community, Euratom and the European Economic Community. Under the presidency of the German, Walter Hallstein, these three bodies were eventually merged to form a single organisation: the European Community. Hallstein – whose name was also given to the doctrine that the Federal German Republic should not recognise the communist Democratic Republic – was its first President. Under his leadership, the new organisation was gradually consolidated and European law began to have a modest, but significant, impact on national legislation.

This required a major change in the continent's way of thinking, since at the start none of the six original member states were inclined to take much account of Brussels and its wishes. National governments and above all national bureaucrats continued to pass legislation which hindered cross-border movement of goods, persons, capital and services and which also created unfair competition. This was the period during which the Commission had to put its foot down strongly against such infringements of the new European law. Its success was due largely to the work of its main ally – the European Court of Justice, which during the 1960s handed down a number of important judgements, with splendid-sounding names such as Van Gend & Loos, Costa/Enel, etc.

As a result of these efforts, Europe was gradually taken more seriously. During the 1970s the Presidents of the Commission were closely involved with the early phases of the great political projects of the decade, such as the European Monetary Union and the European Political Union, based on a report named after the Belgian politician, Leo Tindermans.

However, for several years, these projects scarcely developed beyond the ideas stage. The first oil crisis in 1973 and the second in 1979 brought progress in both directions to a temporary halt. Economic hardship once again caused the member states to place greater emphasis on national interest and for a time Europe only continued to exist as a theory. It was only the President of the Commission who kept the European ideal alive – but it was the member states which momentarily had the upper hand.

France and Germany decided to create the European Council, a forum for the regular meeting of national government leaders and heads of state, but even this was unable to prevent many of Europe's great flagship projects from getting into difficulties. Perhaps most severely affected was the jewel in the Union's crown – the Common Agricultural Policy. After the Second World War, Europe was a net importer of food. One of the first tasks of the European Community in the 1950s was to create a common farming policy which would lead to a significant increase in food production. The architect of the new policy was a Dutchman, Sicco Mansholt. His basic principle was that farmers should be encouraged to produce by receiving a fixed price for their products which was significantly above the world market price.

Initially, the policy worked well. The farmers ploughed dutifully and output rose to the desired level. Unfortunately, Mansholt forgot to take account of one important factor – technological development. The farmers mechanised and modernised, so that by the 1970s there was serious over-production. The result was the notorious milk lakes and butter mountains, which gave Europe such a bad name.

Mansholt later admitted his mistake and became a confirmed 'green'. This might also have had something to do with the fact that he got romantically involved with a young trainee from the Economic and Social Committee: Petra Kelly. Kelly was known for her strong beliefs. After having converted Senior Commissioner Mansholt into an advocate of green policies, she founded the Green Party in Germany, thereby changing the political landscape of Europe's most populous country. After Mansholt, she became romantically involved with

Leo Tindemans and Sicco Mansholt: the generation of passionate Europeans.

a retired general. Tired of the world and fearful for its future, the duo committed suicide during the 1980s, using the general's service revolver.

It was only during the mid-1980s that Europe gradually began to recover its reputation. Under the presidency of Jacques Delors, the Union once again began to focus its attention on prestigious, large-scale projects. The timing for such projects was good: at Fontainebleau in 1984, the European Council had finally agreed to reduce agricultural production and to compensate the United Kingdom for the limited benefit it received from the CAP. The 'British rebate' was born.

Spurred on by the solution of this decade old problem, Delors launched his '*Europa 1992*', with the aim of finally implementing the

European Single Market. Various key sectors of the economy were liberalised, such as aviation and telecommunications. This was followed in 1991 by the signing of the Treaty of Maastricht, signalling the first concrete steps towards the greatest European economic project of all: the euro.

Running parallel to these economic developments, there were also significant political initiatives. After the fall of the Berlin Wall in 1989 and the reunification of the two Germanys, the way lay open for the enlargement of the Union and, thereby, the reunification of the whole continent. Delors once again gave the lead and his successors as President completed the work: in 2004 the EU was increased from 15 to 25 member states, with further candidacies still in the offing. In 2007 both Romania and Bulgaria joined, while Croatia and Turkey are still in the waiting room.

The Treaty of Maastricht was signed in 1991. Europe's last great feat of arms.

The European Constitution of 2005 was intended to initiate the final phase in the process of continent-wide integration, the crowning work in the 'Europe of Great Projects'. But Europe stumbled at the final hurdle. This leads to an inevitable question: what are the limits of Europe? How much Europe can the European Union absorb? It is a question which still needs to be answered.

As a result of all these developments, the function of the President has become more important, but also more difficult. In the house of the mandarins, the President is still the be-all and end-all. His opinion is sacred, his word is law. When Delors became President, he was no more than a *primus inter pares*. By the time he left, he was the Union's undisputed leader and figurehead. He had given the position of President a presidential prestige, but had also – together with his merciless executioner, Pascal Lamy – created a political system which allowed him to control the Commission and bend it to his will. His legacy was a Commission which was very firmly in the driving seat, a solid organisation at the heart of the European spider's web.

The treaties of Maastricht (1991), Amsterdam (1997) and Nice (2001) all helped to cement these changes and to further enhance the power of the President. In the past, the Commissioners had fought amongst themselves to decide the allocation of the different portfolios – a difficult process, often compared with Hitler's Night of the Long Knives! This inevitably led to lasting vendettas and feuds. Now the President decides the allocation of portfolios. He can even shuffle these portfolios mid-term and in extreme cases can request the removal of a Commissioner, if he finds his performance inadequate or his attitude too intransigent.

The Treaty of Nice in 2000. The end of the French-style Union.

In other words, the transformation from prime minister to president is almost complete. A strong President with a clear and realistic agenda, surrounded by competent mandarins, is nowadays almost unstoppable. It is only when the President is weak or his cabinet inept that the Commissioners and their DGs have more scope to act on their own initiative. But this is not generally a good thing: it leads to competing and often contradictory proposals, so that to the outside world it appears as if the Princess is losing her way. Ill-tempered as she is, she needs clear guidance to be provided by the President.

The President is dependent on two external factors to exercise his political function: the European Parliament and the European Council (the leaders of the national governments). Once again, Delors set the trend. Throughout his presidency he enjoyed the approval of both the Parliament and the two most important national leaders: the Chancellor of Germany and the President of France. This gave him a basic core of support on which he could build his great 'prestige' projects. His successors have sometimes found it more difficult.

Partly as a result of Delors' initiatives, Parliament has acquired much greater powers. In particular, it has the power to vote out the Commission, whereas the Commission does not have the power to dissolve the Parliament. This has led to a political imbalance, which in practical terms means that it is now very difficult for the President to say 'no' to the Parliament, without incurring irreparable political damage. In 1999 the Santer Commission resigned prematurely, because it was afraid of being voted down in Strasbourg. The Commissioners were so scared of the Euro-MPs that they preferred to commit political suicide rather than to go down fighting.

Finding support amongst the member states has also become more difficult. To some degree, this is an inevitable result of the Union's enlargement. There are now so many different member states and so many different national interests, that it is impossible to keep everybody happy. Yet this is precisely the aim of the President – to keep everyone moving in the same direction. He is the Union's great conciliator and reconciler. It is his task to heal dangerous rifts and to soothe damaged national egos. This requires him to be highly flexible, often to the point of turning a blind eye to his own rules. Some years ago, the governments in Paris and Bonn decided that they no longer wished to honour the terms of the Growth and Stability Pact. In other words, they intended to allow their national budget deficits to exceed 3%.

If a smaller member state had dared to do such a thing, it would immediately have received a letter of warning from the Commission: small states are expected to follow the rules. However, the same principle does not apply to the big boys. If a major EU player breaks the rules, the President will attempt to persuade them to see reason, but he has no power to compel them. In other words: if small member states violate the rules, their policies must be changed; but if bigger member states violate the rules, the rules will be changed.

This is what happened with Germany and France. The President argued with them passionately to respect the terms of the Growth and Stability Pact, but everybody knew that he was simply 'going through the motions': if France and Germany no longer wished to stick to the rules, the rules would be revised. This is symptomatic of the weakness of the President's position. His point of political reference is no longer his own Commission, but rather the European Council. He is strong in his own house, but weak outside it.

But if the President lacks power beyond the walls of the Princess's castle, he does not lack prestige. He is the Princess's ambassador, the public face of the European Commission to the outside world. This allows him to sit at the same table as the world's most powerful leaders. He has summit meetings with the presidents of Russia and America and he attends the great international conferences, such as the G8.

Yet even here, he does not have the field to himself. The leaders of the important national governments and the important supranational organisations all do much the same thing. He even has 'competition' from within the European Union's own ranks, in the shape of the European Council's High Representative for Foreign Policy. This Representative attempts to mediate between warring factions in international conflicts, such as the Lebanon. The aim is to provide a common European position on such matters, but this does not prevent the President and various national foreign ministers from also trying to put across their own points of view. As a result, most international peace conferences are attended by whole busloads of European delegates, each with his or her own agenda. Yet in the final analysis, this lack of a common policy is not important: the important thing is 'being there': 'flying the flag,' as the British used to call it.

In this respect, the first-ever High Representative, the Spaniard Javier Solana, was the ideal man for the job. He defended the European Union's position in his own peculiar version of English and French which was almost completely incomprehensible, apart from a few key phrases such as 'important', 'peace' and 'co-operation'. In these circumstances, the lack of a common European position was not a major problem: nobody could understand a word that he was saying anyway! This is, of course, (and unintentionally in Solana's case) the highest form of diplomacy: saying something that means nothing.

Moreover, he also possessed the ideal diplomat's second essential quality: cordiality. Solana was a 'backslapper' and a 'hand-shaker' – everybody liked him and everybody wanted to be in the photograph with him. Whenever the cameraman clicked his shutter, you could be guaranteed that Solana would be standing in the middle of the group. The world's conclusion: 'Europe is present, Europe is playing a role.' It was the message that everyone in Brussels wanted to hear.

Of course, in the international arena Europe has another very important trump card: money. It has at its disposal vast resources which it is prepared to spend in order to acquire a high political profile in areas of conflict. In this respect, the division of responsibilities in the world's war zones is fairly clear: America fights, the United Nations feeds and the European Union funds. Europe is an advocate of 'soft power', the power of persuasion linked to the power of the euro.

However, this is a concept with limitations. Many national leaders in Asia, the Middle East and Africa are the products of 'hard' power. In these countries, power is often a question of life and death and these national potentates have no interest in Europe's essentially liberal and humanitarian concepts – they are only interested in Europe's cash. True, they will often pay lip-service to these concepts – but only as long as they are being paid. 'Soft power' is a product of a 'soft' culture: it is the politics of naivety and good intentions – 'if we are kind and understanding, we can help to make others kind and understanding'.

Sadly, this is not the way the world works. In 2003, for example, the Commission received a visit from the Libyan leader, Moammer Ghadafi. During the 1980s, Ghadafi had been the world's Public Enemy No.1 – the main sponsor of international terrorism and the man personally responsible for the Lockerbie bombing. Yet now he was welcomed and feted in Brussels as though he was one of Europe's greatest friends. 'To be or Lockerbie – that is the question,' scoffed some of the newspapers. Europe's answer was 'to be'. It wanted to see Libya return to the international fellowship of nations and was prepared to pay the Libyan dictator large sums of money to convince him.

Did it work? In a speech to the Organisation of African Unity in 2006, 'Mad Moammer' threatened to take no steps to prevent the stream of illegal immigrants crossing from Africa to Europe, unless the Union continued pay him 10 billion euros each year. He also had Bulgarian nurses sentenced to death for crimes they did not commit. However, in return for some hard euros the execution could be discussed.

This is the problem with 'soft' politics: its intended targets are anything but soft. On the contrary, they are as hard as nails and as vicious as a school of piranhas. As a result, Europe continues to nourish the monsters who are seeking to devour it. The Third World still sees Europe in terms of the last days of the Roman Empire: a corrupt and disintegrating system, with the President in the role of the Emperor Nero, fiddling while the whole edifice burns around him.

But at least the President does not fiddle alone. In addition to the High Representative, there are many other mandarins involved in foreign affairs. The Commissioners of the so-called Relex Family occupy themselves with a wide range of matters relating to international relations, development policy, aid projects, foreign trade, cross-border finance, etc.

However, this can – and often does – lead to conflicts of interest. For example, the role of the Commissioner for Development is limited to the drawing up of policy matters. The practical implementation of these policies is the responsibility of the Commissioner for International Relations, since it is his or her budget and personnel which make possible the necessary work on the ground. This means that two separate hierarchical lines, each with its own commander, are intimately involved in the same project, which they both view from a completely different perspective. In these circumstances, disputes are almost inevitable.

To complicate matters further, the Commissioner for International Relations also has to take account of the activities of the High Representative, who is responsible for the foreign relations of the European Council. Add to this the input of the President himself, who likes to maintain a high profile in all international matters, and it is clear that

European foreign policy is a classic example of 'too many Chiefs and not enough Indians'.

During the 1970s, the famous American Secretary of State, Henry Kissinger, used to complain that he never knew who to call in Europe in the event of a major international crisis. He said that he wanted 'just one number'. Thirty years later, things have only improved marginally. The Secretary of State can now call the High Representative, who is supposed to co-ordinate Europe's diplomatic response, but if Europe is not united – which is usually the case – the Secretary might still find himself being telephoned by a whole host of European officials, each anxious to give his own view of the situation. As a result, the superpowers – America, Russia and China – simply choose whichever opinion most suits their own ideas. By the time Europe has finally reached a common position, the crisis is usually over!

This 'overpopulation' in the field of foreign affairs is set to become even worse, if the European constitution ever comes into force. In these circumstances, the European Council would appoint a European president – who would also want to have his say in the international arena. This could only be to the detriment of the position of the Commission President. In their enthusiasm, the mandarins have already built a new palace for their European president – an imposing mansion in the Wetstraat in Brussels, opposite the Charlemagne Building, where the Relex Family is housed. However, for the time being this building must remain empty, since the electorates of both France and the Netherlands rejected the draft constitution in national referenda. This is the eternal problem for the mandarins and their President: Europe would be easy to run if it wasn't for the people! Whatever the final shape of European foreign policy, it is to be hoped in the future that Relex will become more relaxed!

Taking account of all the above, it is clear to see that the President really has a dog's life. His task is to try and please all the people all the time, but without the power and the resources to do so. The only things of which he can be certain are too little sleep, too much stress, too much cholesterol – and tons of criticism. Even so, there is never any shortage of applicants to take on this almost impossible job.

Why? On the positive side, it brings with it prestige, a high media profile and powerful friends in high places. In general, the President of the European Commission is regarded throughout the world, certainly the Western World, as being 'one of the good guys'. But like most good guys, he has little or no real power. Europe is a kind of institutionalised talking shop. Everyone has a right to their say, but nobody has the courage or the strength to decide. Even so, the glamour and glitter of the President's position continue to attract famous candidates. Vanity may be one of the Seven Deadly Sins, but is still the driving force behind most politicians. And Europe offers the bonfire of all vanities.

I had the opportunity to follow the campaigns of two famous politicians in their efforts to become President of the European Commission. On both occasions the campaigns were unsuccessful – although I hasten to add that this had nothing to do with me!

The first time was in 1994, when the Dutch Prime Minister, Ruud Lubbers, put forward his name as a possible successor for Jacques Delors. I was then a political editor for the *NCR Handelsblad* newspaper and was asked to monitor Lubbers throughout his campaign. It was obvious that Lubbers had been planning to make a bid for the top job in Brussels for quite some time. He had been re-elected premier in 1989 for a third – and almost certainly – last time. Consequently, he was on the look-out for a new job to end his political career: preferably an international position of high prestige. Naturally, he denied his ambitions categorically but the signs were evident from an early stage. During the European summit in Edinburgh in 1992 he was extremely conciliatory towards the Spanish, who were demanding a significant rise in contributions to the Cohesion Fund. Spain was one of the largest beneficiaries of this fund and the Netherlands was one of the major contributors

The result of this was to risk an impressive overall net increase in Dutch contributions to the EU, since for a number of years thereafter the amount of agricultural subsidies received by The Hague would also fall rapidly. I wrote an article linking these two issues, suggesting that in Edinburgh Lubbers was attempting to buy goodwill for the furtherance of his future political career; a hypothesis which was confirmed to me by the then Deputy Minister for European Affairs Piet Dankert.

Lubbers was greatly irritated by this suggestion and quickly telephoned to my editor-in-chief, inviting him for 'a cup of tea and a chat'. Lubbers repeated his denials, both about Edinburgh and about his desire to go to Brussels. My editor conceded that the premier 'had a point', but he probably had little alternative. Lubbers was then at the height of his power in the Netherlands and everyone – and certainly every newspaper – wanted to keep on the right side of him. His charisma was legendary and it certainly seemed to have worked on the Dutch media establishment. However, as a good Calvinist, I had always distrusted the Catholic Lubbers – too many Jesuitical tricks by half!

My suspicions were confirmed when Lubbers put forward his name as a last minute candidate for the President's job in May 1994. The appointment of Delors' replacement was scheduled to be made by the European Council during a meeting on the Greek island of Corfu in June, and it was clear that Lubbers was hoping to surprise them into a quick decision following a blitz campaign.

I was asked to cover the story and didn't need to think twice. I was always doubtful about Lubbers' chances. It seemed clear to me that the German Chancellor Helmut Kohl would oppose him: he had not forgotten the negative comments made by Lubbers about German reunification at the Strasbourg summit in 1989, immediately following the fall of the Berlin Wall. True, the French president Mitterrand, the British prime minister Thatcher and the Italian premier Andreotti had all made similar comments, but Kohl had little option but to forgive the 'indiscretions' of these large and powerful countries.

It was a different thing all together to accept such criticism from a small and vociferous neighbour with a long history of anti-German feeling. A few weeks after Lubbers announced his candidature, a small article by John Palmer appeared on the front page of the British *Guardian* newspaper, with the title 'Kohl and Mitterrand want Dehaene'. To my mind, this sealed Lubbers' fate: if the French and Germans were pushing for the nomination of the Belgian prime minister, Lubbers' chances were zero. Because when Kohl said 'no', he really meant 'no'.

Lubbers, however, remained confident. He invited me for an interview in the aptly named Little Tower – the prime minister's poky office in the Binnenhof. He told me in detail about the support he expected from Spain (premier Felipe Gonzalez), Italy (premier Silvio Berlusconi) and a number of smaller countries. He said that it was time to stand up to the 'Directorate' of France and Germany. It was not right that these two European superpowers should have an almost automatic right to rig the appointment of the Commission President. The small countries also had a right to be heard and he wanted to give them a voice. Once chosen, he would follow an independent line, not simply agreeing to the policies put forward by the Big Two.

By now, I had listened to more than enough of his campaign propaganda, so I interrupted him abruptly.

'Mr. Lubbers, thank you for inviting me but I think you are looking at things the wrong way. You need to face the political realities of the situation. You are never going to be elected against the wishes of France and Germany.'

This was true, but it was cheeky of me to say it. I could see that Lubbers was not impressed. Nor was the Director of his Information Service, who was also present.

'Tut, tut, young man: you are speaking to the Prime Minister of the Netherlands!' Lubbers tried to counter my arguments: 'Why shouldn't I be elected? There are lots of small countries who will back my candidacy.'

The Director of the Information Service shot me a warning look, but I ignored it. 'It's the big boys who call the tune,' I replied. 'There is no such thing as a coalition of small countries. Sooner or later they are going to fall into line behind France and Germany. At the crucial moment they will all desert you – and not even Italy and Spain will be able to help you then!'

I expected to be thrown out at this point, but still Lubbers tried to persuade me that his analysis of the situation was correct.

'You'll see,' he said. 'I have wide support and there are many countries which are no longer prepared to accept orders from Bonn and Paris.'

He was probably thinking of Great Britain, but in the European Union British support can often be a mixed blessing, if not a curse. We finally agreed to disagree, but I left my first – and last – interview in the Little Tower with the certain knowledge that Lubbers was a lame-duck candidate. If Jean-Luc Dehaene was nominated, then either Dehaene would win or neither of them would.

A week later, the Christian-democrat grouping held a meeting in the European Parliament Building in Brussels. I drove down from The Hague to watch the spectacle and it was well worth the ride. The meeting began with a little piece of slapstick: Chancellor Kohl tried to enter quietly through a side door, only to find it locked. He stood there banging on the glass panel, shouting *'öffne die Tür'*, while someone rushed off to find the key. When he finally managed to gain access to the packed meeting hall in the Paul Henri Spaak Building, he immediately made his way to Dehaene's side. The two greeted each other like long-lost brothers, laughing and slapping each other on the back. It was a public display of what the Germans call *Männerfreundschaft*. Lubbers watched this demonstration in quiet dismay.

It was now clear that he did not belong to the big boys' club and he should have realised then that his candidacy was going to fail. However, he did at least have the satisfaction of bringing his rival down with him. At Corfu, the heads of government were unable to reach a decision. Lubbers received insufficient support – as expected, although not by himself – but Dehaene was blocked by a British veto. The President's post was eventually offered by Helmut Kohl personally to a third, compromise candidate: the Luxembourg prime minister, Jacques Santer.

Kohl and Dehaene laughing. No laughing matter for Lubbers.

Later, Lubbers also put forward his candidacy for the position of Secretary General of NATO. Once again he was unsuccessful. The Secretary General is traditionally a European, but he has to work closely with the Americans and, in most cases, to do what they tell him. During a preliminary interview in Washington, the ex-Dutch premier was so vague and evasive in his replies that the Americans decided more or less on the spot that they didn't want him. 'Woolly,' was how they described him.

Success finally came in the year 2000, when Lubbers was appointed as the Commissioner for Refugees with the United Nations in Geneva. Sadly, his international career was not destined to be crowned with glory. A few years later he was forced to resign from his post in disgrace, for having pinched the bottom of one of his female assistants. If he had picked an Italian or French assistant, he would probably have been OK: at worst, he might have got a slap across the face or at best an invitation for a romantic evening. However, he made the mistake of choosing an American: she took him to court, went to the press and demanded huge compensation for what is now known as 'sexual harassment in the workplace'.

Precisely ten years later, I was able to witness at close quarters the failure of the attempt of another Belgian prime minister to become President of the European Commission. This time the unfortunate candidate was Guy Verhofstadt and he made precisely the opposite mistake to Lubbers – he relied too heavily on the support of France and Germany.

Like his Dutch counterpart, he also denied for many years that he had any ambitions to enter the European arena. However, it came as no surprise to me when he put forward his name for the vacant President's post in 2004. I knew that he had been lobbying secretly for quite some time and that he had visited most of the countries whose support he hoped to attract. By this time I was a mandarin myself and I did not look forward to the prospect of a Verhofstadt presidency.

Two years earlier he had successfully attempted to close down a column I was running in the *De Standaard* newspaper. I had been subjected to his wrath after I had published an article on him and his working methods in Belgian politics. I wrote that he tended to launch too many projects simultaneously, without ever finishing a single one. Even worse: he could not stand criticism of his failure and simply kept on messing up. The 19th century British prime minister William Gladstone once described his rival Benjamin Disraeli as 'The Grand

Corruptor'. I did the same with the Belgian prime minister. Needless to say, he was not amused by this title and ordered his staff to contact the Commission President, who advised me, in no uncertain terms, to 'discontinue' my contribution for 'the foreseeable future'. The affair had eventually blown over but I knew that the arrival of this man in the Berlaymont could only have one outcome for myself: the premature termination of my career!

For this reason, I followed his campaign with some anxiety, but to my great relief he made even more mistakes than Lubbers. After the expansion of the EU to 25 countries, the support of France and Germany alone was no longer sufficient to ensure success. There were now ten new countries in the voting equation and the relative strength of the Big Two had diminished accordingly. To make matters worse – from Verhofstadt's point of view, not mine – he had violently opposed the war in Iraq. He was even instrumental in passing a Genocide Law through the Belgian Parliament, which would have allowed American ministers and generals to be tried for war crimes in Brussels. There was even talk of subpoenaing President Bush Senior, Secretary of Defence Donald Rumsfeld and Israel's Prime Minister Ariel Sharon! Verhofstadt called the Genocide Law 'a mark of civilisation'. Most of the Washington diplomatic corps regarded it as the mark of an idiot and they looked forward to a Verhofstadt presidency about as much as I did. But, unlike me, they had the power to do something about it.

This view was reinforced when he launched a proposal to create a European army based in Brussels. This army was intended to act as a 'counter-balance' to NATO – the organisation by which the Americans had financed and guaranteed the security of Europe for almost sixty years! Verhofstadt even went so far as to invite the German chancellor, the French president and the Luxembourg prime minister to a special summit in Brussels to discuss the matter. This was the so-called 'Praline Summit', named after the world-famous Belgian chocolates. However, this was too much for the many pro-American nations amongst the member states, particularly Great Britain, Italy, Spain, Portugal and the Netherlands. They wanted nothing more to do with Guy and his box of chocolates and began to work actively against his candidature.

Their biggest ally was Verhofstadt himself, who continued to shoot himself in the foot on a regular basis. He did not believe in God and therefore objected to Him being mentioned in the proposed European Constitution. This instantly cost him the support of the Catholic and God-fearing Poles, since the then Polish Pope had demanded that God should be mentioned in the European Constitution on the grounds that Christianity is one of the main features of European culture. In a last-ditch effort to garner Polish support he travelled to Warsaw and told his counterpart that he had changed his mind and would now be prepared to inderde God in the Constitution. But the Poles were not convinced by his last minute conversion and they kept on opposing his candidacy.

It didn't do him much good either with the Christian-democrats – by far the largest grouping in the European Parliament. Verhofstadt had a great dislike for the Flemish Christian-democrats, primarily because they had kept him in opposition for twelve years. He found it hard to hide this dislike from the wider European Christian-democrat movement. This was to cost him dearly, since the Christian-democrats made sweeping gains during the 2004 European elections.

In particular, the German CDU under Angela Merkel wished to have nothing to do with the Verhofstadt candidacy. Consequently, they were instrumental in putting forward the name of the British Commissioner, Chris Patten, as an alternative candidate. This was not a serious nomination – Patten learned about most of the details from the press – but was designed exclusively to torpedo the Verhofstadt campaign.

Matters came to a head during the meeting of the European Council of Ministers in June 2004. Would the national heads of government choose Verhofstadt or not?

Once again, the Belgian premier and his advisers made a serious miscalculation. They were convinced that in the final analysis the Verhofstadt supporters could outvote the Verhofstadt opponents and they lobbied with this aim in mind. But they failed to take account of the fact that the appointment of the President is seldom put to a vote. There is either a consensus in favour of a candidate – or there is not. In Verhofstadt's case, there was no such consensus. Yet even when this was clear to everyone else, the Belgian still refused to give up his ambitions. He held the leaders of Europe hostage until deep into the night, putting forward argument after argument in his own favour.

It was only after the French president had personally explained to him that his cause was irretrievably lost, that he finally agreed to throw in the towel. The other national leaders departed for home, but a disappointed Verhofstadt remained behind in the conference room for a further thirty minutes. What was he thinking during that solitary half hour? Who can say? Perhaps he was blaming himself for the mistakes he had made. For at the end of the day he had only himself to blame.

Like Lubbers before him, he had brought about his own downfall. Perhaps this is the inevitable fate of national politicians who try to step into the international arena at the height of their power in their own country. Surrounded by 'yes men' at home, they sometimes lose sight of the subtle balances of power which exist in the wider world.

Guy Verhofstadt wanted to be President, but fell into a pit which he dug for himself.

I was pleased but not surprised at the rejection of Verhofstadt's candidacy. People who mess about with God usually get punished. Besides, the Princess deserves to be something more than just a feather in the cap of a political careerist. Lubbers and Verhofstadt both badly wanted to become President of the Commission, but for the wrong reasons. As a result, they failed to realise their dreams and the glittering prize fell into the hands of someone who hadn't really sought it. And this is how it should be. Serving the Princess is an honour – not just a reward for 'services rendered'.

7| Offside

The group of twenty Swedish businessmen stared blankly at the Commissioner, with the kind of enthusiasm – or lack of it – usually found in a dentist's waiting room. We were in the stylish surroundings of the Conrad Hotel in Brussels, where the boss was giving a speech entitled 'Europe at the crossroads'. The first of our Scandinavian guests fell asleep after about fifteen minutes. He was quickly followed by most of the others. The few who remained awake looked longingly towards the bar.

The Commissioner carried on regardless, ploughing his way through the turgid text, threaded with technical jargon that even many of my mandarin colleagues would have had difficulty in understanding. He was so intent on his notes that he didn't notice that the Swedes had mentally 'left the building' a long time ago. When he reached a section over 'solvency-liquidity requirements', even he began to realise that he didn't have the faintest idea what he was talking about. He had little option but to read the remainder of his prepared speech 'parrot-fashion'. It was about as interesting as watching paint dry.

As soon as he had finished, the Swedes made a run for the door – and the bar. The Commissioner was visibly disappointed.

'Who writes this rubbish?' he enquired, as we made our way back to our car. 'Speeches are usually prepared by the DG and approved by the director-general,' I replied. 'And doesn't anybody else look at them?' he continued. 'Yes – you do! Or at least you're supposed to. But usually there isn't much time. The DG delivers the speech as late as possible, just to make sure you can't change anything.'

The Commissioner was getting irritated. 'This is intolerable. I'm being forced to read speeches that even I don't understand. God knows what the public make of them. Not very much, I imagine.' He complained that the texts were always so dry and uninteresting. 'They never contain a single joke or historical parallel. Nothing.'

I told him that that was what the director-general intended. Normally, the first draft is made by the official responsible for the dossier. This will usually contain a few lighter references, perhaps even a joke or two. However, this draft is then passed on to the head of unit, the deputy-director-general and the director-general for approval. The director-general, in particular, was notorious for scrapping all humorous comments. For him, the texts had to be business-like and informative: the future of Europe was no laughing matter. Possibly not, but the results were predictable. The speeches were unbelievably boring and totally incomprehensible to anyone who didn't possess a university degree in political science.

In contrast, the director-general's own speeches were light and witty – as a result of which, they were reported more frequently in the press than the Commissioner's own efforts! Just coincidence?

'This is no longer acceptable,' said the Commissioner, gathering together his papers and handing them across to me. 'From now on, I want you to look after my speeches. I have no intention of reading this kind of drivel for the next five years. It's like trying to skate on yoghurt.'

Speech-writing was nothing new to me. In fact, I had been doing it from quite an early age. My dad was a member of the local village council and as a teenager I was already helping to prepare texts on his behalf.

This is not the way it used to be. In the old days, the mayor and the councillors used to put nothing down in writing – except for very brief minutes of the local council meetings. When I enquired why this was so, the mayor replied: 'It's actions that count, sonny, not words. And certainly not bits of bloody paper!' However, all this changed in the mid-1960s, when there was an 'incident' during one of the council meetings. A gentleman-farmer with a liberal background wanted to make clear to the mayor – a stylish, almost aristocratic figure, who was a member of the Christian Historical Union (CHU) – that the reallocation of agricultural land had been botched.

This reallocation was a highly sensitive issue in the local farming community. The idea was that pieces of land should be exchanged and re-distributed, in order to allow more efficient country planning and to guarantee safe water drainage for everybody – a key requirement in a low-lying country like the Netherlands. However, there were always people who felt aggrieved at the resulting redistribution and it was a subject which was always calculated to make tempers boil. And so it was on the evening in question. Feelings were running high and during the heat of debate the gentleman-farmer shouted at the mayor: 'Just admit it – you've fucked the whole thing up.'

This might sound fairly mild by modern standards, but it was not the kind of thing we were used to in the 1960s – and certainly not in the conservative and Calvinistic village of Bronckhorst! The mayor was genuinely shocked and hardly knew what to say. The reaction of the village registrar was even more dramatic – he fainted on the spot! This gentleman was a member of the orthodox Protestant State Reformed Party – which meant that he was against votes for women, against television and in favour of the death penalty. When he came to our house with papers for my father, he always stood pointedly with his back towards the television set. The television was 'a tool of Satan' and definitely not in keeping with the State's Bible, the biblical translation of 29 July 1637, from which his party still drew most of its political ideas!

When the registrar had regained consciousness, the mayor suspended the sitting and had the council chamber cleared. He also had a quiet word with the village secretary, to make sure that the offending term was not included in the minutes of the meeting, and then rushed off to persuade the reporter of the local newspaper to do the same thing. The registrar eventually recovered, but he was never quite the same again. Nor was our village politics. A new mayor was appointed, this time from the Anti-Revolutionary Party. This party was also strongly Protestant, but the new mayor liked to think of himself as 'a man of the times'. Consequently, he tried to introduce changes which he thought were more in keeping with the spirit of the enlightened and democratic 1960s.

One of these changes was that the annual budget speech of each councillor had to be submitted to the mayor in writing. This was not my dad's strong point and so he set me to work. The speeches dealt with a wide variety of subjects, ranging from the famous land re-allocation issue to the creation of a new camp site for German tourists, from traffic lights and footpaths to measures to promote fertility in cows. The same issues kept coming back year after year, and I was repeatedly required to try and find a new angle of approach to the same old problems. It was ideal training for my later career with the Commission!

The mayor was impressed with my speech-writing abilities and eventually told the vicar of our local church. Why did the mayor do this? Because he knew that the vicar had a very serious problem: he couldn't write a sermon for love nor money. Or rather he could write a sermon, but it took him about twenty hours to do it. And for those of us sitting in the pews each Sunday, it seemed like it took about twenty hours to listen to it!

When I was young, going to church was still the focal point of everybody's Sunday. I was there every week, sitting on the second row, immediately behind the members of the church council. The seats next to me were occupied by several elderly ladies from the village and it was their habit to eat a peppermint during the vicar's sermon (they were kind enough to give me one as well). They preferred peppermints to boiled sweets – or so they told me – because peppermints didn't get stuck under their false teeth. This could be dangerous, and on one memorable occasion one old lady's bottom plate flew out during the singing of Psalm 119, which is a particularly long and intricate psalm.

The sermon usually lasted about the length of time the ladies needed to suck their way through their peppermint, but sometimes they needed to take a second one – and so we began to categorise the vicar's efforts in terms of the number of peppermints: a one-peppermint sermon, a two-peppermint sermon, etc. Thankfully, three-peppermint sermons were a rarity, but not completely unknown!

When he learnt of my hidden speech-writing talents, the vicar asked me to come and see him at the vicarage: a large, white house on the edge of the village. After a preliminary cup of tea, he came to the point.

'Young man, you sit in church each week amongst the veterans of the Lord. What do they think of my sermons?'

I wasn't sure that the old ladies would like being described as 'veterans' and I wasn't sure how I should answer this delicate question. I decided that a vicar would prefer me to be honest.

'Vicar, they think your sermons are too long. The seats in our church are very hard, and even though most of your veterans are well-padded in those regions, two peppermints' worth of preaching is a bit too much for most of them.'

The vicar raised his eyes heavenwards and sighed. 'Yes, I thought so. I have always had problems with my sermons.' He asked if I could help him and we went through a number of his old sermons, trying to make them shorter and more interesting.

The vicar made the mistake which many people make: he wanted to say too many things at the same time. As a result, his speeches, or rather sermons, were much too long and difficult to follow. I suggested that he should try and work to a fixed format: 1,500 words or fifteen minutes. This would force him to be more selective in his subjects and more concise in his expression.

The vicar found fifteen minutes too short – almost as short as the sermons given by the priest in the Catholic church on the other side of the village! He didn't want any 'Roman trickery' in his church, with short services and people just coming in at the end to light a candle! 'In our faith, the Word is central, young man,' he reminded me. As a compromise, we agreed on twenty minutes or 2,000 words.

In all honesty, writing speeches for the Princess was not so different from writing sermons for the vicar. The basic principles are the same. You take an old sermon out of the cupboard, dust it off, mix it about – and suddenly you have a new sermon. In the first year of his five year mandate, the Commissioner gave a speech entitled 'Europe at the crossroads'. In the second year he gave much the same speech, but this time with the title 'Europe: time for action'. A year later, the new title would read 'Europe: the plans for tomorrow'. In year four we decided on 'Europe: new challenges on the horizon'. And we finished off in style in our fifth and final year with 'The Future of Europe'.

The Commissioner faced much the same problems as the vicar. There are only so many things you can say about Christmas, Good Friday, Easter, Pentecost, etc. The same is true of the Internal Market or any other European topic. Sooner or later, you are bound to end up saying the same things over and over again. The trick is not to make it too obvious.

I consulted regularly with the Commissioner about his speeches, especially if they were intended for translation and wider circulation. Often these speeches – or extracts from them – would be sent to the press or would be 'launched' via a specific channel, such as the opinion page of a particular newspaper. The Commissioner was strict – much stricter than the vicar had ever been. The basic material was still provided by the DG, but in a raw form. The officials responsible for the dossiers were delighted with this new development, since it meant that they no longer had to spend weeks preparing a text which would then be cut to ribbons by their superiors. This was now my privilege.

I reworked the DG material into a usable draft and passed it on to the boss. He went through it with a fine tooth-comb – or in his case, a fine, red pen. Line by line, word by word. By and large, it was worth the effort. Between us we produced a range of amusing and understandable speeches on subjects which were not intrinsically all that interesting: financial services, pensions, postal services, patents, etc. The key to our success was a light and humorous approach – the only way to keep an audience's attention. If only our vicar had tried this approach thirty years earlier with the veterans of the Lord, my youth would have been so much happier!

After a year of doing speeches together, mainly on technical dossiers, the Commissioner one day suggested something slightly different. 'Now I'd like to do a speech about the future of Europe.'

I was surprised: this was not in keeping with the traditional 'programme of events' for a Commissioner.

'Already?' I queried. 'Are you sure? You're only in the second year of your mandate. Most of your colleagues reserve that kind of speech until their final year.'

I knew that a debate about the long-term future of the Union could only lead to friction with the other Commissioners and, above all, with the senior mandarins. Everyone had been pleased with our 'Europe at the crossroads' speech, because it said very little of substance. The Commissioner – like hundreds of others before him – had simply pointed out that there were still many problems to be solved, but had said nothing about how we should solve them. I sensed that he now wished to move on to more specific proposals, not necessarily connected with his own portfolio. When I told the head of cabinet he looked at me gloomily and the spokesman did not seem too happy, either. He did not think it was a good idea.

However, the Commissioner was adamant: now was the time to speak out. 'What's the point of waiting until my mandate is almost over? I want to make my contribution to the debate while I'm still in a position to do something about it.'

He was determined to throw a big stone into the Brussels' pond of complacency and political correctness. What's more, he thought that he had found the perfect platform to do it. A week earlier he had received an invitation from a Dutch newspaper to give a speech in the Grote Kerk (Great Church) in The Hague. This was a very Dutch way of doing things: in the Netherlands politicians, even from the non-believing socialist and communist parties, all give their keynote speeches from the pulpit of a church – probably something to do with their upbringing.

From the Commissioner's point of view, the timing could not have been better. The recent European summit at Nice had not been a success and the closing treaty had only been able to secure very limited changes, whose long-term future was far from certain. His theme for his speech was therefore 'Europe after Nice'.

I went through the broad outlines of the speech in the Commissioner's office one afternoon. We worked according to our usual routine. I drew up a text and the Commissioner made his comments in the margin. I drew up a revised text and the Commissioner added new comments in the margin. And so we continued, until we eventually arrived at a final version. The Commissioner was meticulous: every grammatical error, every spelling mistake was removed with a quick stroke of his famous red pen. But this time, he was equally stringent about the political content. He wanted to make a statement and his statement was that Europe now needed to make some difficult choices: otherwise, there was a grave risk that the entire European project might 'disintegrate'.

At this time, 'disintegration' was a dirty word in Brussels. Every mandarin was working 24 hours a day to secure greater European 'integration'. The last thing they wanted to hear was a prophet of doom talking about 'disintegration'. 'Disintegration' was the equivalent of heresy: it displayed a complete lack of faith in the European ideal and the European mission. Above all, it suggested that Europe was moving too quickly and doing too much.

In many ways, I could sympathise with the Commissioner and his arguments. The European Union stood on the threshold of an enlargement which would welcome ten new countries as member states. However, it was clear to many of us that the European institutions had not yet been sufficiently reformed to accept this massive new influx. Several existing member states would quickly discover to their cost that the new arrangements did not work in their best interests.

Chief amongst these nations would be France. The Commissioner quoted from the French newspaper *Le Monde*, which had recently published an article with the title 'Europe – no longer France's own back garden.' The article suggested, correctly, that France's relative strength in the European Union could only be weakened by the enlargement and that the French would become more Euro-sceptic as a result. The days when the famous Franco-German axis decided everything in Europe now belonged to the past. Instead, future decisions would be taken on the basis of 'single issue coalitions'.

Not content with alarming France in this manner, the Commissioner also put the boot into the Dutch, the Belgians and the Germans. He criticised the behaviour of the Netherlands' prime minister in Nice, where he had tried to secure one more vote than Belgium in the new voting structure. He also hammered the Belgian premier, Guy Verhofstadt, and the German Foreign Minister, Joschka Fischer, for their

Joschka Fisher, German foreign minister and great European federalist.

naive views with regard to the future of a truly federal Europe. For the Commissioner, the 'United States of Europe' was an illusion, a dangerous fantasy which destroyed more than it created. Moreover, it threatened to undermine the legitimacy of Europe, since this kind of 'pie-in-the-sky' thinking would not go down well with the European electorate in the national referenda which must inevitably follow. According to the Commissioner, the EU would one day face the wrath of the voters, if its leadership kept on daydreaming in their ivory towers.

However, the Commissioner saved his *piece de résistance* for last. Immigration, he argued, was the greatest of all the problems facing the European Union. There was an urgent need for a clear immigration policy along the lines followed by countries such as the United States and Canada, which were more familiar with the difficulties associated with 'undesirable aliens'.

The end of his speech read as follows: 'Already today, a third of the population of Amsterdam and Rotterdam is made up by people of non-European ethnic origin. In fifteen years time, these groupings will have acquired a majority in most of the built-up urban areas in Europe. This can only lead to very serious problems of cultural, social and economic integration.'

This was political dynamite – especially if one remembers that the speech was given at the beginning of 2001: before 11 September and the murder of Pim Fortuyn.

Dynamite usually leads to an explosion, and the explosion was not long in coming. The day after the speech I was summoned to the cabinet of the President. I was treated to a long lecture by the head of the cabinet, the essence of which was that the Commissioner's message was 'a pile of crap'.

The fact that he was a Frenchman might have had something to do with his anger, but he warned me to expect trouble from other quarters as well. He was not wrong. The Dutch prime minister sent a personal fax, explaining why it was important that the Netherlands should have more votes than Belgium in the Council of Ministers. The Belgian prime minister was equally miffed about the sneering references to a federal Europe and henceforth he refused to invite the Commissioner to lunches with European liberal leaders, organised at his official residence in Brussels. Even the press were against us, accusing the Commissioner of 'another bout of wog-bashing'.

The Commissioner had planned to throw a stone into the Brussels' pond, but he hadn't expected the tidal wave of reaction it would provoke. Neither had I.

MINISTER-PRESIDENT

No: 's-Gravenhage,

Geachte heer

Deze week heb ik kennis genomen van de ANP-berichten over uw ontbijtsessie met journalisten.
Ik ben daar bijzonder ongelukkig mee. Uw uitspraken over bevriende staatshoofden en
regeringsleiders dienen niet het belang van Nederland. Evenmin zijn deze uitspraken goed voor
de positie van de Commissie, in een periode waarin de Nederlandse regering beoogt de positie
van de Commissie te versterken. Ik acht ze ook niet passend voor het gezag dat past bij het ambt
van Commissaris. Ik moge u daarom dringend verzoeken om u in de toekomst van dergelijke
uitspraken te onthouden.

                                    Hoogachtend,

An angry letter from the prime minister to the Commissioner. One of many.

's-Gravenhage,

Dear Sir,

*This week my attention has been drawn to the ANP communiqués relating to your
breakfast sessions with journalists. I am extremely unhappy with this situation.
Your comments about friendly heads of state and government leaders do not serve
the best interests of the Netherlands. By the same token, these comments also do a
disservice to the Commission, at a time when the government of the Netherlands is
seeking to strengthen the Commission's position. Furthermore, I do not think that
such actions are compatible with the dignity of your function as a Commissioner.
For all these reasons, may I urgently request you to refrain from making such comments in future.*

Yours faithfully,

In the past, I had translated the Commissioner's speeches into English and French, but now I had to have versions made in a whole range of European languages. Everyone wanted to read it, but nobody wanted to talk about it. During the next meeting of the College of Commissioners there was hardly a reference to the speech, apart from one Commissioner who described it as 'interesting'; a European euphemism for 'brave, bordering on the suicidal'.

As I had feared, we had not only aroused the anger of several European governments, but also the wrath of most of our EU colleagues. It is an unspoken rule that the Commissioners do not interfere with each other portfolios – and my Commissioner had now broken this golden rule ten times over!

There was a similar atmosphere of gloom and doom within our own cabinet. The head of cabinet was furious at this breech of European etiquette. Every mandarin knows that honesty is never the best policy and on this occasion the Commissioner had been brutally honest.

'It's going to take months to repair the damage,' he growled. I could see from the nodding heads around the table that most of his staff thought the same.

New measures were immediately 'agreed' for the processing of future speeches, which would henceforth be submitted to the entire cabinet. The first victim of this new procedure was Joshua, a colleague of mine, who in my absence had just completed a draft on another subject for the Commissioner.

Many of our cabinet members suspected that Joshua was not a 'committed European'. He had previously worked for the leader of the British Conservative Party, Ian Duncan-Smith, and many of my fellow mandarins still regarded him as being a cross between the American

Barry Goldwater (right), the hero of my fellow-speechwriter Joshua. All the European mandarins distrusted him.

Republican, Barry Goldwater, and the British Tory, Norman Tebbitt (which, even I must admit, is a fairly terrifying combination). As a result, Joshua's text was examined with a microscopic precision worthy of the McCarthy Committee – but I only learned about it later. I had not been invited to take part and was clearly being excluded from the full cabinet for my failure to control the Commissioner in his 'Grote Kerk' speech.

This is how things work in the Commission, both in the College of Commissioners and also within the individual DGs and cabinets. If you have been a naughty boy or girl, you are banished temporarily to the wilderness. Here it is expected that you will work quietly and diligently on your dossiers, without causing any fuss and bother. Once you have done this for the required period (which is generally longer than the biblical forty days and forty nights) you will be allowed back in to the fold. And then you can start sinning all over again...

Or this, at least, is how the Commissioner saw it. He had little option but to lay low for a number of months and this he duly did. However, once the heat had died down, he was on the lookout for new opportunities to proclaim his own personal vision of Europe. His next target was the anti-globalisation movement, which at that time was holding a series of violent and destructive demonstrations in cities throughout Europe.

He asked me to start work on a speech, which would be given in Zurich, where he had been invited by the top Swiss newspaper, the *Neue Züricher Zeitung*. The organisers had assured me that the auditorium in Zurich City Hall would be packed with major politicians and bankers, allowing me to neatly kill two birds with one stone: a large and influential audience and front page coverage in the Swiss national press. It seemed almost too good to be true.

The Commissioner and I flew to Zurich on a Thursday afternoon, arriving at the amusingly named Kloten International Airport – at least we found it amusing: 'kloten' in Dutch means 'bollocks'. We were met at the foot of the aeroplane steps by one of the organisers and he rushed the Commissioner to a waiting car.

The man was so busy with his VIP guest that I didn't even get a welcoming hand shake. I had to make my own way towards the giant Mercedes and I only just managed to jump into the front seat before it roared away. Our host sat in the back with the Commissioner, talking nineteen to the dozen. He instructed the driver to take us to one of the hills overlooking Zurich and I must admit that it was an impressive sight: the elegant city was beautifully lit – it was nearly Christmas time – and the grey mass of the lake, with its huge fountain, lay shimmering in the darkness. We then made our way to the city hall, which was equally impressive.

The auditorium was ideal and in my mind's eye I could already picture the Commissioner's triumph. With an audience of 1,000 grey-suited capitalists, a speech against the excesses of the anti-globalisation activists was guaranteed a warm reception. The applause would be loud and long, the television coverage would be prime time and tomorrow's newspapers would shower us in praise. What could possibly go wrong?

At this stage, the only irritation was our guide: he just wouldn't stop talking. Here was a man who gave whole new depths of meaning to the phrase 'verbal diarrhoea'. Even as we walked from the changing room and stepped out onto the stage he was still chattering away. However, what we saw caused all three of us to fall silent. And what exactly did we see? Well, nothing – and that was the problem. Instead of a hall full of Swiss bankers, we stood staring at 970 empty seats (the organisers themselves had at least managed to fill the first row).

'Are you sure we're in the right hall?' I asked our escort. For once, he was at a loss for words. 'I don't understand it,' he stammered. 'We sent out hundreds of invitations and I was certain that everyone would come.' 'Did you put the right date on the invitation?' I enquired. He blushed bright red but assured me that he had. 'This is ridiculous,' I whispered to the Commissioner and started to look around for the exit.

But the Commissioner wouldn't hear of it. He had come to Zurich to make a speech and that was what he intended to do – even if it was only for thirty people! I went and sat in the second row in a desperate attempt to make the room look fuller, but the whole thing was a fiasco. The Commissioner's words sounded hollow, my carefully-crafted jokes all fell flat and the applause at the end was even briefer than the Swedes had given us in the Conrad Hotel. It was not the devastating attack on the anti-globalisation demonstrators that we had planned and I expected the Commissioner to be furious. To my surprise and relief, he remained calm and relaxed. 'Oh, it doesn't really matter. Once when I was an MP in Holland, I gave a speech in Aalten to eight farmers and a sheepdog. It's all part of the game.'

We drove back to the hotel for a meal, still accompanied by our guide. Now that he was trying to be apologetic, he talked more than ever. Suddenly, it all became too much for the Commissioner.

'My dear sir, when we are in the hotel, do you think you could arrange a small conference room for us? I need to talk urgently to my assistant here.'

Now I was really worried. Was he planning to sack me for this evening's disaster? At the hotel, our talkative Swiss friend did as the Commissioner had asked and we soon found ourselves alone in a small but comfortable meeting room. I prepared myself for the worst, but instead of giving me a rocket, the Commissioner sank down into a chair and let out a sigh of relief.

'Thank Christ for that,' he exclaimed. 'I don't think I could stand another minute of that mindless chatter.' All he wanted was a bit of peace and quiet. He was more bothered about our garrulous escort than by this evening's empty hall.

I was less happy about the empty hall and at dinner I buttonholed the chief editor of the *Neue Züricher Zeitung*. I told him that his newspaper had put my Commissioner in an embarrassing position and that I held him personally responsible. I demanded adequate compensation, in the shape of full front-page coverage for our speech. He agreed, but it was two weeks later before anything appeared, and even then it was only on page two.

This was not unusual for the *Neue Züricher Zeitung*. When the Third World War eventually breaks out, it will still take at least two weeks before it is reported in Zurich: the Swiss papers only exist to serve the interests of the bankers – the bankers who we had never seen. We left for Brussels the same evening, still amused by the name of the airport: *omen est nomen*, as the Romans used to say. The next morning I told the head of cabinet about our failed attack on the anti-globalisationists. He was visibly relieved. 'An empty room: that's the perfect audience for a speech by the Commissioner. It's a shame we can't always arrange it like that ...'

It was obvious that the Commissioner was trying to set a political agenda with these speeches. The subjects were not always (i.e. almost never) portfolio-related and everyone knew that he was trying to promote his ideas to a wider public through the media. His views on the state of affairs in Zimbabwe were by no means portfolio-related but I fully agreed with him that it was a telling example of political hypocrisy.

Not too long ago, many prominent European politicians were strong advocates of the current President of Zimbabwe, Robert Mugabe. Once an icon of liberation, Mugabe had turned into a devious dictator, skimming off the fat of his country. However, his former admirers remained silent and the Commissioner intended to point the finger at them.

He asked me to draft an article for the Dutch daily *De Volkskrant*. I did with some conviction, because I had just visited the country and I was shocked by what I had seen. The newspaper published the article which intentionally aimed a blow at several so-called progressive politicians, some of them members of the European Parliament. The Commissioner thought the article 'an absolute hit' but the members of parliament concerned were not amused.

Instead, they filed parliamentary questions to the President of the Commission, asking whether the Internal Market Commissioner reflected the position of the Commission on Zimbabwe? Obviously, this was not the case. The President's spokesman asked me to stop annoying members of Parliament, because in the end 'they could sack us all'. In the world of the mandarins polemic actions are never appreciated. Language is a tool to assuage, not to ignite. The Zimbabwe operation irritated our own cabinet, our own spokesman and most of the fellow Commissioners. But none of this ever seemed to worry my Commissioner. In fact, he didn't seem too concerned about who he upset.

On one occasion, he used the Mansholt Lecture (named after the former European Commissioner) to argue that the majority of Mansholt's policies were complete nonsense – and this while most of Mansholt's surviving family were sitting in the front row! In particular, he poured scorn on Mansholt's belief in the 1970 report of the Club of Rome, which suggested that by the year 2000 Europe would be drowning in a sea of pollution, while the communist countries of the Soviet bloc would be enjoying a purer environment. Precisely the opposite was true: advanced western technology had ensured that fish were once again swimming in the Rhine, while the Soviet Union's legacy to the world was an environmental disaster: Chernobyl.

In a similar vein, he used the Drees Lecture (named after a former Dutch prime minister) to give a ringing affirmation of his privatisation policies to an audience largely made up of trade unionists and socialists. Drees had always been a realistic socialist and had left the party at the beginning of the 1970s. Using quotations from Drees's own writings, the Commissioner tried to show that the old premier would now be regarded as being on the centre-right of the political spectrum. Drees had argued for limited state interference in the economy and the Commissioner thought that this excellent example should be followed by the present-day leadership of the Dutch socialist movement – all of whom were in attendance in the Red Hat Church in Amsterdam, where the speech was being given. Yet another church!

I could give dozens of other examples. Another classic was his performance at the Institute for Economic Affairs in London. During the 1980s, the Institute – under the leadership of Lord Harris of High Cross – had been one of Margaret Thatcher's leading think-tanks and was instrumental in formulating the reformist policies by which the Iron Lady had put Great Britain back on its feet.

It seemed like the perfect place to discuss reformist policies for Europe and so the Commissioner unveiled his proposals for the increased use of nuclear power in Western Europe as part of a Common Energy Policy, in order to reduce the EU's reliance on gas and oil imported from Russia and the Middle East.

As always with the Commissioner, what he said made perfectly good practical sense. Nuclear energy had long been a taboo subject within the European Commission and several of his colleagues, led by the Environment Commissioner, were baying for his blood when he arrived back in Brussels. However, some of these doubters were later prepared to change their minds, when President Putin decided to turn off the gas taps for a day – proving once again that in politics a small practical demonstration can sometimes achieve more than a grandiloquent speech.

Often, the Commissioner was ahead of events, trying to open people's eyes and to prepare European policymakers for major changes. But he learned the hard way that in the European Union words are rarely followed by action. Europe only reacts when it has to, forced by outside events like the interruption of its energy supply.

There were three major issues outside his own portfolio which particularly interested the Commissioner: the euro, Turkey and immigration. He had strong opinions on all these issues – and they were opinions he intended to express, no matter who he offended.

He first became seriously involved in the euro debate when Germany and France announced that they no longer intended to honour the terms of the Growth and Stability Pact. This meant that they were planning to allow their budget deficits to exceed 3%. If a small country had attempted to do such a thing, it would have received an immediate letter of warning from the President of the Commission. However, because France and Germany are major European powers, it was understood that the rules would simply have to be changed. Instead of sending a letter of warning, the President of the Commission uttered conciliatory remarks in an interview with the French daily *Le Monde* about 'exceptional circumstances' and 'justifiable exceptions'.

This inequality of treatment irritated the Commissioner. Not only was it blatantly unfair, but it also threatened to undermine the reputation of the euro as a 'hard' currency, based on sound economic and monetary practice. In the Netherlands, the Commissioner had had a long fight to persuade the Dutch prime minister to honour the 3% deficit figure – and now the President was planning to wipe out these hard-won gains via the backdoor of Europe!

'I just can't accept this,' he told me on more than one occasion. 'And I'm going to say it.' I knew that he meant it, and so it was with a sense of foreboding that I tuned in to his appearance on the Dutch television programme, *Buitenhof*, a few weeks later. The Commissioner argued as passionately as ever for a hard euro, but the TV presenter was ready with his reply. 'Your President doesn't seem to agree with you, does he? He thinks that there is room for some flexibility.' To which the Commissioner replied: 'Then I disagree with the President. On this matter, he's got it wrong.'

I almost fell off my chair: this time (to quote our American friends) the shit was really going to hit the fan. And the fan was working full blast!

The next day, we were scheduled to travel to Strasbourg for a meeting of the European Parliament. I was travelling by car; the Commissioner intended to fly. I had just passed Metz when he called me on his mobile phone.

'Guess what. I've just had the President on the line. He's not very pleased with me. He seems to think I'm being disloyal. I don't know what he's going to do next, but there's a chance he might kick me out of the Commission. Well, let him get on with it. The euro is too important – I'm not going to back down.'

For the second time in two days, I again almost fell off my chair. 'Kicked off the Commission'! This was bad news indeed. If the Commissioner was sacked, then I would be sacked as well – and unlike him, I was not yet ready to go into early retirement!

I told the driver to step on the gas and get us to Strasbourg as quickly as possible: I needed to do some damage limitation – and fast! To my mind, the only way to get us out of this mess was to find as many other supporters for the Commissioner's position as I could. If we could create a broad front, we might just survive.

I called first on the cabinet of the Spanish Commissioner, since the euro was part of his portfolio. The head of cabinet said that they were keen to 'maintain strict criteria for the euro'. It was a good start, but one ally was not going to be enough – especially a wobbly Spanish one.

I next moved on to the two German cabinets. Their support was vital and I knew that for them the crux of the matter revolved around the definition of the term 'inflation'. The Italian President of the Commission had a very relaxed attitude towards inflation. In fact, all Italians have a very relaxed attitude towards inflation. For them, it's a bit like rain. It comes, it goes – and afterwards the sun always shines. Besides, this was still the era of the lira, when the Italians were used to paying for everything in huge figures. When a cup of coffee costs 10,000 lire, you tend not to notice when the price goes up to 10,100.

This would not have been the case in the Netherlands. For a Dutchman, inflation is the work of the devil. The guilder had been a strong currency for over three hundred years and that's how everyone wanted it to stay. The guilder was a currency you could build on – literally. Its stability had allowed millions of Hollanders on relatively low incomes to take out huge, long-term mortgages to build their own homes.

But if the Dutch hate inflation, for the Germans it is a nightmare obsession. This fear dates back to the 1920s and 1930s, when hyperinflation caused the collapse of the Weimar Republic and paved the way for the political career of a failed artist and housepainter – Adolf Hitler. The two German cabinets still displayed this same loathing for inflation and both thought that the issue needed to be discussed more 'thoroughly' (a favourite German word) – something, in their opinion, which the President had not yet done.

'The President has spoken too soon,' they told me, 'and his views do not necessarily reflect the views of the College.' This was music to my ears. With four Commissioners on our side, our group was large enough to hold its own. The President could hardly sack two Germans, a Spaniard and a Dutchman: this could only lead to the resignation of the entire Commission – and I knew that this was the last thing the President had in mind!

My Commissioner arrived in Strasbourg on the afternoon flight, still fearing for his job. I filled him in on the day's developments and we both went off smiling to the College meeting. We knew we were safe. The President said nothing more about the unfortunate television interview and instead suggested that an information document about the euro should be sent to all interested parties 'to promote further discussion'. Honour was satisfied on both sides and we lived to fight another day.

In fact, the Commissioner lived to fight many other days and eventually made it through to the end of his five year mandate. As a parting shot, he decided to bundle his collective political thoughts in that most flexible of political tools: a book.

Our idea was to conduct interviews with ten leading members of the European Parliament about the future of Europe. The people we chose were European monuments in their own right: politicians such as Willy De Clercq, Mario Soares, Michel Rocard, Hans Modrow, etc.

The Commissioner would write an introduction, giving comments on the interviews and summarising his own thoughts on the matters they raised. It seemed like a neat solution to avoiding any last minute problems with the Commission. Who could object to a book? Who could object to the collective wisdom of so many eminent Europeans, all of them members of the European Parliament? It looked like we were covered all round.

We held the interviews on a monthly basis in the Commissioner's office in Strasbourg. Some of our interviewees were enthusiastic collaborators; others were more sceptical – to begin with. One of these was Hans Modrow, the last prime minister of the old German Democratic Republic. He entered the office almost apologetically, asking 'Is this the right place?'

As one of the few remaining communists in the Parliament, he was probably expecting a surprise attack from the Commissioner, who had once been described as the liberal equivalent of the Hezbollah. After some initial nervousness, the interview was conducted in a relaxed atmosphere, with Modrow demonstrating his clear and precise mind. This is typical of the old guard communists: they all received a decent education at the party school and their survival often depended on having the right ideological answer to the right question at the right time.

I was surprised at the extent to which the liberal Commissioner and the communist Modrow could find common ground on a number of issues – but this tended to be the case with all the interviews. The Commissioner was particularly delighted after the interview with leading French socialist, Michel Rocard. I regarded French socialism as one of the most treacherous forces in European history, but the Commissioner kept on praising Rocard's powers of analysis and sense of logic. Their conversation resulted in a sort of mutual admiration society and the two decided to write a book, just prior to the French presidential elections, on how to reform France.

Hans Modrow, the last communist premier of the German Democratic Republic.

The Commissioner and Michel Rocard. A remarkable entente cordial.

Our own book of interviews was published under the title *The Limits of Europe* and was generally well received. There was only one subject which continued to cause us problems: Turkey.

The European Community first promised full membership to Turkey in 1963. At the beginning of 2007 the Turks are still in the waiting room and after 44 years are gradually beginning to lose patience. As a result, many Turks no longer wish to join the Union – a point of view which the Commissioner would be happy to endorse.

He has always been against Turkish membership and even said so during an official visit to Ankara: not surprisingly, the reception following his speech was not a particularly cheerful affair. His reasoning is that Turkey would cause the European Union to implode. Turkey's huge population (currently 73 million, with an anticipated 100 million by the year 2050) would guarantee it powerful voting rights, while its relative poverty would represent a massive drain on the Union's shrinking resources. In short, the European system would overload and collapse – and all this for a country that many people do not regard as being genuinely European.

Of course, it is not politically correct to say all this – the Princess is always reluctant to upset her neighbours – but at the end of his mandate the Commissioner had few qualms about putting it in his book. And so he did.

The *Financial Times* quickly picked up on the matter. They requested an interview with the Commissioner, on the basis of which they concluded that he wished to see Turkey as a buffer state – not as a member state. They splashed the headlines all across the front page, referring to the text of the full interview on page 5. But what did we find when we turned to page 5? Nothing. Nothing at all! They had forgotten to print the interview! Even the running of Europe's most prestigious daily newspaper is subject to ordinary human failings!

Not that it mattered. There were soon to be plenty of other opportunities to get ourselves back in the press on the Turkish issue. The next one arose when the Commissioner was asked to give a speech to mark the opening of the academic year at the University of Leiden.

He asked me to write a speech comparing the European Union with the old Austro-Hungarian Empire, which had collapsed at the end of the First World War. I set to work with enthusiasm and had soon completed a first draft. Historical parallels are not only interesting and instructive, but can also be politically useful. They allow you to suggest comparisons which would be labelled as 'heretical' if they were linked to contemporary issues.

We decided that the title for the speech should be: *The Multinational Union*. The more we thought about it, the more we came to see the similarities between the Hapsburg Monarchy and the European Union. The Hapsburg Empire also contained a wide variety of different nationalities, which were conquered and absorbed at a speed with which the political institutions of the monarchy were unable to cope. In particular, the eight million German-speakers feared being overwhelmed by the 20 million Slavs within the Empire's new boundaries. This would certainly have been the case if the Slavic peoples had been granted the same voting rights as the Austrians and the Hungarians – and so the Austrians and Hungarians made sure that these voting rights were never granted, creating still greater internal pressures within the Empire as a result. An explosion would have been inevitable, if the First World War and the Treaty of Versailles had not intervened.

The proposed membership of Turkey threatened to put the European Union in exactly the same position – at least according to the Commissioner. The original founder members of the EU were in danger of being outvoted and bled dry by the poorer countries they had taken under their wing. However, it was very difficult for the Commissioner to say this openly as the representative of a Commission which had voted to continue negotiations with Turkey by a majority vote of 19-1 (although he was the single vote against, much to the disgust of our head of cabinet, whose motto was 'never alone and never first').

In the final analysis, the Leiden speech boiled down to a single question: how could we point a finger at the Turks without actually naming them? We solved this question by reference to a quotation from an expert in Islamic history, Bernard Lewis. He believes that if present demographic trends continue, Europe will have become an Islamic continent by the end of the 21st century.

'Europe will become part of the Arabian West, stretching from the Magreb Desert to the Atlantic Ocean.'

This allowed the Commissioner to add in his speech: 'If Lewis is correct, the liberation of Vienna in 1683 will all have been for nothing.'

It was a neat solution. The reference to the raising of the siege of Vienna was also a clear reference to Turkey's last serious effort to conquer Europe, but we had managed to avoid using their name – or so we thought.

Unfortunately, we forgot to take account of the press's ability to ignore or alter facts which don't suit their own purposes. Instead of printing what the Commissioner actually said, they all quoted him as

1683: Vienna is liberated from Turkish encirclement. Is history repeating itself?

saying: 'If Turkey joins the EU, the liberation of Vienna in 1683 will all have been for nothing.'

This controversial and confrontational statement appeared in papers in Europe, the Middle East and the United States – and there was nothing we could do to stop it. As always, however, the Commissioner was not really too concerned. Unlike his head of cabinet, he is always happy to be both first and alone, if the situation demands it. He has the courage of a pioneer, not the calculation of a mandarin.

We sent copies of both the book and the speech to all the other Commissioners, but not one of them reacted. They all have their own portfolios and they were only too happy to avoid the hornet's nest which my Commissioner had stirred up.

This taught me an important final lesson about the European Union. In the world of the mandarins, crucial questions about the future of the continent are seldom debated. The only thing which can arouse the passion of the Princess's servants is the discussion of technical details – details which are essentially irrelevant to Europe's continued existence.

The possible accession of Turkey to the Union is a subject for discussion in every newspaper and every bar from Lisbon to Latvia. In fact, the only places where it is not being seriously discussed are the higher European circles of Brussels and Strasbourg. Perhaps this helps to explain why the mandarins are so surprised when the voters of Europe try to signal their fear of Turkish membership by other means – such as the votes against the European constitution in France and the Netherlands. In both countries, the future enlargement of the Union was a much bigger issue than the nuts and bolts of the constitutional mechanism.

Yet the mandarins refuse to see this, even when the facts are staring them full in the face. The gulf between the European elite and the European people has never been as great as on this issue of Turkish membership. The people are dead against it, but still the elite continues to press forward and will doubtless do so, until the next referendum produces the next defeat.

Surely it is time for the Princess's servants to realise that countries such as France, Austria and the Netherlands will not vote in favour of Turkish membership. Not now. Not in ten years time. Not ever. But perhaps it will not come this far. Perhaps Turkey will finally get tired of waiting and will pull out of the negotiations of its own accord, angry and hurt. In some ways this would be a shame – but there would be a huge sigh of relief in most of the capitals of Western Europe.

8| The Mother
of all Parliaments

The European Parliament was my first lover and I have never been unfaithful to her. After my job as assistant to several Euro-MPs, I left her for a while to enter the world of journalism. But even then I kept returning to the scene of our most memorable romantic encounters: the bar in the European Parliament! When I was working for both the Dutch *NRC Handelsblad* and the Belgian *De Standaard* newspapers I had plenty of opportunities for making European trips: and this usually meant to the Parliament's dual headquarters in Brussels and Strasbourg.

Writing about Europe as a journalist can sometimes be difficult. On the one hand, most editors have little interest in Europe, because they find it a dull subject. On the other hand, the journalists themselves are constantly besieged by politicians from Brussels and Strasbourg, all anxious to get their names in the newspapers. As a result, a reporter of European affairs often finds himself between the devil and the deep blue sea. Those responsible for Europe wish to inform the public, while those responsible for newspapers don't want to bore their readers to death.

A journalist can return from Brussels and Strasbourg with a whole sackful of interesting stories, only to find that his work is given the lowest priority by his bosses. Often he has to fight, just to get one or two pieces into actual print. This means that the poor old journalist loses out on all sides. His editors complain that he is always moaning about Europe and the Euro-politicians complain that he never uses the 'excellent' information they were 'kind' enough to give him. Little wonder that many Euro-journalists, like many Euro-MPs, end up suffering from Euro-sclerosis. They become frustrated at their inability to get their work published and seek solace in the company of their fellow sufferers in one of the Parliament's many bars. This leads to the development of a group mentality amongst the Brussels/Strasbourg press corps. 'We're all in the same boat together,' they think and so they gradually begin to adopt each other's ways of talking and reasoning. This is 'pack journalism' at its worst. In the end, they all say and write exactly the same things.

When I was working for the *NRC Handelsblad* I was once temporarily 'banned' from doing further European stories. During the plenary session of the Parliament in May each year, there is traditionally a celebration of the asparagus harvest in the village of Hoerdt, near Strasbourg. This is quite a famous event in the region and busloads of European politicians (and their staffs) are driven out to take part in the festivities, which involve copious quantities of asparagus, ham – and wine.

As a dedicated reporter, I felt that it was my duty to tag along and watch the Euro-MPs at play. To get a real 'feel' for my story, I also felt it was my duty to partake of the aforementioned asparagus, ham and wine. I later wrote a piece about '*Our men in Strasbourg*'. I described the Euro-MPs in the following terms: '*Le Parlement Européen; on y mange, on y danse et on y parle*', which means 'The European Parliament: they eat, they dance and they talk'. This was a reference to the Prince De Ligne's famous comment about the Congress of Vienna in 1815. When asked by a friend how the Congress was progressing, he replied '*Le congrès ne marche pas, il danse*': it does not progress, it dances.

I thought that this was a nice allusion, but it was destined to rebound on me with a vengeance. During the celebrations, I had failed to notice the presence of a film crew from the British Broadcasting Corporation. The British are always keen to show Europe in a negative light and it was no different on this occasion. The resulting report – shown a week later on English television – was full of images of drunken politicians and reporters, all enjoying themselves at 'the taxpayer's expense'. Unfortunately, I was one of the reporters who was caught in the act. My editor was not impressed to see me dance my way across his television screen, even though I was doing a very respectable attempt at a polka! The next morning he summoned me to his office. 'Journalists must keep their distance. If politicians want to make fools of themselves, it is our job to watch them from the sidelines – not to join in with them!' I was banished to the Africa Desk.

Happily, this banishment did not last very long and I was soon back reporting European affairs – although I decided this time to take my editor's advice and adopt a more critical approach. I had heard rumours about a Dutch Christian-democrat Euro-MP, Jimmy Jansen van Raay. He was a huge man, famous for his extravagant and lavish life style – certainly by Dutch standards. Jimmy first became a national celebrity in Holland at the end of the 1970s, when he was involved in a legendary row with the Dutch European Commissioner, Henk Vredeling in the Sofitel Hotel in Strasbourg.

Both men liked a glass of whisky and both always liked to have the last word. On this occasion, their 'discussion' got out of hand. To prove the validity of his well-reasoned arguments, the socialist Vredeling picked up an ashtray and threw it at the head of the right-wing van Raay. In a rare moment of awareness and lucidity, Jimmy was able to duck the heavy metal object, which flew into a very expensive mirror hanging on the wall. A member of Vredeling's cabinet immediately paid for the damage, in the hope of keeping the incident quiet: but it leaked out. Via Jimmy.

Jimmy in his favourite pose: at the centre of media-attention.

As time passed, Jimmy's fame gradually turned into notoriety. According to some sources, he was recommending parliamentary lobbyists to employ the services of a particular legal firm – a firm of which he was also a silent partner. The lobbyists had to pay the firm a large sum of money for 'advice', following which Jimmy would ensure that an amendment reflecting the lobbyist's wishes was submitted to Parliament. It was also reputed that Jimmy asked money in return for favourable speeches, which is not really a part of the job-description for a Member of the European Parliament! I decided to look into the matter and so I phoned Jimmy. He immediately invited me for a massive lunch.

'My dear friend, let's first go and eat,' he said in his well-known jovial manner. He always had a fine sense of the dramatic and some suggested that his legendary appetite was the result of his stay in a Japa-

LIFE OF A EUROPEAN MANDARIN

nese prison camp during the Second World War. Jimmy once said that after this experience he never wanted to go hungry again. Judging by the size of his waist, he had been true to his word. 'I know an excellent fish restaurant,' he told me. 'Let's give it a bash!'

Jimmy ordered a taxi and his assistant Anneke came along for the ride. I delayed putting my question about his possible conflict of interest until the end of the meal. I didn't want to ruin his appetite – or spoil a good lunch. According to Jimmy, the restaurant he had chosen was much better than the more famous *Le Crocodile*, where politicians of the Spinelli-type came together to discuss the future of Europe.

'The portions at *Le Crocodile* are too small,' said Jimmy with the voice of someone who had clearly made an in-depth study of the matter. 'If I go to a restaurant, I don't just want to talk. I want to eat.'

As if to illustrate the point, he ordered most of the things on the menu. We started with fish soup, into which Jimmy poured a stiff glass of brandy: 'Just to improve the flavour, you understand.' This was followed by the 'speciality of the house' – a huge fish dish which was presented on a special display unit in three different layers. The whole structure was so big that I could no longer see Anneke sitting on the other side of the table!

I had no idea how we were ever going to get all this food inside just the three of us, because there was enough to feed a small army. But Jimmy didn't see a problem. 'This is what they call a *plat consistent*. It really sets you up for the rest of the day.'

It would have set me up for the rest of the year, but Jimmy began to demolish it all more or less single-handedly. As he did so, he told me about his great efforts in Parliament, about the deficiencies of his colleagues in the Christian-democrat grouping and about the incompetence of the grouping's leader, Hanja. Jimmy was against just about everyone and everything. 'Loyalty' was not a word which seemed to figure highly in his political vocabulary.

To my amazement, Jimmy finished off every last morsel of the main course. To my even greater amazement, he was still not satisfied! '*Garçon*, bring me the dessert menu!' By this time I had had more than enough and politely declined. Even the faithful Anneke said 'no'. Throughout the meal she had behaved like the perfect assistant, nodding agreement at his comments, laughing at his jokes and even wiping his chin when he spilt something. But dessertin that was taking faithfulness a bit too far! Jimmy shrugged his shoulders and ordered a double-portion of *crème brûlée* and another cognac.

I felt that this was the moment for my question about Jimmy's supposedly doubtful practices and so I asked him point-blank: 'By the way, is it true that you get money for tabling parliamentary amendments through your legal firm?'

He froze with a spoonful of custard half way to his mouth and I expected an explosion of anger. But the good meal had put him in a good mood: he popped the spoon into his mouth and turned to answer me with a smile.

'My dear sir, look me in the eye. I would never do such a thing. I am as innocent as the Lamb of God. Before you sits an honest man – I swear it.'

I wasn't sure whether to believe him or not. He wouldn't have been the first lawyer ever to have told a pack of lies after having sworn a biblical oath. But Jimmy seemed more interested in finding out where the rumours had come from.

'I bet I can tell you,' he said, with his finger in the air. 'It was that no-good nurse, wasn't it?' This was clear reference to Hanja, who had been a member of the medical profession before moving into politics. Like a good reporter, I defended the secrecy of my sources, but we both knew that Jimmy was not exactly a million miles off target.

Suddenly, he looked at this watch. 'My goodness, is that the time?' And indeed, more than three hours had passed since we first sat down at table, what now seemed like a lifetime ago.

'I'm afraid I'll have to leave you, old boy. Time for a nap in the Sofitel, I think. But I enjoyed our chat – and the meal. *J'ai bien mangé* as our French cousins say!'

With that, he rose from his chair, paid the bill and went off for his 'nap' with Anneke. I would have liked to follow them, but found that I was no longer capable of movement: I had eaten and drank far too much! With a superhuman effort, I eventually managed to get to my feet and staggered off to a waiting taxi, which took me back to the European Parliament Building. The basement contained a sauna complex and I spent the rest of the afternoon trying to sweat off the inches that Jimmy had added to my waistline. As I sizzled gently in the steam, I went over the lunch in my mind. Was Jimmy really on the take? I supposed that I would never find out. And I didn't. Nobody did.

Jimmy was a much too slippery customer ever to get caught, even if the allegations were true. Later he changed political parties and moved back to Dutch politics, serving for six months as an MP for the Pim Fortuyn grouping. I often thought of him and imagined that the change from the richly-filled tables of Strasbourg to the bread-and-cheese politics of The Hague must have been a huge shock to his system. Perhaps he even lost weight. Then again, perhaps he didn't.

Years later I returned to the European Parliament – but in a totally different capacity. I was no longer a reporter – on the outside looking in. I was now a cabinet member of a European Commissioner – on the inside looking out.

This was, indeed, a complete reversal of roles. In the old days, I was trying to sniff out the secrets of Strasbourg. Now I was trying to make sure that all these secrets remained firmly under lock and key. In the old days, it was the MEPs who were trying to keep me sweet: they wanted to speak to me and so I decided which ones I spoke to and which not. Now, I needed the support of the MEPs and so it was me who had to keep them happy and contented. In the old days, I just wandered down to the Parliament bar for a drink and a chat, hoping that I might pick up some useful tit-bits of political gossip. Now, it was my task to make solid political alliances for the Commissioner and to protect him against attacks from the alliances of others. And these attacks were not long in coming.

My Commissioner had an outspoken – one might even say controversial – political style, which made him a 'soft' target for parliamentary criticism. In short, he was the quickest and easiest way for most Euro-MPs to get their names in the newspapers – a kind of political punch-ball: whichever way you hit him, he just kept coming back for more.

My Commissioner was involved with the work of two parliamentary committees: the Internal Market Committee and the Economic Monetary Committee. As chance would have it, the chairmen – sorry, chairpersons – of both these committees were women: the one a passionate Spaniard, the other a fiery German. Being an old-fashioned gentleman at heart, the Commissioner at first tried to win over these ladies with a little old-fashioned flattery and charm. This was not a great success, since the ladies in question were both hardened career women. There is a popular theory which says that women are much better in politics than men: they appreciate the other person's point of view, they are good listeners, they can work better with others, etc., etc. Perhaps I was just unlucky, but I never came across any women of this type during my time in Brussels and Strasbourg.

On the contrary, I have never encountered such ruthlessness and ambition as I encountered in the large majority of female politicians. True, they do act as a counterbalance to traditional male weaknesses, such as laziness, favouritism, excessive drinking, etc. True, they are hard on themselves – but they are equally hard on others. Moreover, they can be jealous and vengeful in a manner that you will seldom find among their male colleagues.

Men can usually settle their differences over a drink in the bar, but women can let their political feuds drag on for years – even decades, if it is with another woman. Like so many other things these days, it is not politically correct to talk about the fierce rivalry which can sometimes exist between female politicians, but it is nonetheless a useful piece of information for a male mandarin. In fact, it can very often be his salvation.

The Commissioner wanted to build up good relations with both women and so he began by inviting them for a cup of tea and a chat in his office. He praised their leadership qualities, their tireless effort, their political insight. In short, he laid on the flattery with a trowel. And it seemed to work. Soon both the chairpersons were giggling like young school girls: luckily, the hard outer shell of every female politician hides a soft centre. The Internal Market Committee and the Economic Monetary Committee both wanted to hold a joint meeting with the

Commissioner in Strasbourg to discuss the European Union's future economic strategy. During the tea visit this seemed to pose no problem. The dark-haired Spaniard and the red-haired German smiled and nodded politely at each other and everything seemed to be arranged. Until the ladies went back to their own offices.

Then things mysteriously started to go wrong. Neither of them could agree with the other. One of them wasn't really happy with the timing. The other wasn't really happy with the agenda. Their staffs weren't happy with either the timing or the agenda: a joint meeting always meant lots of MEPs, all of whom wanting to have their say. The Commissioner suggested a compromise: he would just give a short introduction, so that there would be plenty of time left over for the MEPs' questions. Moreover, he would keep the whole evening free for the debate and would spend the night in Strasbourg. Surely, this would please everybody?

It did, but as soon as the meeting started other problems began to arise. In particular, there was the delicate question of who was going to take the chair. Both ladies thought it should be them – and neither was prepared to budge an inch. They whispered at each other furiously in broken English, while the Commissioner sat between them, turning from one to the other, like a spectator at a bad-tempered game of tennis. Finally, he interrupted them and proposed that the Spanish lady should chair the first half of the meeting, with her German colleague taking over for the second part.

They reluctantly agreed, but the agreement didn't last long. There was a group of MEPs at the back of the room (men, of course), who were laughing and making jokes. The meeting had begun at 8 o'clock in the evening, after a fairly lengthy reception, and there was also a bar invitingly close, just along the corridor. In other words, the boys were just beginning to get warmed up. This was not to the liking of the German lady, who grabbed the microphone and told them to be quiet. Her Spanish colleague was furious.

'I'm leading the first part of the meeting!' she shouted. 'It's up to me to decide who should be quiet!' 'Well, if you're supposed to be the leader, why don't you lead?' snapped the German. 'We can't hold a meeting with all this racket going on.'

For the second time in five minutes, the ladies began muttering heatedly in English, with the Commissioner looking on in embarrassment. This was testing his diplomatic skills to the full. 'Ladies,' he suggested, 'why don't we start again. We will adjourn the meeting for five minutes and then reopen it as if nothing has happened. And this time, *I* will request the room to be quiet.' It wasn't necessary. As soon as the Commissioner began his speech, everyone fell respectfully silent and the meeting progressed according to plan.

Sadly, it was not always as easy to keep the European Parliament under control. The Parliament now has almost 800 members, divided into five main groupings (Christian-democrat, Socialist, Liberal, Nationalist and Green), but with a whole host of minority splinter groups and factions. Before he can pass effective legislation, a Commissioner has to somehow persuade a majority of this diverse assembly to support his proposal. This is a difficult task at the best of times, and the situation is complicated further by national differences. All Europeans share the same continent and the same basic European culture, but this is about all they share. For the rest, they are as different as chalk and cheese. A Greek will look at the world differently from a Finn. A Bulgarian will approach a matter differently to a Portuguese. The British will always do their own thing and nobody can understand the Poles. In short, there are only a small number of loose factors which can bind them together.

Right from the very beginning, appearances were against my Commissioner. His portfolio was concerned with the liberalisation of the markets for goods, services and capital. Parliament is the natural enemy of liberalisation, since one of its key roles is the protection of existing rights and privileges. There are many groups of 'citizens', ranging from unions to lawyers, and from artists to doctors, who have strong lobbies in Brussels and Strasbourg. And behind every lobby there are many different levels of grassroots support.

This means that anyone who attempts to liberalise important sectors of the economy is likely to run into the resistance of Parliament, since the Euro-MPs think that this is the best way to protect their own electorate's best interests. The liberalisation of the post had already created a lot of bad blood between the Commissioner and Parliament. The first reading of the draft proposal in Strasbourg had been a harsh verbal battle which left lasting scars on both sides.

After this confrontation, I advised the Commissioner to change tactics. 'Look, we're a year into your mandate and our relations with the Parliament are at rock bottom. They're automatically voting against your proposals, not because the proposals are bad, but simply because they are *your* proposals. We've got to try and charm them. There is no other way.'

The Commissioner agreed. With four years of his mandate still to run, he was in desperate need of parliamentary support. We didn't have to like Parliament. We didn't always have to agree with Parliament. But we did need a majority on the floor of the chamber. Otherwise dozens of potentially useful measures would be lost, for personal and political reasons, rather than for reasons of principle.

'OK,' he said. 'So let's charm them.' It was against his Anglo-Saxon way of doing things, but he understood that there was no alternative. And so we launched *Opération Charme*.

We went to lunch with Members of Parliament. We invited Members of Parliament to dinner. We visited each of the political groupings to engage in 'constructive dialogue'. During speeches in the chamber we heaped praise on the Euro-MPs by the bucket-load. 'You'll be asking me to send them bunches of flowers next,' joked the Commissioner. Things were going well, but we were hampered by the fact that the Commissioner's portfolio was essentially 'unsexy'.

The media and a majority of the Euro-MPs found it difficult to work up much enthusiasm for the fifth motor-vehicle insurance directive or a debate on the Collective Investment of Transferable Securities. As a result, discussion of our measures was usually scheduled in the evening session of Parliament between 9 o'clock and midnight. This meant that, if we were lucky, there might be ten to fifteen MPs in the 800-seater chamber, with no press and no public. It was not what we wanted, but it was better than nothing.

The chamber was only really full during voting sessions. The Commissioner was sometimes required to be present at these sessions, which meant that he was also required occasionally to defend or explain the proposals of his fellow Commissioners which were under discussion. Usually, he did this by reading from the notes provided by the DG of the Commissioner involved. However, this was not a foolproof method. On one occasion he was given a note to read by a mandarin from DG Public Health. The note was about BSE, but I saw

Opération charme: *shaking hands, massaging egos and satisfying appetites. Kilo after kilo.*

that the name of the disease was written out in full and in English: Bovine Spongiform Encephalopathy. I doubted whether the Commissioner would be able to get his tongue around that mouthful – and I was right.

'We don't understand! Say it again!' shouted 700 highly amused Euro-MPs. Each new version got further and further away from the correct pronunciation. 'Again!' they screamed. Eventually, the Commissioner gave up. 'Let's just call it Mad Cow Disease,' he suggested, amidst howls of laughter from the floor of the chamber. The incident won him some sympathy with the parliamentarians and was therefore good for *Opération Charme*.

In fact, *Opération Charme* was good all round. It certainly stopped dislike of the Commissioner from spreading any further and it helped us to push through a number of less contentious proposals. We knew, however, that we would still be in for a rough ride on more controversial dossiers.

One of the most difficult dossiers was the Takeover Directive. The Commission had been trying for twelve years to get Parliament to agree to a set of common rules which could be applied to company takeovers in all EU countries. Most member states tried to prevent takeovers by means of protective measures, such as 'the golden share'.

The holder of 'the golden share' – often a national government – did not necessarily own a majority of the company's shares but nonetheless had a statutory right to block any proposed takeover. In a Europe with free movement of capital, it was only logical that investors would buy shares in foreign companies. It was therefore equally logical that a majority of these investors should be able to decide all aspects of the company's future – and this irrespective of nationality and the existence of a 'golden share'.

This idea was not popular with a diverse group of opponents: member states, governments, unions, politicians, etc. They all feared, for example, that a leading German company could be taken over by the British or – even worse – the Americans. In these circumstances, the existing holders of the status quo all had something to lose. The existing national government feared a loss of national prestige. The existing company management feared being given the sack. The existing union leadership feared loss of influence and loss of jobs. The only people who had something to gain were the shareholders, whose money was keeping the company afloat. But nobody seemed too interested in their rights. Nobody, of course, except my Commissioner.

Initially, everything went according to plan. The draft proposal for the directive passed its first and second readings in Strasbourg without difficulty. The proposal secured increased rights for shareholders and reduced the number of permissible protective measures. The international takeover of companies was made much easier and the Commission was even prepared to challenge the legal validity of the 'golden share' by taking Germany to the European Court of Justice. True, there were still a number of minor differences between Parliament and the Council of Ministers, which needed to be settled during the so-called 'conciliation'. This is a consultative process between Parliament and the Council, with the Commission acting as honest broker. Negotiations between delegations from Parliament and the Council were already underway and the outlook for a successful compromise agreement was looking promising. Then something happened.

This 'something' was the takeover of the German steel giant Mannesmann AG by the British Vodafone company. The Takeover Directive had always been a sensitive issue for the Germans. Most German companies are run by an unholy alliance between the management, the banks and the unions. In most countries, these three elements are usually enemies of each other, but not in Germany. There they work together hand in glove to dominate the nation's economic and commercial life: sitting on the board of directors, doing business with each other, ensuring each others succession through a system of co-option, etc.

The likelihood of a legal case in the European Court of Justice against the Volkswagen golden share had already created unease in Germany, but the 'loss' of one of their flagship companies to an aggressive British takeover bid was the final straw. The managing directors of several of Germany's largest conglomerates, including BASF, Volkswagen, Mercedes and BMW, all telephoned to the German Chancellor in Berlin, asking him to do something to prevent this from happening again.

At this time, the Chancellor was a socialist, but this didn't stop him from being known as *Genosse der Bosse* (the Bosses' Friend) or *Der Kanzler aller Autos* (The Car Chancellor). The managing directors knew that they could expect a favourable response and they were not disappointed. The Chancellor regarded their appeal as a signal to mobilise his political forces. He summoned leading German figures from the European Parliament to Berlin and instructed them – even at this relatively late stage – to liquidate the proposed directive. With a typical German respect for authority, all 99 German MEPs did a complete 180 degree about turn and started to oppose the Commissioner and his plans.

This was bad news indeed, since it meant that we would now have to do battle with the European Union's largest member state, if we wanted to see our measures succeed. The Germans normally do their lobbying via the European Parliament, since their 99 seats mean that they are by far the largest national group. What's more, these seats are evenly distributed among the major political families, which at that time were the Christian-democrats, the Socialists and the Greens. Within each family – particularly the Christian-democrats and the Socialists – it is the Germans who pull the strings.

They decide who gets the nice jobs – parliamentary rapporteur, chairman of a delegation, even President and Vice-President of the Parliament as a whole. They also decide who gets the not-so-nice jobs or no job at all. There are very few career-minded parliamentarians who can afford to go against this display of German power, particular as the Germans are renowned for their long memories and their belief that revenge is a dish best served cold. And at the very top of this hierarchy stands the German Chancellor himself. Kohl and Schröder were both well-known for phoning instructions to the Christian-democrat and Socialist factions in Strasbourg and several other Chancellors have exercised a veto on European proposals in a similar fashion. It was a powerful weapon – and one that was now being pointed directly at the Commissioner and myself!

We soon noticed that the conciliation process was starting to get more difficult. The parliamentary rapporteur for the Takeover Directive was (of course) a German. Suddenly, he was seeing problems where none had existed before and he was able to persuade the French and the Italians to support him. Only the British remained on our side and it looked like the Commission's proposal was running into serious trouble.

The Commissioner was visibly worried that the accumulated work of twelve years was about to be thrown out of the window and he did all in his power to try and turn the tide in our favour. He suggested that it might be better to try and contact the doubters by telephone at home. Away from the stern gaze of the German rapporteur, they might be prepared to be more conciliatory. I made the necessary arrangements and the Commissioner began dialling. And it looked as though it might work! A number of conciliation committee members agreed to change their votes (yet again) and at the end of the day we were able to secure the narrowest of majorities: 6 votes for, 4 votes against.

Yet even now, our worries were not at an end. The recommendations of the conciliation committee still needed to be approved by a simple majority in a plenary session of the Parliament. And it was in Parliament that the German steamroller was potentially at its strongest.

The initial battle lines were quickly drawn up: it was a straight fight between the Germans and the Commission. Germans of all political persuasions were unanimously against, and they could also rely on substantial support from the Socialists (minus the British) and the Christian-democrats (minus the British and the Spanish). In a reversal of their traditional historical roles, the smaller green, communist and trotskyist factions also backed Berlin. The Liberals were the only major grouping to openly favour the Commission's proposal – there were no German Liberals at this time – and it seemed that our only hope of securing the necessary majority lay with the splinter groups, including the fringe nationalist and religious movements.

I had originally thought of lobbying these groups, but they were the kind of people I never felt comfortable with – either politically or

Jean Marie Le Pen, the eternal rebel.

socially. One evening I was dining alone in the Hilton Hotel, when I suddenly noticed that the tables on either side of me were occupied by fringe leaders. To my right sat Jean-Marie Le Pen, leader of the French *Front National*. He ordered a steak 'with plenty of blood' (as one might have expected). To my left sat the Northern Irish Protestant minister, the Reverend Ian Paisley. Paisley was accompanied by his assistant, but he ate his meal and then read his newspaper without speaking a single word to her. I imagined that my reception would be equally cool, and so I decided not to approach them to ask if they would consider supporting the Commission's proposal. It was a missed opportunity.

As the vote approached, unanimity of support within the Commission for the proposal also began to waver. The Commissioners saw that the vote could go either way, and so they looked for a means to cover their own backs in the event of possible defeat. Several of them stopped lobbying within their own political families. Even the President began to express doubts about certain aspects of the planned directive. Everyone was happy to share the fruits of any possible victory, but nobody wanted to be associated with the humiliation of defeat. It was an important lesson.

The actual vote was preceded by a day's debate on the recommendations of the conciliation committee. The Germans were present in force and made clear their open hostility. More disturbingly, many other MEPs from other countries also lined up to attack the directive. One Spanish member said that the Commission was planning 'to let the Wall Street sharks into Europe', which would result in a 'feeding frenzy on our European companies'. His comments were greeted with loud applause – criticism of the Americans is always good for a standing ovation in Strasbourg.

The Luxembourg socialist Robert Goebbels was also fiercely opposed to the Commission's proposals. He spoke of the rising tide of aggressive capitalism, which he compared to a plague of locusts. Bankers in London and New York would seek to make the ordinary workers of Europe eat bread and cheese, just to boost their own greedy profits back home. My Commissioner had known Goebbels since the 1980s, when both had been ministers of foreign trade for their respective countries. During one famous European meeting, the French chairwoman, Edith Cresson, had called Goebbels to the speaker's platform. But instead of saying 'I would now like to invite Mr. Goebbels to speak' she had said 'I would now like to invite Mr. Göring to speak'! During the Takeover debate I was sitting next to the Commissioner and I could see that he was toying with the idea of deliberately repeating this

Edith Cresson: was it Goebbels or Göring?

legendary *faux pas*. In a chamber already full of hostile Germans, this would have been a fatal mistake (perhaps literally!). 'Remember,' I told him, tapping with my wedding ring on the desk to underline the point, 'his name is Goebbels, Goebbels, Goebbels – not Göring!'

The Commissioner behaved himself and fifteen minutes later the vote was taken. We watched anxiously as the results were announced and to our amazement we saw that the vote was a tie: 273 votes for and

273 votes against. But a tie is not a majority, and so the draft directive was rejected. After twelve years of trying, it was back to square one for the Princess.

Or was it? As we were gathering together our papers, a British Euro-MP asked if he could say something. 'Madam President, I didn't see you cast a vote. Did you forget?!' The French President of the European Parliament turned bright red and was forced to confess that she had indeed not cast her vote, but that she had not forgotten – she simply wished to abstain. This was the final insult: before being appointed as President, she had been one of the parliamentary rapporteurs for the Takeover Directive – and one of its greatest supporters! Even she felt powerless to resist the German steamroller.

Our last chance had gone and we left the chamber in disappointment. This disappointment grew when we learned later how narrow our defeat had actually been. One British conservative had been planning to vote for us, but was absent on the day in question, because he was receiving a delegation of constituents from home. Another was sitting on the toilet when the vote was taken. Even the Flemish Block would have been prepared to support us, if only we had asked them. I saw two of their members as I was leaving the Parliament Building.

'Why didn't you come and see us? We're always happy to help, if we can fuck things up for the Socialists. We'd probably have been able to persuade Jean-Marie and the Reverend (Paisley) as well.'

I had had my chance and I hadn't taken it. I had been stupid, but it taught me yet another important lesson. If you want to succeed in politics, you must sometimes be prepared to forget your principles – and accept support from anyone, if need be from the devil himself!

Another key to political success is to forget your defeats as quickly as possible. We still had plenty of other important proposals in the pipeline, but we knew that we would get nowhere unless we could repair our damaged relations with the large German delegation. We decided once again to opt for the culinary approach and so we began by inviting the German Christian-democrats to a lunch in Strasbourg. They came – all of them. When they arrived, it was an impressive sight. They were huge men, well in excess of 100 kilos. During the 'wining and dining' of *Opération Charme* the Commissioner and I had both put on a bit of weight, but so far we had managed to remain under the 100 kilo mark. It seemed that in Germany it was an essential criterion for a political career that you should go as far beyond this mark as possible! Physical weight reflected political weight.

However, in my experience big people have one huge advantage: they eat, they drink – and they don't bear grudges. After two hours of serious dining, we parted as friends. We had lost, and admitted it; they had won, but were gracious in victory. They followed the maxim which Otto von Bismarck had laid down for Prussia 150 years before: 'We must win, but we must not be seen to triumph.' Two years later the Commission put forward a new Takeover Directive, which the Germans this time felt able to support. *Opération Charme* had not been in vain.

Another great battle was destined to be fought over the Services Directive, although by this time the Commissioner was already enjoying his pension. There has never been so much parliamentary resistance to a directive which was passed so easily through the Commission.

Following in the footsteps of Jacques Delors, the Commissioner wanted to complete the liberalisation of the internal market before he retired. He had already been instrumental in creating the free movement of goods and the free movement of capital, but the free movement of services was still just a theory.

In principle, it was already possible for a company to offer its services to customers in other member states, but in practice each national government protected its own market by means of a series of bureaucratic measures, such as work permits, compulsory registration, special taxes, etc. In other words, it was effectively impossible for an architect, a dentist, an estate agent or a computer specialist to offer his services in another country, because the cost of the national restrictive practices meant that it was economically not viable – it simply cost too much.

'We have to finish Delors' work,' said the Commissioner during a cabinet meeting. 'There is one last great task: the internal market for services.' This was one of the fastest growing sectors of the economy and was a source of much employment. Nowadays, about seventy percent of GNI (Gross National Income) comes from service-related activities. A European-wide market for services would create more jobs and more growth.

The DG set to work and produced a draft proposal which would sweep away the national practices which hindered the free movement of services, in much the same way as Delors had done for goods. The basic idea was as follows: if a provider of services is officially recognised in one member state, then he should be allowed to offer these services without further restrictions in all member states.

In some respects, this was a limited proposal, which did not go as far as existing practice already allowed. In 1998 the Court of Justice had already passed a number of judgements (Kohl, Decker, Watts) which allowed patients to make use of the free traffic of medical services. As a result, medical insurers were obliged to refund the costs of medical treatments carried out elsewhere in the European Union. It was yet another example of how the European Court of Justice can sometimes act as an alternative legislative power.

The draft proposal passed easily through the various stages of approval within the Commission. The other DGs had no objections. There was only one 'special chef' required to obtain unanimous cabinet support, with just one amendment: a request from the Spanish Commissioner to make an exception for games of chance, in order to protect the famous Spanish national lottery – to which we happily agreed. Even the Legal Service was in favour, since the completion of the internal market was a clear treaty obligation. The Hebdo saw no problems with the proposal and in the College it was passed as an A-point. Everybody happy, no discussion necessary. From the point of view of a European mandarin, this was a textbook example of how legislation should be created. So why did it all go so horribly wrong? And how? And where?

Certainly not in Parliament – or not initially. When the Commissioner defended the proposal in Strasbourg in September 2004, there was even applause. The press was also favourable, with hardly a negative article to be seen.

Things first started to get difficult during the campaign for the referendum on the European Constitution in France. It quickly became clear that this referendum was not so much about the constitutional mechanism, but was more a kind of public debate about the future of the European Union as a whole. It was the French unions who first opened fire on the proposed Services Directive, because it was an easy way to mobilise their own grassroots support.

The unions in France and Belgium have been losing members for years and they felt that it was necessary to find a 'common enemy', in order to scare their membership into closing ranks. The draft proposal was an obvious target. The unions claimed that the proposed legislation would allow Polish workers to work in France and Belgium for Polish wages and under Polish conditions of service. This was a blatant lie, but if a lie is repeated often enough, it can sometimes create a new truth – and this is what happened in this case.

The propaganda machine of the unions was louder and more effective than that of the Commission and public opinion gradually began to turn against us. At the same time, there was also growing political resistance. The socialist leader in Wallonia, Elio Di Rupo, used the directive as a means of winning support for his own campaign for the European elections. The ultra-liberal image of the Commissioner made him a perfect fall-guy for Di Rupo, who called the draft proposal 'the work of Frankenstein'.

Yet even now, things seemed unlikely to get out of hand. The directive – which had been approved by an essentially left-wing Commission at the beginning of 2004 – survived the European elections with ease. Resistance at this stage continued to be confined to Belgium, where there were one or two minor union demonstrations in Brussels. I happened to see one of these demonstrations while I was out shopping: the banners called for the head of the Commissioner on a platter and represented him as being some kind of monster. But it all seemed somehow irrelevant: 'full of sound and fury, but signifying nothing,' to quote Shakespeare. Shortly thereafter – and a full two months after the elections – the Commissioner was applauded out of Parliament, out of the Commission and into retirement. We still seemed to be 'on track'.

It was the referendum in France which really got us into trouble. The unions and the strong left-wing political groupings mobilised all their resources to portray the directive as a typical example of 'asocial Europe' and the dangers of globalisation. These were opponents of a different calibre to the Belgians and their publicity machine succeeded in convincing the ordinary man in the street that the directive was the symbol of a giant European super-state, which threatened the French way of life and its social model. Public resistance grew and political support waned.

The Services Directive was an A-point in the Commission. But not in Europe.

LIFE OF A EUROPEAN MANDARIN

It was at this point that a number of weaknesses in the Commission's strategy became apparent. The first mistake was that the Commission had made little or no effort to explain the proposal to the general public. The proposal was an A-point, every mandarin's dream – why bother explaining it if nobody was against it? It might have been better if there had been opposition at an earlier stage, as with the postal directive. This would have led to a public debate and to a proper consultative process, which could only have resulted in a stronger and better balanced draft proposal, which would have taken account of people's legitimate fears and objections.

As it was, the Services Directive was a hot-house plant grown exclusively by the mandarins, with the result that very few of the Commissioners actually knew what they had voted for, even though they were unanimous in their support! When public reaction finally came, they were overwhelmed by the strength of feeling against the proposal and found that it was too late to change the popular perception of the legislation as being 'a bad thing'.

As opposition increased, it also became apparent that the timing of the proposal was all wrong. The Commission had tried to push through the directive towards the end of its mandate period. As a result, the existing Commissioners were already looking for new jobs, while the Commissioners-Designate regarded it as the work of others. In other words, there were very few Commissioners, either present or future, who felt strongly committed to the Services Directive. When it was publicly attacked, they all found that it was better for their future careers to quietly withdraw their support – which is precisely what happened. It was an object lesson for all future Commission Presidents: major projects must always be launched at the beginning of a mandate period, as central elements in a political agenda which has broad and active support. This is what Delors had done and this is why he was successful – in spite of all the opposition he faced.

By now, everybody knew that the ship was sinking and it was left to my retired Commissioner to try and salvage something from the wreckage. He defended the directive at a press conference in Paris but it soon became evident that he was fighting a lone battle. He telephoned me one day to say that nobody was prepared to help him. His former director-general refused to provide him with the latest background information, the Dutch Embassy in Paris refused to arrange a hall for him and the other Commissioners were all avoiding him like the plague. In the end, he travelled to Paris alone by train and met the media in a room hired for him by an American journalist. It was here

The Polish plumber conquers the single market.

that the mythical 'Polish plumber' was born, the prototype of a worker from a new member state who wanted to come and provide services in an old member state. But the unions of old Europe had no interest in the services offered by new Europe, even though there was a desperate need for them.

The French had their own plumbers – not very many and not very good ones – and the unions intended to see that their privileges were protected. The Poles were ready and able, and there was more than enough work for them to do – but they weren't allowed to do it. The French unions were so angry at the Commissioner that they even cut off the electricity supply to his holiday home in France.

Defeat was inevitable and it was only a matter of time before the European Parliament also turned against the proposal. People who had once been fervent supporters of the directive now became self-appointed leaders of the resistance. Typical was the reaction of a Belgian member of parliament. Until recently, he had been a member of the Commission and had voted in favour of the directive in the College. In Parliament he was now one of its most vociferous opponents and voted consistently with the 'no' lobby.

The Commission itself was the next group to desert. The new Internal Market Commissioner, an Irishman, was worried by the growing bad publicity and proposed to Parliament that they should draw up an amended Service Directive which he would automatically approve. For the first and only time in her history, the Princess abdicated her legislative responsibility and refused to defend a proposal which had been created in her name. She ought to have been ashamed of herself.

The outcome was predictable. The Parliament scrapped from the directive the basic principle on which the internal market has always been based: that a product or service which is approved in one EU member state may be offered to customers in all other EU countries. A Danish cheese can be sold in France. It is therefore only logical that a Copenhagen architect should be able to practice his profession in Paris. But the European Parliament doesn't always deal in logic. Like most elected parliaments, it is more susceptible to public sentiment and public opinion. As a result, the Services Directive was neutered in Strasbourg and the clock for the free movement of services was turned back to 1958. What had begun as an A-point ended as an all-time low-point.

Could it have been any different? Some suggested that a separate directive should have been drafted for each particular service, but this again ran contrary to the basic principle of uniformity of treatment. When dealing with the free movement of goods, Delors didn't make one directive for cheese, one for socks, one for condoms, etc. He reasoned (correctly) that condoms which work in Germany will also work in France. The sectoral approach would have resulted in dozens of directives, which would have sent the Commission's administrative machinery into overload. Moreover, the service sector is constantly changing, with new services being created every day. The legislative structure would never have been able to keep pace with these rapid developments.

The failure of the Services Directive was therefore attributable to two factors: its preparation was too easy and its end product was not defended. This allowed the European Parliament to create a 'compromise' solution which was effectively a car without an engine. What's more, it was a car of 1950s vintage, an old-timer which should no longer be allowed on the motorways of modern Europe.

One sunny spring afternoon I was walking through Strasbourg. The Services Directive was on the agenda for the Parliament and the unions had mobilised their troops in force. A month earlier, the city had been rocked by a demonstration of angry dockers, who had broken the windows of the Parliament Building in protest at the liberalisation of harbour services. As a result, most members of Parliament, like the scaredy-cats that they are, got frightened and immediately threw out the planned liberalisation. Dozens of dockers, mainly Belgians, were arrested by the French police.

Now the streets of Strasbourg were once again full with busloads of union activists from France, Germany, Belgium and Holland.

Once again they marched on the Parliament Building, shouting angry slogans against the directive and carrying banners which proclaimed 'Europe wants to rob us of our pensions' and 'Brussels wants to lower our wages'.

The mood was excitable but there was no hint of trouble. For most of them, it was just a day out with the lads. I pushed my way through the crowd, heading for the Hilton Hotel – the last haven of the European mandarin. I said nothing and pretended that I was just another tourist. I avoided Belgian buses for fear of being identified by Belgian union leaders.

I had never imagined that the work of a few mandarins in Brussels could bring so many misguided people out onto the streets. Where did the fault lie? With the people or with the mandarins? I had no intention of asking the people – at least not at that particular moment – and

I knew that the mandarins would not have the answer either. Several of my colleagues in Brussels had already said to me: 'How is this possible? It was an A-point in the Commission...' Yes indeed, it was an A-point. Precisely that was the problem!

9| The Boss of all Bosses

.

'The European Council was a success for the Commission.' These were the words with which the head of the President's cabinet always introduced his de-briefing to the other cabinets following a European summit meeting. The wording always remained the same, even when the meeting had obviously been a flop. On these occasions the head of cabinet at least had the honesty to accompany his words with a cynical laugh and a knowing look, but for the outside world the summit had to be regarded as a triumph – even if it wasn't. In the Princess's realm, black is sometimes white and night is sometimes day.

For the average European mandarin, a meeting of the European Council is a distant event in a far-off place. Even the Commissioners are not invited to attend, unless one of their portfolio subjects is on the agenda for discussion. In these circumstances, the Commissioner will be kept waiting in a small side room, until his 'turn' comes. He will then be led into the meeting hall, where he says his piece. As soon as he is finished, he will be expected to depart as quickly as he came – as though the prolonged presence of a mere mortal in such exalted company might be harmful to them both.

The Princess has reserved the European Council for the President, his head of cabinet and the Secretary General of the Commission. They are the chosen few. They are the ones allowed to sit at the same table as the great and the good – although they are not allowed to say very much. The President, however, is at least allowed to appear in the group photograph.

The European Council was created during the 1970s. It was a typically French initiative. The French love ceremony and protocol, flag-waving and fine-sounding declarations – and this is what the Council was

Valéry Giscard d'Estaing, the uncrowned emperor of Europe.

supposed to embody. The French president, Valéry Giscard D'Estaing, agreed with the German chancellor, Helmut Schmidt, that the leaders of Europe should meet together on an informal basis – 'for a cosy fireside chat' – to discuss the continent's problems. And at that time, there was plenty to discuss. The first oil crisis of 1973 had divided the member states and led to a revival of nationalist politics. The Commission seemed powerless to stop this trend and so it was intended that the Council would provide Europe with some much needed guidance and leadership.

And indeed, throughout the years there have been some memorable meetings of the European Council, which have achieved much: Fontainebleau in 1984 (reduction of agricultural subsidies), Strasbourg in 1989 (fall of the Berlin Wall), Maastricht in 1991 (political reform and the euro), Amsterdam in 1997 (further political reform), Berlin

Helmut Schmidt, the best German Chancellor in my time.

in 1999 (European budget under the name Agenda 2000), Lisbon in 2000 (Lisbon Agenda for the modernisation of Europe by 2010), Nice in 2000 (more political reform), Brussels in 2004 (enlargement of the Union) and Brussels in 2005 (financial perspectives 2007-2013). Equally, there have been many meetings of the Council which (quite rightly) have been consigned to the dustbin of history. Perhaps the best publicised recent failure was the inability of the Council to reach agreement on the war in Iraq in 2003.

To be honest, the European Council is now an outdated concept which has long outlived its shelf life. However, for the time being there is no valid alternative. Some people would like to see a European president, thinking that this would help to pave the way towards a United States of Europe – although experience suggests that a more likely result would be the Disunited States of Europe. But the 'no' votes against the European constitution in France and the Netherlands mean that this idea has temporarily been put on 'hold' and so the European Council will continue to meet for the foreseeable future.

My Commissioner always thought that the Council was a complete waste of time. On more than one occasion he was kept waiting in the small side room, but he was never called to address the full meeting. 'The worst run institution of the organisation,' was how he described the European Council.

The Dutch writer, Gerrit Komrij, went even further. He compared the travelling circus of the national heads of state to 'a bunch of well-dressed pimps'. This is perhaps a little harsh, but it nevertheless contains a grain of truth.

The start of a European summit always reminds me of Prague, a city I was fortunate enough to visit in 1983 for a youth conference. During a speech by Yasser Arafat I slipped away from the main conference hall and was taken to visit some of the country's dissidents – this was still during the Soviet era. They told me about the Czech leadership, who were flown back to the national capital by helicopter each Sunday evening, having spent the weekend in their comfortable dachas. The people never saw them, the people never knew them, the people never influenced them. All they heard were the helicopters once a week.

A meeting of the European Council is not so very different. On Thursday afternoon the Brussels police cordon off the streets around Schuman Square. Accompanied by a cavalcade of police motorcyclists, the national leaders are driven in heavily armoured limousines to the Justus Lipsius Building, where they are quickly rushed inside by armed security men. They have come to discuss 'the Europe of Citizens' but the people never see them or hear them. They have come to promote 'a United Europe' but they spend most of the time arguing, usually about money. They are 'Supporters of the European Ideal' but they are happy to give Europe and the Princess the blame for just about everything. The national leaders have become isolated figures, completely shut off from the outside world. Appropriately, the Council Building looks more like a fort than a People's Palace. Most of these leaders have trouble maintaining a parliamentary majority in their own countries, but while they bungle at home they continue to play the role of big shots in Europe.

Like my Commissioner, I never had much time for this travelling circus. A meeting of the European Council is followed by the issuing of a document entitled the Council's Conclusions. Followed? 98% of the so-called 'conclusions' are decided well in advance. These conclusions do not 'follow': they precede. Giscard D'Estaing's original idea of a 'cosy fireside chat' has now become something comical. With 27 national leaders in attendance, it must either be an extremely big fireside – or else some of them must be left sitting in the cold.

In terms of structure and organisation, the European Council has become a monster. If every national leader speaks for just ten minutes, the meeting will last a minimum of four hours. For this reason, the organising country has to make backroom deals on most of the agenda points long beforehand. If everyone is in agreement, the Council rubber stamps the decision. If there is no consensus, the matter is quietly dropped. As such, the European Council has been reduced to a kind of glorified photo opportunity.

Jacques Chirac and Gerhard Schröder, the Romeo and Juliet of Europe. Or should that be Tom and Jerry?

In 2003 France and Germany reached a deal on agricultural expenditure up to the year 2013. The farming French were keen to keep spending at reasonable levels and the Germans were prepared to support them. The deal was struck in the Conrad Hotel in Brussels between President Chirac and Chancellor Schröder. The two leaders immediately took a liking to each other, perhaps united by the fact that they were both in trouble politically at home. During the European Council's closing photographic shoot they embraced each other like long-lost brothers. It was like a scene from a Disney movie.

However, this deal reveals one of the hidden truths about the European Council. It can only function if there is a degree of chemistry between a sufficient number of the national leaders. In practice, this means between France and Germany. They are often the Council's big buddies. Giscard D'Estaing and Schmidt were friends. Kohl and Mitterrand were contemporaries and shared the common experiences of a generation.

In contrast, the British are usually the ones trying to break up these cosy little groupings. They have spent five centuries pursuing a policy of a 'Disunited Europe' and in all that time they have become rather good at it. If Europe is divided, the British prime minister usually goes home a happy man.

Nowadays, the task of the British is that much easier. With a group of 27 national leaders, it is much harder to develop the close personal relationships which have worked so well in the past. Does the prime minister of Portugal know who the prime minister of Latvia is? Can the Irish premier spell the name of his Greek colleague? I fear not. The group of national leaders has become much larger – and therefore much more anonymous. It has become more difficult to understand each other – and therefore much harder to reach agreements.

Another destabilising element is the uncertainty of national domestic politics. Democratic leaders can appear and disappear very quickly, so that the composition of the European Council is seldom the same for two consecutive meetings. It is like a puppet show with constantly changing puppets. This makes continuity difficult to achieve. For example, it was very difficult to obtain final agreement on the text for the draft European constitution, precisely because this is a long-term issue and few of the current national leaders were involved in the initial stages of the process.

Yet if the success of Council meetings is often dependant upon close personal relations, its failures can sometimes be caused by individual blunders.

Champion in this department was the Italian president, Silvio Berlusconi. He single-handedly destroyed the December 2003 summit in Brussels. He arrived at the Council Building by helicopter and saw many demonstrators in the streets below. He thought it might be amusing to drop a few hundred euro bank notes amongst the crowd and so he instructed the pilot to fly lower. The pilot – clearly a political analyst in an earlier life – suggested that the crowd might be much happier if Berlusconi was dropped out of the helicopter!

The Italian told this anecdote at the beginning of the meeting, to break the ice. In a similar vein, he suggested to the German chancellor that he might like to tell one or two jokes about the women in his life. The chancellor had just been married for the fourth time and was now known as the 'Audi-man' in his own country, where the symbol for the famous Audi motorcar is four intertwined rings. His foreign minister, Joschka Fischer, had been married five times and was therefore known as 'Olympia-man'. The Germans were not amused and the summit was doomed to failure before it had even begun.

This was by no means a one-off for Berlusconi. He spread chaos and confusion wherever he went. I once had the chance to see him 'at work' in Strasbourg, where we were both staying in the Hilton Hotel. Berlusconi occupied the Europa Suite and swept smilingly out of the lift each morning, surrounded by a phalanx of bodyguards. He was awaited by a posse of pressmen and women, whom he addressed while still moving through the foyer. Whereas it was not unusual to see the prime ministers of countries like Sweden and Finland standing at the reception desk to pay their own bills, Berlusconi strode out of the building in true presidential style. Instead of just one car, he had ordered a whole convoy of limousines, which departed with sirens screaming in the direction of the Parliament Building. He loved attention and was very good at attracting it.

But this was just the start of his performance: the best was yet to come. I accompanied the Commissioner to the plenary of the Parliament for a vote on the draft directive for public procurement, but we were forced to wait because smiling Silvio had still not finished his speech.

As always, he insisted on trying to be funny, even with people he regarded as his political opponents. In the past, he had had more than one confrontation with the German socialist, Martin Schulz, and it was Schultz he now turned to address.

'I used to watch an American television series about prisoners of war. One of the characters was a *Capo di Campo,* a camp guard – he was also called Schulz. It would be an ideal role for you. I think you would make a very good *Capo di Campo*.'

Berlusconi laughed at his own joke, but his foreign minister, Gianfranco Fini, went visibly pale at his side. Schulz could hardly believe what he had heard. Telling a German that he would make a 'good camp guard' is like telling the Pope that he would make an excellent rapist. Schulz took off his headphones and asked the people sitting near him if he had perhaps misunderstood the translation. No, they all confirmed that Berlusconi had used the words *Capo di Campo*.

The resulting diplomatic row was impressive, even by normal Berlusconi standards. The Italian was eventually forced to apologise and Schulz's political career was given a new impetus: he was given the preferential no.1 position in the list of socialist candidates for the forthcoming German elections and ultimately became leader of the socialist group in Parliament. Unfortunately, he developed a rather authoritarian leadership style and still tends to address his fellow socialists like a Prussian officer. Some of his colleagues think that Berlusconi was right after all! And our public procurement directive? It was passed (notwithstanding 450 amendments), but it never made the press. Silvio was much better at attracting attention...

A European summit is a two-day merry-go-round. The national leaders travel to Brussels with their own national agenda. This means that they either want more money from Europe or they want to pay less. At the end of the meeting, this horse-trading is dressed up in the elegant-sounding rhetoric of a closing declaration. This declaration seldom mentions anything so dirty as money and always refers to the high ideals upon which the European Union is supposed to be based. To underline this myth, the declaration often launches a 'process' named after the location where the summit was held: Cardiff, Barcelona, Lisbon, Hampton Court, etc.

These processes usually have a life expectancy of four to six months, following which they are quietly locked away in the Brussels cupboard of broken promises. Occasionally, a process might survive for a little longer – like the Lisbon Agenda – but after a time nobody really knows what to do with it. These processes are the paper crown on the head of the European Council, just like in a party game. Moreover, it is a game which suits the national leaders very well. It gives the impression that 'something' has been decided, whilst committing them to do precisely 'nothing'.

Of course, the game continues even when the meeting has finished. The national leaders immediately hold press conferences to tell their national electorates how they have 'triumphed in Brussels'. And the press is happy to play along, reporting the outcome of the summit meetings as if they were football results: England won 300 million euros – Germany lost 200 million euros. They even add the appropriate 'changing room gossip': who tackled who, who fouled who, who tricked who, etc.

Once the leaders have returned home, it is much the same story. They assure their parliaments that they did not 'surrender to the mandarins' and that they defended the country's interests to the last eurocent. The pattern is always the same. In front of the camera, the national leaders behave as though they are the best of friends, complete with back-slapping, hand-shaking and smiles. Behind the scenes, their diplomats and officials conduct a savage fight about money.

Just about the only person who is not involved in this sordid grab for money is the President of the Commission. He is just happy that he is allowed to talk part. For a few brief days, it makes him feel like a national leader. Not that he has any tangible power, of course. The real national leaders regard the Commission as little more than a secretariat, whose task it is to carry out the instructions handed down by the European Council – the boss of all bosses.

If anything, the European Council is more dependent upon the Council of Ministers than upon the Commission. These groups of national ministers – there is, for example, an Agricultural Council, a Finance Council (Ecofin), a Transport Council, etc – are the people who do the real work: amending proposals, making deals, taking decisions. If they are unable to agree, the matter will be referred back to the members of the European Council. If *they* are unable to agree, the dossier can drag on for years and years. Sometimes even for thirty years or more.

This being said, there is a strange contradiction between the European Council and the Council of Ministers, which often puts the President of the Commission in a difficult position. The decisions of the European Council are framed within the context of grandiloquent declarations, such as the famous Lisbon Declaration of the year 2000. This enthusiastic – some might say over-optimistic – document suggested that by the year 2010 Europe should have the most modern and the most competitive economy in the world, better even than the United States. This could only happen if the key economic sectors, such as transport, energy and post, were fully liberalised.

The implementation of this liberalisation was the task of the individual ministers for these different sectors, working within the Council of Ministers. However, if these ministers fail to agree – which is often the case – the whole process grinds to a halt. This, for example, is what happened with the Community Patent dossier. It has taken so long to reach a decision on this crucial matter that most inventors now go to America to register their ideas. A Community Patent is just too expensive, because of all the associated translation costs. So why not use just one language for patent applications? English, for example? Because the French will not accept English as the single working language. And if the French will not accept it, then neither will the Spanish. Nor the Italians. Nor the Germans, etc., etc. Europe becomes paralysed by its own national symbols and by wounded national pride.

It is the job of the Commission President to try and sort out this mess. The President talks, talks and talks again with national ministers, hoping to create a moral climate in which some kind of decision can eventually be taken. In other words, the national leaders in the European Council hide behind fine-sounding principles, while the President is left to get on with the difficult job of creating a political consensus. The national leaders moralise for Europe. The President has to persuade, coax, cajole and lobby for Europe.

It is a task in which the President is assisted by his own Commissioners and their cabinet staffs. This meant that the Commissioner and myself were often sent abroad on lobbying visits – something which I always used to enjoy. Our most frequent destinations were London, Paris and Berlin. If you are looking to secure agreement for any European proposal, you have to start with the Big Three. If they are for it, the rest will follow. If they are against it, you might as well forget it and start again.

Occasionally, it might also be necessary to offer an additional sweetener to a troublesome minor country. For example, the savings directive required unanimous support before it could become law. This was an ideal opportunity for a country such as Italy to demand extra compensation on the milk quota issue. In a similar fashion, the Belgians insisted on an extension of their preferential tax programme for companies. In my experience, it is often the most supposedly 'pro-European' countries who are the fiercest negotiators behind the scenes.

A visit to London was always an adventure. I once went with the Commissioner to discuss the savings directive with the British Chancellor of the Exchequer, Gordon Brown. Brown's official residence is No.11 Downing Street, immediately next door to the Prime Minister's mansion. This was an impressive but ultimately impractical building, full of wide colonial corridors and ageing imperial furniture: Britain might now possess one of the most modern economies in Europe but for most Europeans it still remains what it has always been – a giant, open air museum.

Brown received us cordially and cracked the ice with a few jokes (in Berlusconi fashion), which he laughed at himself (also in Berlusconi fashion). But there the comparison ends. Brown is a clever politician and a shrewd negotiator. He told us point blank that he could never agree to the proposal for the taxation of savings at source: this would be political suicide for a socialist minister in an essentially anti-European country.

He therefore suggested substituting taxation at source with a free exchange of information. In other words, the bank in the country where the savings were held would pass on information to the country where the saver was resident, so that the home country could then levy the required tax.

This allowed the British a neat get-out from taxation at source, but it created a new problem for countries such as Luxembourg, where a large part of the national economy is based on the secrecy offered by its banks. After a bit of Kissinger-like shuttle diplomacy, flying backwards and forwards between London and various other national capitals, a traditional European compromise was eventually reached: both systems would be introduced, with the member states free to choose their own preference.

Europe's British friends. All smiles in Brussels, all frowns at home.

Trips to Paris were also a regular occurrence, usually to the Ministries of Finance or Economy. The French still adopt a very interventionist approach to their national economy, regarding the state as the 'guardian' of the nation. Our mission was once again *parler, parler et encore une fois parler* but the style of negotiations was very different from in London. French ministers have an air of self-importance which is unequalled anywhere else in the world. They are little deities in their own right but like most deities they have no idea what is happening in the real world. I remember that Prime Minister Jospin sent letter after letter to my Commissioner, arguing that Brussels' liberalising ideas represented a serious danger to *le service publique*. According to Jospin, public services were the ultimate expression of a truly civilised society. Just to prove it, every time we went to Paris we were welcomed in Renaissance palaces furnished with Louis XIV furniture and various other priceless bits of art. At first I could hardly believe it. A minister in the Netherlands who surrounded himself with this kind of opulence would immediately be called to account – and probably be accused of corruption.

But not in France. There everything is larger than life. The luxury is staggering. The rhetoric of the ministers is staggering. Most staggering of all (at least in my humble opinion) is the beauty of the female French assistants. It was sometimes hard to remember what we had actually come for! This, of course, is part of the French *mystique*: they can sometimes be tricky customers to deal with, but nobody can deny that they have style.

'Style' is not a word that I associate with my visits to Germany. 'Difficult' is the word that I would use. I had always imagined that Germany was a free market economy which did all it could to stimulate business activity. Nothing could be further from the truth. Germany is a corporatist country where the politicians, the unions and the banks form an unholy alliance, an unlikely *menage à trois* which benefits them all but strangles commercial development. The economy is severely over-regulated and ideas such as the free market, the free movement of capital or the free movement of people are just illusions. In this sense, modern Germany is the inheritor of the Prussian legalism of the 19th century. This often led to problems between the President of the Commission and the Chancellor in Bonn (or later Berlin).

On one memorable occasion a Chancellor referred to a member of the College of Commissioners of his day as a *scheisshund*, which is more or less the equivalent of 'a piece of dog shit'. My own Commissioner was described by the same Chancellor as a 'miserable Hollander', who was trying to bombard Germany with the devilish ideas of Von Hayek.

A meeting between us and the Chancellor was out of the question, but we often had discussions with his ministers, who were more reasonable men and women. They gave us one piece of golden advice: 'whatever you do, keep your hands off Volkswagen.' This, of course, is precisely what the Commissioner did not do: one of his most hotly-disputed measures was his procedure against the 'golden share' of the German government in its nation's leading car manufacturing company.

We were always able to give as good as we got in our dealings with Germany, partly because we always maintained good relations with the right people. On another occasion, the Chancellor refused to appoint a Christian-democrat politician as a member of the European Commission. Against all tradition, he proposed a Socialist and a member of the Green Party, thereby excluding the candidate of the popular CDU/CSU Party.

This party was temporarily in opposition and therefore its leading lights were denied a national platform for their talents. As a result, many promising Christian-democrat politicians from the federal German regions visited Brussels, in the hope of acquiring a European profile. And who did they visit? Not the Chancellor's red and green lapdogs, but the 'miserable Hollander' with his liberalising ideas. We were happy to see them and to help them, because we knew that one day soon they would be back in power – and then they would be able to help us.

And this is exactly what happened. The Chancellor lost election after election in the federal states, often to the same CDU/CSU politicians whom we had just welcomed in the Kortenberglaan. And who were these politicians? Well, amongst others *Frau* Merkel, *Herr* Merz, *Herr* Stroiber, *Herr* Wulff and *Herr* Koch. In politics, it is never a bad thing to have friends in high places.

The German Chancellor Angela Merkel. A gracious lady and tougher than she looks.

LIFE OF A EUROPEAN MANDARIN

A Commissioner who wants to succeed in his negotiations with national ministers must possess three essential qualities: perseverance, personal charm and political insight.

He must defend the Princess's cause with dignity and resilience and must seek to be on the same wavelength as his conversation partner. Above all, he must know who are the coming men and women, the leaders of tomorrow with whom he will be able to work. Sadly, these leadership figures are becoming harder and harder to find: one of the great dilemmas of modern Europe is that it no longer possesses visionary leaders of substance.

Too often, the Princess's vessel of state is being steered by men without a compass and with very little baggage – intellectual or otherwise. The European Council contains too little substance and too much trivia. It does not bode well for the future. Europe deserves a better fate.

10| The sleeping Beauty

For the past several years, the 12th floor of the Berlaymont Building has offered me a splendid view of both Brussels and Europe. To the left, I could see the Charlemagne complex, the home of the Relex mandarins, the 'happy family' which occupies itself with the Princess's foreign affairs. Behind the Charlemagne stands the building which is intended to become the new headquarters for the President of Europe – if we ever get one. His palace is ready, but the rejection of the European constitution means that it is destined to remain empty for the foreseeable future.

Further on lies the damp and often murky city of Brussels, half of which is European and half of which is rapidly becoming Islamicised. In the distance, the impressive steel globes of the Atomium tower over the Heizel, once a symbol of hope and progress in an age when nuclear energy was still not a taboo subject. In its shadow, the park of Laken, the tropical gardens and the royal palace nestle side by side. How will it all look in 2030? How will Europe look in 2030? Will there still be a Berlaymont? Will there still be a European Union? Or will it have collapsed under its own weight? Or been torn apart by internal pressures and disagreements? These are existential questions.

I recently attended a meeting at which many of the Princess's leading courtiers were present. The mandarins were invited to ask questions and one of them, a Dane (I think), raised his hand: 'I came to Brussels to work for European integration. But the constitution has been rejected and the Commission no longer seems to know what to do. What is our mission now? I, for one, do not intend to work for a kind of Yugoslavian federation of Europe.'

These comments were greeted with loud applause by most of the 200 mandarins in the hall. Clearly, the Scandinavian had touched a sensitive nerve. These are mandarins who had once been proud to serve the Princess, but who now feel that their efforts are increasingly in vain and that the great project of which they once dreamt is gradually slipping through their fingers. They have, indeed, become mandarins without a mission. The Princess's court is gripped by a kind of *fin de siècle* feeling, even though the new century has only just started.

However, it is far too early to give up hope. Europe has faced much greater crises than this. It has survived economic disasters and endured terrible wars, but it has always managed to rise phoenix-like from the ashes, albeit sometimes weaker than before.

The Second World War marked the end of the European nations as great powers. After 1945, the Old Continent was forced to seek a new

The French and Dutch 'no' was an unexpected slap in the face for the European mandarins. The people can sometimes be so ungrateful…

role in the world. European co-operation was not so much an indication that the peoples of Europe had learnt the need for co-existence; it was more a necessity for economic recovery.

It was with this aim in mind that European Community was set up in 1957, precisely fifty years ago. The founders were passionate in their belief that this was the best way forward for the new continent, but they represented only a small section of the national elite in an equally small group of key countries. This was a weak foundation on which to build the mighty European edifice and the rejection of the constitution in France and the Netherlands, combined with growing opposition in other countries, shows that the limitations imposed by this narrow base of support have not yet been fully overcome.

The population of Europe fears for the future. By this, I mean that there are deep-rooted anxieties about the consequences of globalisation and immigration. The world is moving faster and faster, but Europe is struggling to keep up with the pace. There is an increasing desire for isolation, for the creation of a kind of safe haven, where it might still be possible to shut out the unpleasant things happening elsewhere on the planet. Most Europeans regard the national state as the geo-political entity most likely to provide this safe environment. They do not think that the European Union is capable of providing it. On the contrary, they see the European Union as a key promoter of globalisation and immigration.

Most Europeans cherish three illusions, which act as a kind of self-protection mechanism.

1. Our peace is guaranteed, because for the past 60 years all major conflicts have taken place beyond the boundaries of Europe. The violent disintegration of Yugoslavia was simply the exception which proves the rule, a belated settling of old scores left over from the Second World War. In future, our best defence will be no defence. We are kind to the rest of the world, so the rest of the world will be kind to us. Global terrorism is essentially an American creation and an American problem. Spain and Great Britain were only subject to terrorist attack because of their support for the Americans in Iraq. If we leave the radical leaders alone, they will leave us alone.

2. National governments will continue to provide prosperity, thereby ensuring our level of income. The welfare state is the highest expression of human civilisation: we are earning more than ever before and we have more free time to enjoy it. No matter how old we are, we are all mentally preparing ourselves for our pensions. We have the mindset of senior citizens: no more change, no more innovation. Europe is no longer the centre of the world and is being overtaken by new and more dynamic societies. In fact, Europe has become the largest retirement home in history. But who cares, as long as there is money to pay our pensions? Just leave us in peace to do our own thing, or tell the rest of the world to slow down a bit.

3. Isolation is the best defence against globalisation. In this respect, Europe is living in cloud-cuckoo land: the continent is being overrun by wave after wave of immigration, while its own populations are gradually shrinking, particularly in Italy, Germany and Poland. From 2010 onwards, more Europeans will die each year than are born. Midwives will become unemployed, while funeral homes will become big busi-

ness. The situation is precisely the opposite in North and West Africa and the Middle East. These areas have all witnessed a demographic explosion in recent decades, sometimes with a doubling of the population as a result. Moreover, these areas are economically 'poor', while Europe is (still) economically 'rich'. In these circumstances (as history has repeatedly shown) a movement of peoples away from poverty and towards prosperity is inevitable. This is not a problem, say most Europeans. We will build a fence to keep out the immigrants we do not want, but we will let in some of the cleverer ones, so that they can work for us and help to pay for our pensions.

Europe is a continent which is rich in diversity and rich in history, but it no longer believes in its own future. We have lost our 'can-do' approach to life and have replaced it with the culture of inertia. We have no idea how we are going to cope with the storms which will inevitably break over our continent and so we bury our heads in the sand: our desire for isolation is greater than our urgency to find viable solutions to our dilemma.

Even the Princess has fallen asleep. She has become a modern-day Sleeping Beauty. The rejection of the European constitution in 2005 torpedoed her next great project before it ever really got started. As a result, her economic and political agenda was reduced to chaos. She had just begun the reforming programme agreed in Lisbon, but suddenly the fruits of victory were snatched from her grasp – by her own electorate!

There followed a period of reflection, and gradually the Princess is trying to get back on her feet. However, she is moving very carefully, step by step. For the time being, there are no great initiatives, no great deeds, no great declarations. What is the point, she says, of trying to run before you can walk? For this reason, the measures which she currently proposes have to look good and sound good. They must be popular, since they are designed to cheer up the people and restore their faith in the European ideal. That being said, these measures lack cohesion and unity of purpose: it will simply take too long to reap tangible results. It is clear that the Princess no longer knows in which direction she should be dancing. Her every next step could be a *faux pas*.

The European Union is unique in the history of the world. It is the only major geo-political grouping which has consciously attempted to promote the greater general good. It is the Empire of Good Intentions. And it has undoubtedly achieved much. The generation before mine lived in a very different world – and viewed this world in a totally different light. As teenagers, my parents experienced the Nazi occupation of the Netherlands. My parents-in-law were children during the Siege of Moscow. The parents of most of my German colleagues served in the *Wehrmacht* or the *Hitlerjugend*. Everybody was fighting everybody, everybody hated everybody. Post-war European integration has become the basis for a better and more peaceful continent.

Few of the modern generation realise this fact. For most of them, history began in the 'fun' decades of the 1960s and 1970s. By this time, everybody loved everybody. For this reason, they regard the enlargement of the European Union into Central and Eastern Europe as 'normal'. In fact, it is little short of miraculous. If a journalist had written in 1980 that by 2007 Poland, the Baltic States, Hungary, Rumania and Bulgaria would all be members of the EU and NATO, he would have been laughed at by his colleagues – and sacked by his boss. It was inconceivable, yet it is precisely what happened.

In other words, Europe was responsible for a key change in the way international relations were conducted. After the war, protection against the Soviet menace, the preservation of democracy and the rebuilding of economic prosperity were the key motivating factors behind European co-operation. However, these goals have all been achieved, so that the European Union now threatens to become a victim of its own success.

The world vision of its citizens is changing under the influence of new challenges, such as globalisation, the continued viability of the welfare state and the fear of immigration. They feel that Europe has not found suitable answers to these increasingly pressing questions. They think that the European Union has become too big, a situation which the possible accession of Turkey is set to make worse.

In fact, the majority of Europeans no longer feel at home in this Europe. As a result, their own national identities are becoming stronger – and not weaker – as the Union grows. Europe is no longer a part of the solution – it has become a part of the problem. For this reason, people are tending to look inwards as a reaction to threats which are essentially external. The European elite recognised this phenomenon much too late. Many of them have still failed to recognise it.

The 'no' vote against the European constitution has led to a discussion of what until recently was a taboo subject: what are the boundaries of Europe? This, in turn, has led to a further question: will the integration of the continent now be followed by its equally rapid disintegration?

'Disintegration' is a word that we are not allowed to use in the Commission. If anyone is unwise enough to mention the phrase, they are instantly branded as a 'non-believer', a heretic, a pessimist, an anti-European, etc.

For me, Europe was a place of work, where I attempted to achieve realistic ends through practical politics. A policy of rhetoric alone, without concrete benefits, will ultimately lose its legitimacy. For most of my colleagues, however, Europe has become an article of faith. That makes it very difficult to discuss the future of the Union. For them, the debate about Europe is a question of black and white. You are either for it or you are against it. You are a either a 'good European' or a 'bad European '. It's as simple as that.

As a consequence, a debate on Europe is more theology than politics. I am a believer in European integration but, given its history, I am wary of Grand Designs. For European believers the introduction of a European Tax is the pinnacle of integration. They say that a European Tax will bring citizens closer to Europe. I tend to disagree. The opposite is more likely. Too often the introduction of new taxes has ignited revolution. A European Tax will bring the heads of European leaders uncomfortably close to the chopping block.

During my days in the Berlaymont, I often asked myself if the European Union (notwithstanding all its good intentions) is not inevitably subject to the same process of decline as history's other great empires: the Roman Empire, the Chinese Empire, the Ottoman Empire, the Hapsburg Empire and the Soviet Union. All these empires have one thing in common: they all reached a point of imperial 'over-stretch', from which no recovery was possible.

It is also striking that none of the imperial leaders of the day realised that this fatal moment had arrived. When they did eventually become aware of what was happening, it was too late to do anything about it.

Their empire was already on the slippery downward slope, with only one possible outcome: decline and disintegration. Why should the modern European empire be any different?

There were many reasons for the fall of the Roman Empire and it is still a subject for heated debate amongst modern historians. In his epic work *The Decline and Fall of the Roman Empire* (1787), the British historian Edward Gibbon attributed this disaster to moral decline amongst the Roman elite, coupled with the need to hire foreign mercenaries to keep the invading barbarians at bay. 'Prosperity helped to ripen the seeds of decline. The factors contributing towards her destruction were magnified with each successive conquest of new territory. As soon as time or accident removed the artificial pillars on which the imperial edifice was constructed, the entire system was destined to collapse under its own weight.'

Other historians have offered different opinions. In 2005, the British historian Peter Heather published his *Fall of the Roman Empire*, in which he not only alluded to the threat posed by the barbarian invasions, but also to the growing Persian threat from the East.

This meant that Rome had to devote a higher proportion of its already dwindling resources to fight a war on two fronts. The struggle against the Persian Sassanids was every bit as costly as the struggle against the Huns and the Visigoths. This was a strain which the political and economic system of the Empire was unable to withstand: tax pressure rose, leading to a crisis in agriculture and depopulation. Inflation spiralled, the currency depreciated and the people and their leaders lost the will to defend the city.

From this point on, the immigration of the Germanic peoples was unstoppable. Rome had reached the point of imperial over-stretch long before the last emperor was finally toppled from his throne. The Romans had conquered an empire that was too large for them to govern effectively. Their system became brittle, cracked and eventually collapsed.

Similar questions have been asked about the European Union in recent years. Has the Union not become too big – and therefore unmanageable? What are the likely consequences of demographic decline and migration? Can Europe keep the euro strong or will it be subject to rising inflation, as national governments allow their budget deficits to grow in order to keep paying their citizens' pensions? With an ageing electorate, the politicians have a stark but simple choice: pay up or be voted out. History never repeats itself precisely, but it is clear that there are lessons to be learnt from Ancient Rome.

The Chinese Empire was older, more modern and larger than Europe when Marco Polo first visited it in 1266. However, it was only a century and a half later, under the Ming Dynasty, that China first engaged in world trade and territorial expansion. In 1405 the empire dispatched a fleet of 317 ships, with a crew of some 28,000 soldiers and sailors, to explore the Asian seas. Admiral Zheng He led this impressive armada across the Indian Ocean and the Persian Gulf, eventually reaching the coast of Africa. Everywhere the admiral landed, he set up new trading posts. Rulers in Asia and Africa were impressed by this display of wealth and power and soon bowed to China's supremacy.

Within decades, the Emperor in Peking had become the effective ruler of half the world. However, one of his successors brought this empire to a sudden and abrupt end. In 1525 he recalled all the ships and had them destroyed. Plans for new ships were burnt and China turned its back on the maritime skills it had only so recently acquired.

The reason behind this decision remains one of the great mysteries of history. Did it have something to do with transfer of the capital from Nanking to Peking in 1521? Was it a purely financial decision (the Emperor needed to strengthen and extend the Great Wall to keep the Mongols at bay)? Or did it signify a return to a purer form of Confucianism, whose basic principles were against the creation of a trading empire? It was certainly true that mandarins at the court of the Emperor were fierce opponents of these foreign 'adventures'. In particular, they were afraid that foreign trade would lead to foreign influences and contact with foreign 'barbarians'. It was much better for the Middle Empire to cut itself off from such 'contamination'.

It was a disastrous decision. China turned inwards on itself, became weak and ignorant, and eventually fell pray to the colonial politics of the West. This was the opposite of imperial over-stretch: self-isolation. It was, however, equally damaging. From the 16th century onwards, it was not the Chinese but the British and Dutch fleets which dominated Asian trade. China was reduced to an irrelevancy, a nation of civil wars and opium addicts.

It never regained the position it had voluntarily surrendered in 1525 and it is only now, nearly 500 years later, that China is once again making use of its vast potential to become a world power. The emperors have long gone but the new communist mandarins intend to make sure that this time China maintains its position.

The collapse of empire is not purely a historical phenomenon. As recently as 1989, the Soviet Union showed how modern empires can still be subject to the same destructive forces.

Viewed from beyond the Iron Curtain, the Soviet Union seemed impregnable. When the French writer Hélène Carrère D'Encausse published her book *L'Empire éclaté* (The Imploding Empire) in the 1970s, suggesting that ethnic tensions in the Caucasus would lead to the break up of the Russian empire, she was ridiculed by most respectable critics. Yet within 15 years her predictions came true – albeit for different reasons.

The main cause of the disintegration of the Soviet state was economic stagnation, so that it was no longer able to meet the expectations of its many disparate nationalities. Leaving aside the fact that the Soviet Union was a one-party state, whereas the Europe Union is a voluntary association of democratic nations, the two systems have much in common in terms of symbolism and internal dynamics.

The Soviet Union wanted to harmonise as much as possible within a single political framework; this is also the mission of the European Union. The Soviet Union was administered by a political elite; so is the European Union. The Soviet Union saw itself as a utopian state; European federalists have much the same views. The Soviet Union had a single bureaucratic centre; likewise the European Union. The Soviet Union was dominated by a powerful Secretariat General; so are the European institutions. The Soviet Union had party ideology; the European Union has legal principles. The Soviet Union wished to create a viable society through a series of official procedures; so does the European Union. The Soviet Union had *apparatchiks*; the European Union has mandarins. The Soviet Union had a Five Year Plan; the European Union has a work programme. The Soviet Union saw socialist integration as an 'irreversible process'; the EU sees integration as the means to an 'ever closer Union'. The Soviet Union claimed to act on behalf of the mythical worker; the European Union has its mythical citizen. The Soviet Union wished to surpass the United States; the European Union has been trying to do the same thing for years.

With all these bureaucratic and political similarities (albeit in a highly exaggerated form in Moscow), it is worth looking more closely at the reasons for Soviet collapse. The Soviet regime's main problem after 1980 was that it was no longer able to keep the promises it had made to its peoples after the end of the Second World War. Official state statistics continued to show indisputable progress, in accordance with the best Marxist theories of historical inevitability. But the citizens on the streets knew better. The country was living in a fantasy world. The facades created by the party newspapers were in stark contrast to the harsh realities of daily life.

The crucial turning point came at the start of the 1980s, when the Soviet Union effectively 'missed' the electronic revolution. For the Politbureau, even a humble fax machine was regarded with suspicion; in such an ideological atmosphere, the use of a personal computer was unthinkable. As a result, the Soviet economy began to stagnate. While the citizens spent hours in long queues in front of near-empty shops, prosperity in Europe and the United States increased dramatically as a consequence of computerisation. The USSR quickly began to fall behind its main rivals, both in economic and military terms. Moscow was unable to keep up with the rapid pace of technological change and the population began to lose faith in its leaders and their promises. By the time Gorbatchov tried to reform the system, it was already too late. The Berlin Wall fell and the rest, as they say, is history.

What were the key factors which made this disintegration inevitable? In my opinion, it was the utopian idealism of the Soviets and their obsession with bureaucracy as an end in itself which led to final disaster. The Soviet Union did not possess the self-criticism and the self-correcting mechanisms which are typical of democratic states. Their pretended utopianism led the Soviets to ignore the true facts of the situation until they were already fatal. Their bureaucratic short-sightedness meant that they were unable to get themselves out of the mess they had created.

Once again, this gap between rhetoric and reality sounds uncomfortably like the present-day European Union. The European constitution was approved with a large majority in the European Parliament and in almost all the national parliaments. However, it was rejected by the populations of two of the most pro-European countries: France and the Netherlands. The ratification process was stopped, because further referenda seemed likely to follow the French and Dutch examples. There is a clear difference between the European elite – which thinks it knows what is best for the people – and the people themselves.

The Roman Empire, the Middle Empire and the Soviet Union: the current architects of the European Empire of Good Intentions would be wise to study these examples.

Politics, like physics, is subject to repetitive patterns of behaviour. Whoever seeks to deny this fact – no matter how good his intentions – is like the foolish man in the Bible, who built his house on sand instead of rock: sooner or later, the whole edifice will come crashing down.

My problem with the European federalists is not their faith, or their aspirations or even their ideals: it is their lack of political insight. The

European constitution is a good example of this naivety. I was present at the European Convention which drew up and approved the text for the constitution, following which Beethoven's Ninth Symphony – the European anthem – was played. The members of the Convention, led by Valéry Giscard D'Estaing, Guiliano Amato and Jean-Luc Dehaene, raised their glasses to toast the 'New Europe'. Some convention members actually hugged each other, as if they had just arrived at the Promised Land. It was a display which bordered on the surreal. I had to pinch myself to make sure that I wasn't dreaming, but I dared not say what I was thinking. Doubting the wisdom of the constitution was viewed as a betrayal of the European ideal.

The event and its product were not open for discussion – let alone doubt. If you opposed the constitution, you were sentencing yourself to long banishment in the deserts of Euro-scepticism. Europe had reached the stage in its development where the truth was no longer convenient – and therefore could not be spoken. This is not a problem – as long as there are no problems.

Even the very term 'constitution' demonstrated a total lack of political reality on the part of its creators. All the member states already have their own constitution, written or unwritten. Why, then, was it necessary to call a new European treaty between the member states 'a constitution'? It implied that the French or German or Dutch constitution would now be superseded by a bigger, better European version. Federalists saw the constitution as an irreversible step towards a federal Europe. The oldest nation states in Europe – France and the Netherlands – saw it as a threat to their national existence. And so they voted 'no'.

The European Parliament approved the constitution with a large majority. Of course, there was one dissident who voted 'non'.

The federalists thought that the nation state was an outdated concept. But they were wrong. As Europe gets bigger and more anonymous, most European citizens feel the need to strengthen their identity. And this is predominantly a national identity: not a European one. If you compare the situation to a building, the European nation states are the upper storeys and European culture is the foundations. There is no European identity which is capable of replacing national identity, but there is a European culture which nurtures and feeds national identity.

European cultural history is the product of many different streams of thought: Christianity, Greek philosophy, Roman law, the Enlightenment, German Romanticism, nationalism, dialectic materialism, etc. These streams of thought – some more than others – have contributed to the development of our various political-cultural communities. We are all the product of European cultural history – not of Chinese or Arabian cultural history. At the present level of European culture, inalienable rights and civil liberties are the common features of a group of democratic states, built around communities based on a common language, culture and history. The identity and loyalties of Europe's citizens are related to these various individual communities and not to a European legal construction based in Brussels.

This is perhaps even truer of several of the new member states, such as Poland, whose recent history of foreign oppression makes them more determined to express their national identities. They are not opposed to Europe per se but they are certainly opposed to a Europe which seeks to patronise them. Most of all, they are suspicious of a Europe which seeks to dominate all aspects of their national life. They have already had experience of this kind of 'union' during the period of Soviet domination.

Europe is only able to act as an *Ersatznation* in countries where there is no clear national frame of reference. This, for example, was the case with West Germany after the Second World War. German politicians looked to Europe as their *Neue Heimat* (New Home). This tendency declined after German reunification in 1990, when the post-war generation once again 'dared' to be German.

The situation is slightly different in Belgium, where Europe still acts as a surrogate nation. There is no such thing as a Belgian language, culture or education. The national anthem cannot be sung in

The fall of the Berlin Wall in 1989. A turning point in European history.

football stadiums because it is not possible to sing the tune in Dutch and French at the same time. Belgium is populated by Flemings, Walloons and Brusselaars – a diversity which leads them to have more in common with Europe than with each other. They hope that Europe will help to solve Belgium's internal problems and thus they preach the doctrine of a federal Europe of 27 nations, while they are unable to make a federal state of three regions work at home. Belgium is not really a nation – and for this reason is all the more missionary about Europe.

The political architects of the European structure often take too little account of these factors. Instead of grand designs, they should build more systematically – and then rebuild and consolidate. They must

LIFE OF A EUROPEAN MANDARIN

concentrate on a limited number of key tasks in the fields of economic, monetary and political union – and not try to legislate for everything under the sun.

In some areas of policy (agricultural and regional policy, for example) there is a positive excess of interference, whereas other areas have been left more or less untouched for too long, such as the common energy policy and a coherent approach to the problems of immigration. The first is over-regulated, while the second is still in its infancy. A European cow receives enough subsidies to fly around the world (in business class), but we still haven't got a clue what to do with a bedraggled immigrant washed up on the shores of the Canary Islands.

European integration is too focused on symbols and not enough on substance. Europe's main problem is not the fact that it does not yet have a president, but rather that it is saddled with a political agenda which belongs to the past. Nevertheless, the chief tenets of this agenda have once again been confirmed in the budgetary arrangements for the period 2007-2013. There is too much support for both agriculture and regional development: two key areas where several of the richer national governments are capable of helping themselves. There are too few resources for common energy, immigration and research policies, which are always running ten to fifteen years behind the times. Europe has a tendency to be progressive in terms of its symbols but obsolete in terms of its policy. The result is a wide gap between what is desired and what is achieved, which gives the citizens of Europe the uncomfortable feeling that Europe no longer has the answers.

The European Union is currently facing three main problems:

1. *Institutional paralysis.* The European Union has expanded rapidly in a relatively short period of time, but its institutions have not been amended to reflect this changing situation. As the number of member states has increased, so the decision-making process has become more difficult. Most European institutions are too big, too slow and too top-heavy. In short, they have lost their sense of urgency. With a Europe of 27 countries, the Union has reached the absolute limit of its capacity to function effectively.

2. *Fear of economic reform.* Europe is losing the battle for economic modernisation. Its economic foundations – the free movement of goods, services, people and capital – are far from complete. Seven years after its launching, the so-called Lisbon Process, which was designed to transform the European economy into the most modern and most competitive in the world by 2010, has been watered down to such an extent that it has become almost meaningless. In the meantime, costs for the care and maintenance of an ageing population have risen dramatically in most member states. Many Europeans long for their pensions, but there are doubts whether in fifteen years time the European economy and the European currency will be strong enough to pay them. Europe needs to adjust urgently to the economic realities of the world but is afraid to do so. And it is often the most 'European-minded' countries – especially Germany, France, Italy and Belgium – which are most hostile. All these countries need to pay for their pensions from current resources. If things are difficult economically, their argument is: 'Reform? Begin with the others!' If things are prospering economically, they retort: 'Reform? Why? Things are going well!'

3. *Cultural capitulation.* During the next twenty years, immigration will have a major impact on Europe's traditional cultural basis. As history teaches us, demography is the mother of all politics. Falling birth rates in many European lands, combined with a population explosion in Northern and Western Africa and the Middle East, will result in a wave of migration towards an ageing Europe. During the nineteenth century, the Industrial Revolution changed the sociological structure of Europe, with a rural/agricultural society rapidly being replaced by an urban/industrial one. During the twenty-first century, the new waves of immigration have the potential to exercise a similarly dramatic effect. The key question is whether Europe will adjust to the newcomers, or whether the newcomers will adjust to Europe. As the most important cultural value of the majority of the newcomers is their Islamic faith, this question can also be put another way: will Europe become a more Islamic continent or will Islam become a more Europeanised religion?

It is time for Sleeping Beauty to wake up. These three questions are critical to the future of the continent – and need to be answered now. If Europe makes the wrong choices, by 2050 our region will have become economically stagnant and culturally barren. Europe will no longer be a major player on the international scene, but rather an object of pity for others and an object of despair for its own population.

As 2007 dawns, the period of reflection within the European Union is gradually coming to an end. The German Presidency unveils the first tentative proposals to restart the process of European integration via the Declaration of Berlin. Germany has both the political weight and the will to kick-start the process. These proposals must lead to a new Inter Governmental Conference (ICG) which should produce a revised treaty – the term 'constitution' has been dropped – to be ratified by the year 2009. This is also the year in which the next European elections will be held and in which the next new Commission will be appointed. In this respect, many pro-Europeans are already looking forward to 2009 as a kind of new start. But in what direction will this new start take us? What are the main objectives for the new Europe?

1. First and foremost, in my opinion, is the question of institutional reform. The European Commission now has 27 members – an absolute maximum. The increasing scale of the College of Commissioners has changed its nature as an institution. In the past, the President had a prime ministerial role. He set the broad policy guidelines, but there was always scope for assertive Commissioners to influence the agenda. This made the Commission stronger, the discussions more relevant and the resulting policy more all-embracing. In a larger College, power has inevitably moved towards the centre, with the President fulfilling a more presidential role. Nowadays he takes decisions following direct consultations with the Commissioner responsible for the portfolio. The other Commissioners are finding it more and more difficult to make themselves heard. As a result, the College has changed from an instrument of government into a glorified debating society, whereas the Commission, initially a policy-making body, has become a think tank.

Moreover, the large number of Commissioners makes the allocation of portfolios increasingly problematical. Several directorates-general have already been split, leading to administrative fragmentation and damaging internal conflicts about areas of overlapping competence. There are endless turf wars throughout the institution.

The Princess is charming ...

... but perhaps just a little top-heavy?

Much the same is true of the European parliament. With 785 Euro-MPs, it has simply become far too large. With 27 national delegations and a whole host of political groupings and splinter groups, it has lost all sense of cohesion. The Parliament always knows what it is 'against', but it no longer knows what it is 'for'. This makes it ever more diffi-cult for Commissioners to secure a majority for important measures

The nearly 800 members of the European Parliament discuss the accession of Turkey – but with little apparent enthusiasm.

LIFE OF A EUROPEAN MANDARIN

– especially if these measures necessitate hard economic sacrifices. Consequently, Parliament usually seeks a majority at the level of the lowest common denominator. The resulting legislation, like the final version of the Services Directive, is often weak to the point of meaninglessness. In short, it is a method of government which achieves little and pleases no-one.

Similar comments could be made about almost every European institution: they are top-heavy and have the structure of a watermelon. The European Court of Auditors has been increased from 15 to 27 members, with the result that most of them have little or nothing to do. Neither the European Economic and Social Committee nor the Committee of the Regions plays an important role in formulating policy. As stipulated in the various European treaties, they provide advice to the Commission, the Council and the Parliament, but this advice usually finds its way into the nearest dustbin or shredder. Both committees have a purely symbolic function and serve as a talking shop for special interest groups.

What can be done? Well, a good start would be to reduce the number of Commissioners to 17, the number of Euro-MPs to 550 and the number of auditors to 10. The European Economic and Social Committee and the Committee of the Regions could be scrapped.

How would this new College of Seventeen work? Each of the six major countries (more than 35 million inhabitants) could be given a permanent Commissioner, while the remaining posts would be rotated between the other member states. This can be expressed as a mathematical formula: X minus six, divide by two, plus six, equals Y.

$$\frac{X-6}{2} + 6 = Y$$

In this formula, X is the number of member states and Y is the number of Commissioners. Following further institutional reform, it is expected that Croatia will be able to join the EU by 2009, thereby bringing the number of member states to 28. The above formula would therefore be applied as follows: 28 member states, minus the 6 major member states, equals 22 member states. 22 member states divided by 2, equals 11 member states, plus the 6 major member states = 17 Commissioners. Eureka!

As stated, the six major member states would each have a permanent Commissioner. The remaining eleven mandates would be divided between the remaining member states on a rotational basis. The permanent representation of the six largest countries may seem a little unfair, but this is necessary to underpin the political legitimacy of the Commission. If smaller member states such as Ireland, Malta or Cyprus were ever in a position to dominate the Commission, it would not be taken seriously by the Big Six. On the contrary, it would encourage the Big Six to try and circumvent the Commission completely. In the world of European power, size does matter; but there are other ways by which equilibrium with the smaller member states could be restored. For example, it might be possible (and advisable) for the President of the Commission to ensure that a fair share of important portfolios is granted to the smaller member states, and not reserved exclusively for the rich and powerful.

In practice, this means that each of the smaller member states would only have a Commissioner in every second mandate period. This could be compensated by the awarding of senior mandarin positions (e.g. director-general) to representatives of the countries who are temporarily 'out of office'. These measures would make the Commission smaller, compacter and more decisive. The directorates-general could be regrouped more logically, within a clear hierarchical structure under a single Commissioner. In particular, the Relex family needs serious restructuring following the inclusion of the High Representative for Foreign Affairs within the Commission framework. Too many tasks have been duplicated, both within the EU and between the EU and the Council of Europe. For example, the EU recently founded its own Agency for Human Rights in Vienna, notwithstanding the fact that the Council of Europe in Strasbourg is already very well-equipped for monitoring human rights issues. It even has its own Court of Human Rights! This kind of replication is both costly and confusing.

The new formula for the College of Commissioners provides a sustainable structure for the future. The accession of new member states will not have any significant knock-on effect on the number of Commissioners. If the six remaining Balkan countries were to join the EU, the number of member states would rise to 34, but the number of Commissioners would only increase to 20. If Turkey were to join, its size would entitle it to a permanent Commissioner post – but even then, the College of Commissioners would be limited to 21 members, whereas present rules would foresee no fewer than 35 members.

Alongside a restructured Commission, a smaller Parliament would force the Euro-MPs to concentrate on important matters, instead of just pursuing their own pet subjects or engaging in mindless nit-picking. The Parliament currently has a massive 785 MEPs – a huge total which could quite easily be cut by 30%. The resulting slim-line Parliament of 550 members would still be sufficient to ensure that the voice of the European people is heard, but would encourage more meaningful debate and fewer boring monologues.

In any new structure, the position of President of the Commission will remain crucial. At the moment, the President is appointed by the leaders of the national governments. This is not a good thing, since it means that the President is not wholly independent. On the contrary, he has to lobby – and bargain – in order to be elected or re-elected. It would be better for Europe if the President could act as a stronger counter-balance to the influence of the national leaders, and for this reason it would be more advisable for the President to be elected by the Parliament. In these circumstances, however, it would also be necessary for the President to have the power to dissolve the Parliament: otherwise he would just end up being a slave to Parliament in the same manner as he is currently a slave to the national governments. Euro-MPs would think twice about voting out the Commission, if they knew that their own highly lucrative jobs were at stake!

A president of Europe is not necessary, or even desirable. In reality, the concept of a European presidency is little more than a fiction, a symbolic dream with no practical benefit. All the president would achieve is to get under the feet of the President of the Commission, by constantly pretending to be what he is not: a president of Europe in the American style. This is an impossibility: Europe is not a state and therefore it does not need to be run like a state. A European president would bear as much resemblance to an American president as a poodle to a pit-bull terrier.

The Council of Ministers and the European Council would also benefit from a degree of restructuring. Given their composition and purpose, it is not feasible to reduce the number of members in either institution. All member states must be represented in the Council of Ministers and must be able to vote according to their qualified weighting. Similarly, all government leaders must be able to speak on behalf of their countries in the European Council. Consequently the structures of both organisations will remain top-heavy. Nevertheless, reform is possible. In particular, the requirement for unanimity of voting in the Council of Ministers for certain key areas, such as taxation, needs to be reviewed. In a Union of 27 member states, unanimity is becoming almost impossible to achieve, which can only lead to a paralysis of the policy-making process. For this reason, it would be advisable to replace unanimity by a system of 'co-decision', whereby proposals would also be subject to scrutiny by the Parliament. If this is a step too far, a possible alternative is to set a lower threshold for member states which are prepared to create a 'coalition of the willing'.

Other practical steps could further enhance the efficiency of both institutions. At present, for example, countries hold the EU presidency for a period of six months, in accordance with alphabetical order. This period of six months is much too short to achieve anything significant. The sustainability of common policies would be better served if a group of member states, such as the Benelux countries, could hold the presidency for a longer period of 18 months or two years. This group could then act as a Council Presidium, preparing and adjusting the political agenda in light of mid-term policy objectives.

2. Once the matter of institutional reform has been dealt with, the next key task for the new Europe will be to convince its citizens of the need for far-reaching economic reform.

This will require courage, since politicians are always reluctant to take electoral risks by proposing unpopular measures. After the rejection of the constitution, a mood of Euro-scepticism took hold of the continent, forcing national leaders onto the defensive. In one sense, this is understandable – politicians can only achieve results if they have power and in 2005 the electorate was wary of further economic reforms: they would simply have voted the reformers out of office. However, both politicians and the electorate would be wise to remember that in the long term an inflexible defence of the status quo could endanger our entire social structure. In the modern world, standing still is often the same as going backwards. If we do not progress, we will stagnate.

The population is becoming economically more conservative as it gets older. This is certainly true of the baby-boom generation of the 1960s, which in recent years has started to take over the reins of political and economic power. It had the best jobs, earned the best salaries and now gets the best pensions (while it incurred the biggest social debts). This generation believes in keeping what it has, and sees the reformers in Brussels as a threat to its hard-won rights. This is an egotistical attitude, which in turn threatens to deny these same 'rights' to future generations.

If the population of Europe insists on standing still, it will no longer be able to compete with the more economically vital regions of the world. Europe risks not only becoming 'old' physically, but also 'old' mentally. Its peoples see change as a danger instead of seeing it as an opportunity and a challenge. This is a perception which the European politicians urgently need to alter – whatever the risk at the ballot box.

It will not be easy. The debate surrounding the European constitution has temporarily paralysed the legislative process. The Services Directive was high-jacked during this debate and was subsequently robbed of its teeth by Parliament. Other proposals crucial to the creation of the single internal market have also been watered down or withdrawn. Several important matters, such as the Community Patent, have been blocked for years, often because of narrow sectoral or national interests. In this atmosphere, the Commission has become more cautious, limiting itself to green papers, info-papers and non-papers.

This is also an attitude which will need to change and there are at least some encouraging signs. The Commission has taken steps to give a lead in the key area of energy policy, issuing a green book for a new energy strategy. Europe is becoming more and more dependent on imported energy, particularly from the Middle East (oil) and Russia (gas). This level of dependency has already reached 50%. If nothing is done, the level will rise to 75% by the year 2030. During the same period, international energy requirements in the rest of the world will increase by 70%. Supplies of oil and gas will dwindle and prices will shoot through the roof. What will be the effects of this gloomy scenario?

High energy prices will place the economy under permanent pressure. Economic growth will remain limited, so that countries will need to start drawing on their financial reserves to maintain their welfare states. Countries which have no reserves (or not enough) will be forced to allow their budget deficits to rise. This will weaken the strength of the euro and will ultimately lead to spiralling inflation – the worst enemy of anyone trying to live on a small pension or welfare benefit.

To make matters worse, Europe's security position will also be weakened. Europe will continue to need energy from Russia and the Middle East and will therefore no longer be able to take a firm international stance in these regions. If it does, the gas and oil taps will simply be turned off. Europe will therefore be condemned to a foreign and security policy based on 'soft' power.

In these circumstances, one might expect the Commission's green paper on energy to promote the potential offered by nuclear power. But it doesn't. Not a single sentence. The subject is still considered to be 'too sensitive'.

Nuclear power is the only source of energy which can significantly help to limit Europe's dependency on the oil and gas giants. Most of France's electricity needs are already generated by nuclear plants. However, many other member states, including Germany and Belgium, have announced their intention to cut back on their nuclear programmes. The words 'nuclear power' have become a taboo in Europe and Europe traditionally avoids its taboos by keeping quiet about them. As a result, the Union plans to concentrate on non-contentious measures, such as the promotion of renewable sources of energy, even though these measures can never hope to have a serious impact on the heart of the matter. Wind power, wave power and solar power are all laudable initiatives, but they cannot produce sufficient electricity to meet our economy's growing energy requirements. Not now and not in 25 years time.

Europe speaks of the need to meet the Kyoto norms, but makes no mention of the source of power most capable of helping industrialised nations to honour these norms: nuclear power. The green paper lists three priorities for its energy strategy: sustainability, competitiveness and continuity of supply. Nuclear energy can make important contributions in all three areas, but for the time being the Princess just doesn't want to know.

This is typical of the dilemma currently facing the European Union. It is confronted with a series of crucial problems, but it does not have the courage to take the hard decisions necessary to solve them. As soon as a subject is deemed to be 'sensitive', it is avoided. 'Soft' power has helped to create 'soft' minds and even softer backbones. What Europe really needs is leaders with determination and powers of persuasion.

3. But if institutional paralysis and fear of reform are serious problems, the consequences of cultural capitulation could be even more far-reaching. During the Convention held to discuss the European constitution, there was a sharp debate about whether the introductory preamble should refer to the Judaeo-Christian roots of European culture. The majority was against any such reference and a compromise was eventually reached whereby a more vague reference was made to the cultural, religious and humanist traditions which have helped to shape Europe. This was simply flying in the face of history. Whether you are a believer or not, it is indisputable that Christianity was the greatest source of inspiration for the development of what we now regard as modern European culture. But Europe's leaders were afraid to say this out loud, for fear of offending anyone. They were no longer prepared – or no longer able – to define their own cultural identity in

terms of simple historical facts. This is symptomatic of a wider crisis of self-confidence in 'old' Europe. The leaders and the national elites no longer know who they are or what they stand for. They are gradually becoming rootless in their own continent, creating a void which others are threatening to fill.

This lack of cultural confidence has been evident on several occasions in recent years. During the row surrounding the publication of the Danish cartoons, the European Union and the majority of member states were happy to leave the Danish government in the cold. Nobody quite knew how to react to the Islamic backlash and so (as always in Europe) they tried to escape from an embarrassing situation by saying and doing nothing. It was only when the Danish embassies in Damascus and Beirut were burnt down that the Union finally took a stance – far too late.

Much the same occurred when Pope Benedict XVI quoted the words of the Byzantine Emperor Paleologos during an address in Regensburg. Paleologos had been comparing the merits of reason and religion and once said: 'Show me what new things Mohamed has brought, and you will see that it is all bad and inhuman. Did he not preach that his belief must be spread by the sword?' Once again, the Muslim world took great offence at what was simply a historical quotation – and once again hardly a single European leader was prepared to defend the Pope. It says much about the current European psyche when the Vicar of Christ is the only person of authority in Europe who is prepared to discuss European culture and European values without fear.

This fear has already begun to result in a form of self-censorship. The Council has even prepared a list of official terms designed to avoid offence or embarrassment. Islamic terrorists are therefore described as 'terrorists who falsely claim to act in the name of Islam'. In similar vein, a recent Commission proposal to set up an anti-terror advice group spoke of 'violent radicalisation'. The word Muslim was avoided because it was thought to be too inflammatory.

In the cases of both the Pope and the Danish cartoons, Islamic reaction was large-scale, organised and violent – both verbally and physically. Moreover, it was carried out by tens of thousands of people who had never seen the cartoons or heard the Regensburg address. Not that this mattered. The organisers of the protests knew how to find the weak spot of the Europeans: make enough noise, act like a victim – and the Europeans will cave in. Why? Because they are weak and lacking in self-confidence. And they were right, of course. The European leaders were almost falling over themselves to apologise for any offence which might have been caused.

If we carry on in this fashion, the Europe of 2050 will be a very different place from the Europe of today. Our present cultural values are in risk of ebbing away. Europeans are constantly asking immigrants to integrate. But integrate with what? The European cultural basis is threatening to become a moral vacuum – a vacuum into which the immigrants will introduce their own cultural heritage. With all due respect to Benedict XVI, today's European politicians are in danger of becoming 'holier than the Pope'. They are so busy trying to see the other person's point of view, they are so anxious not to offend. As a result, they forget to defend the very values on which this essentially 'democratic' and 'humanistic' approach is based.

The moment anyone finally does make an effort to speak up for Europe, they are instantly branded as cultural imperialists, racists, bigots, etc. – and this by the same people who are burning down internationally-protected embassy buildings throughout the Middle East and Asia!

This desire on the part of the Europeans to be 'politically correct' should not be allowed to deflect us from the real issues at stake. Is a theocracy better than a democracy? Is a *sura* better than parliamentary legislation? Is a *fatwa* better than an independent judiciary? The moment a majority of 'Europeans' start answering 'yes' to any of these questions, our continent is in serious trouble.

The discussion about European values is not simply a theoretical exercise for intellectuals. The outcome of this discussion will affect the lives of each and every one of us. Throughout the centuries, the Europeans have anchored their basic human values within a clear constitutional framework: freedom of speech, freedom of religion, equality between the sexes, the separation of church and state, etc. These values must not be made negotiable – even if they do not comply with the letter of Islamic law. The moment we start to compromise, the moment we allow exceptions, a grey area of uncertainty will develop which will undermine European culture from within. Instead, we must be true to our own values and we must be prepared to defend them.

This difficult issue is certain to become increasingly important as the years roll by. Immigration has grown dramatically during the past two decades and will continue to grow in future. Consider the following statistics. Turkey has a current population of 73 million; by 2050 this will have risen to 101 million. Algeria has a current population of 32 million; by 2050 this will have risen to 49 million. Morocco has a current population of 31 million; by 2050 this will have risen to 46 million. Egypt has a current population of 74 million; by 2050 this will have risen to 125 million. Iran has a current population of 69 million; by 2050 this will have risen to 101 million. Senegal has a current population of 11 million; by 2050 this will have risen to 23 million. Ivory Coast has a current population of 18 million; by 2050 this will have risen to 33 million. Nigeria has a current population of 131 million; by 2050 this will have risen to 258 million.

These figures speak for themselves. It is equally self-evident that these countries do not have the economic resources to support populations of this size. So where do we think all these people are going to go? Where is the local birth rate declining? Where are the borders long and indefensible? Where is the nearest haven of tolerance and wealth? If I was an African or an Arab, I would be heading for Europe as well. The first boatloads have already started arriving on the shores of Italy and the beaches of the Canary Islands – and this is just the vanguard.

The European Union has not yet attempted to prepare the peoples of Europe for the likely consequences of this huge wave of immigration. This is a serious mistake. The mental capacities of the average European for integration are fairly limited. European history has been characterised by emigration, not by immigration. As a result, Europeans even have difficulty in accepting each other. When the Austrian-born actor Arnold Schwarzenegger became governor of California, there was much amusement in Europe. 'It could only happen in America!'

was the most common reaction. And this, indeed, is true: it could only happen in America. It could certainly never happen in Europe.

A Frenchman would never be elected in Germany, and vice versa. The Belgians distrust the Dutch, while the Dutch have difficulty in taking the Belgians seriously. The same phenomenon even exists within countries. In Belgium, a Limburger will never become governor of Antwerp. In Germany, a citizen of Bavaria would need divine help in order to become Chancellor in Berlin. National and regional interests predominate, even in the very heart of Europe. If a member state feels that it is not being properly represented, the necessary government delegation will be sent to Brussels to complain. Can a continent with so much institutionalised distrust seriously be expected to accommodate the arrival of millions of foreign newcomers?

Perhaps it can, but only if Europe develops a clear and distinctive cultural pattern into which the newcomers can be integrated. They cannot integrate with nothing. Consequently, there must be a clear set of cultural values which they are expected to learn and respect. This is the American way of doing things. No immigrant to the USA ever has to ask himself whether he must integrate or how. The answers to these questions are patently obvious. The American way of life is omnipresent and unavoidable.

This is not the case in Europe, partly because of the above-mentioned crisis of cultural confidence and partly because Europeans see an insistence on integration as a form of cultural arrogance. This is a misguided perception, since it leads to the isolation of the newcomers in alien enclaves, which in urban environments can quickly grow to become the dominant local culture. Once this point has been reached, effective integration becomes almost impossible.

This situation is not a testimony to the strength of Islam, but rather a consequence of the weakness of Europe. This weakness is rooted in a concept of guilt which is specifically European. Europe is all too willing to see itself as the villain of the piece, while the rest of the world is happy to play the role of innocent victim.

Europe is supposedly 'guilty' of slavery, colonialism, capitalism, globalisation and world hunger. The European 'wrong-doers' confess their guilt in a re-written version of their own history, erecting monuments to those whom they are supposed to have exploited or harmed. The self-appointed victims of these 'crimes' complain ceaselessly about the treatment they have endured and demand an almost never-ending right to compensation for their mental and physical injuries. The Europeans apologise – and pay up. This is an attitude which has led to the development of a very specific form of dialogue between 'villain' and 'victim', a form of dialogue where a spade can no longer be called a spade and where problems can never be discussed on an equal moral footing. The result is a huge gap between facts and policy.

Policy is what Europe needs – a viable, operational immigration policy. Much time has been lost since a common approach to immigration was first agreed in the Treaty of Amsterdam (1997), confirmed by the summit of national leaders at Tampere (1999). The Commission tried to implement these proposals, beginning with the publication of a green book in November 2000. Unfortunately, this book was based on a naïve and ultimately incorrect assumption, namely that it was necessary to keep the channels of immigration wide open, in order to compensate for the ageing European population and to keep economic growth at its existing levels.

A draft directive for the realisation of these plans was drawn up in July 2001, effectively suggesting that Europe should be turned into an immigration union. The draft was sent to the Council of Ministers on 5 September 2001 – just 6 days before two aeroplanes brought the twin towers of the World Trade Centre in New York crashing to the ground. Economic confidence received a severe blow and Europeans became fearful for the consequences of Muslim immigration from Africa and the Middle East. The draft directive was repeatedly blocked in the Council and the Commission finally withdrew it on 3 March 2006.

New proposals are currently under development, but these are still very much in their infancy. It could still be many years before they constitute an operational policy. As the year 2007 opens, there is a policy plan for legal migration, focussing on 'skilled' immigration and the importation of seasonal labour from the Third World. However, this plan is only at the green paper stage. In other words, it only forms a basis for further consultations, conferences and discussions. As always, European policy is lagging hopelessly behind the demographic realities of the situation.

Could more be done? Almost certainly. Any legal form of qualitative immigration for labour purposes (similar to the American green card system) can only help to relieve the pressure. But there are no magic solutions. On the contrary, Europe's own decisions have sometimes made the problem more difficult to resolve – or have replaced one problem with another. Unemployment in the core countries of old Europe is running at about 10%. This is a high figure. Within a few years, the free movement of labour within the Union will finally be realised, leading to a migration of EU citizens from East to West Europe. In addition – if the Commission's proposals are passed – there will also be legal labour immigration from North and West Africa. High unemployment in combination with the encouragement of labour migration? There is something seriously wrong with the policy for the labour market in Western Europe.

The arrival of large numbers of immigrants will also impose an additional strain on the social welfare system. The United States combines immigration with a very limited system of social benefits. Legal immigrants have no rights to benefit payments for an initial period of five to ten years: they are expected to contribute something to the system before they are entitled to start drawing from it.

Europe is much more generous, combining immigration with an extensive network of social support. The first act of many immigrants when arriving in a member state of the Union is to apply for welfare assistance. This is doubly disadvantageous: it increases the social and economic burdens of the already hard-pressed welfare states and it removes the incentive for newcomers to seek work. As a result, they often find themselves trapped in urban ghettos of poverty and unemployment. This leads to social isolation instead of social integration, heightening both the immigrant's sense of grievance and his awareness of his own ethnic identity. Mexicans arriving in the United States want just one thing: to become Americans. Does a Moroccan arriving in Paris or London or Brussels really want to become a European? Current evidence would suggest not.

Could increased development aid help to ease the situation? There is a theory which suggests that increased development aid would lead to increased employment and increased prosperity in the Third World, therefore encouraging more people to 'stay at home' instead of seeking fame and fortune in Europe.

This would be better for all concerned – if it was true. Unfortunately, the facts do not support the theory. Better education and better job opportunities in Third World countries actually make the prospect of emigration to Europe more attractive, not less. Such is the demographic pressure in Asia and Africa that 'skilled' workers will always see Europe as a continent of greater economic opportunity. In other words, increased development aid ultimately results in a Third World brain-drain.

In the Europe of the mandarins, the citizen doesn't always have the last word. Quo vadis, *Europe?*

At the end of the day, Europe must simply accept that a massive wave of immigration is on its way, whether we like it or not. Europe must also recognise that this wave will exceed her current capacity to absorb it, thereby threatening the cultural basis of the entire continent. The only solution is to integrate the newcomers into a newly defined and self-confident European culture, whose political and social values are non-negotiable and applicable to all. Europeans must be proud of their cultural heritage and must seek to defend it. 'New' Europeans, whatever their ethnic origins, must learn to be equally proud of these cultural traditions and to accept them willingly. Only then can we speak of true European integration.

I hope that the leaders of Europe will have the courage to get to grips with this problem – and the foresight to see further than their own next re-election. More than ever before, Europe has an urgent need of leadership with vision, confidence and integrity; leadership which will stand up for Europe and will fight for the values which Europe represents.

Mario Vargas Llosa once wrote of western civilisation: 'Its greatest virtue – and its greatest achievement amongst the many and varied cultures of the world – is its ability to look at itself critically.' This is true, and Europe must also continue to look at itself critically. But this does not mean that we must concede that the other person – or nation, or religion – is always right.

I am convinced that the European mandarins would like nothing better than to give new impetus to the process of European integration. With all their inadequacies and shortcomings, the mandarins still run the engine of Europe. They oil and grease the parts, so that the European vehicle continues to move forward, however slowly. Without their collective knowledge, the European Union could never have survived for half a century. And a Europe without the European Union is almost unthinkable: the result would be a hopeless mishmash of nation states, divided, poor and provincial. In reality, European integration is the best thing that has ever happened to Europe in its long and often troubled history. It has given the continent a collective power it has never before possessed and it has all been achieved by the rule of law – not at the barrel of a gun.

I have always regarded it as an honour to work as a mandarin at the court of the Princess. As my aeroplane for New York climbed out of Zaventem and crossed over Vilvoorde – the home of my good friend, Jean-Luc Dehaene – I looked to my left and saw the Berlaymont, the Princess's star-shaped palace, glistening in the early morning sun. I nodded my head in gratitude and appreciation – and the Princess nodded back.

Good luck, Princess!

Photo credits